The Essential
Windows NT Book

How to Order:

For information on quantity discounts contact the publisher: Prima Publishing, P.O. Box 1260BK, Rocklin, CA 95677-1260; (916) 632-4400. On your letterhead include information concerning the intended use of the books and the number of books you wish to purchase.

The Essential Windows NT Book

Richard Cravens

PRIMA PUBLISHING

Publisher: Don Roche, Jr.

Associate Publisher: Ray Robinson

Senior Acquisition Editor: Alan Harris

Acquistion Editor: Jenny Watson

Senior Editor: Tad Ringo

Project Editor: Jeff Ennis

Copyeditor: Robert Campbell

Technical Reviewer: Jerry Hannis

Indexer: Katherine Stimson

Production: Shawn Morningstar

Cover Design: Vanessa Wong

ISBN: 1-7615-0752-3

Library of Congress Catalog Card Number: 96-70099

Printed in the United States of America

96 97 98 99 DD 10 9 8 7 6 5 4 3 2 1

Contents

Acknowledgments

There are dozens of folks without whom this project would not exist. Unfortunately, I can only thank the few that will fit on this page.

To Howard Myers, Dave Rasmussen, Roger Schuermann, Mike Sullivan, David Peyton, Mike Robertson, and Ross Matheson: do not forget the old days.

An extra big special thanks to Henry Mitchel, Rob Greenberg, and David Bradley for their timely motivation and inspiration. Your tenacious logic, tireless work ethic, fierce loyalty, open minds, and respect for the truth will not be soon forgotten.

It's not often that you get invited to participate in the launching of a new business venture. My thanks to Jenny Watson, Julie Barton, Ruth Slates, Deb Abshier, Alan Harris, Jeff Ennis, Don Roche, and everyone else at Prima for their confidence and incredible patience.

To Steve Stone, Eric Sink, David Ries, Jeanne Balbach, Chuck Isdale, Dan Schrieber, and everyone else at Spyglass: thanks for making me feel instantly at home.

Finally: a resounding, deep, wide, thick, and chewy THANK YOU to my sons Jesse and Ian (who gave up time with me while I fretted over network protocols and other totally silly things) and to my partner and supreme love Diane (your new Pentium is on the way, I swear). I cannot imagine life without you.

Dick Cravens

Introduction

Essential Goals

Welcome to The Essential Windows NT Book. This volume is designed to help you learn the absolutely most important facts and procedures about the newest edition of Microsoft's premier desktop operating system, Windows NT Workstation version 4.0. Please don't expect to find details on every single aspect of NT Workstation (that set of books is much heavier, and it costs quite a bit more). Please do expect to find the most critical information needed to get you up and running quickly.

Although this book focuses on NT on the Intel X86 platform (486 and later), we'll also cover issues on the DEC Alpha AXP, MIPS R4000, and PowerPC platforms where appropriate.

Who Needs This Book?

If you are

- A business professional using Windows NT Workstation for the first time

- An MIS technician, a Help Desk engineer, or an "office guru" administering Windows NT Workstations or considering moving your machines to NT Workstation from other systems

- A "Power User" (at home, in the office, or at your home office) who wants the latest, most reliable, highest-performance operating system

—then you're likely to find much useful information within these covers. This book is designed to quickly acquaint you with the basics of installing, configuring, and operating Windows NT Workstation 4.0 with the minimum fuss and hassle. If you're evaluating different operating systems, this book is a good introductory guide to the overall features and benefits of NT Workstation.

What Experience This Book Assumes You Already Have

This edition isn't really designed for absolute computing beginners and total Windows novices. This book *does* assume you've been around the desktop computing block at least once, and that you've lived with previous versions of Windows or Windows NT, but it doesn't contain the depth of information necessary to be a complete technical reference. If you use a computer daily in your work environment and are a fairly experienced Windows 3.*x* user, with some experience with or exposure to Windows NT or Windows 95, you're going to feel right at home. You may have some homework to do if you're coming to Windows NT from an MS-DOS or character-based UNIX environment, or if you are basically unfamiliar with the general principles of the Graphical User Interface (GUI). If you're comfortable on the Macintosh, you'll probably adjust to Windows NT Workstation's new interface without great pains. If you're an experienced Windows 95 user, not only will you feel comfortable immediately, you have some pleasant experiences awaiting you with NT Workstation 4.0.

We assume you know the difference between RAM and your hard drive, and that you know a serial port from a hole in the wall. If you need some brushing up on your PC hardware or Windows knowledge as you approach NT Workstation, see Appendix F, "Glossary," for a fairly thorough listing of general computing terms and NT-specific terminology (we've included a lot of information on the Internet, as well, since NT Workstation excels as a communications platform).

Who Won't Need This Book

Conversely, this text isn't designed for:

- Support professionals needing extremely detailed product information

  or

- Programmers needing a technical reference

The Essential Windows NT Book does tell you how to find more technical information if you need it, though (see Appendix E, "Windows NT Information Sources").

What This Book Will Do For You

The Essential Windows NT Book is designed to

- Demonstrate how NT is different from other Windows systems

- Show you the basics of using the new NT 4.0 interface

- Give you the most essential information on the most common tasks to make you more productive quickly

- Point you to resources for additional advanced information on NT and related topics

If we've accomplished all that by the time you've covered every chapter and appendix, we'll have both done a good deal of work. This book is designed to allow you to work at your own pace, so feel free to take your time and go through the material at a comfortable rate of speed. Some readers may want to breeze through at a fairly brisk pace to familiarize themselves with the overall structure of the text and then use it as a reference (there's a great index just for that purpose).

What's in *The Essential Windows NT Book*

This book is visually organized much like most other computer books, but the content is set up a little differently. We've kept the first few chapters pretty basic, and put the "heavier" topics toward the end of the book (you could say the material becomes progressively more complex as you go). If you're just looking to get an overview of NT, you can do so easily in the first four or five chapters, without dealing with much of the really chewy technical stuff. If you want to sink your teeth in, you can keep going as deep as you like, right down to the references to strictly technical resources in Appendix E.

General Contents

Chapter 1, "A Brief History of Windows NT," will tell you how NT was developed, how its basic design goals emerged, and how NT has evolved since its initial release in 1993. We'll also touch on some of the primary differences between NT and its cousins, Windows 3.*x*, Windows for Workgroups, and Windows 95.

Chapter 2, "Welcome to Windows NT Workstation," covers what's new in NT Workstation 4.0, including the new user interface, new applications, Internet tools, messaging systems, security features, and lots more.

Chapter 3, "Introducing the NT 4.0 Desktop," is a thorough primer on the basics of operating the new Windows NT Workstation interface. If you've never used Windows 95, you'll want to be sure to spend some time here. If you're a Windows 95 veteran, you'll be able to get up to speed very quickly and learn some of the subtle but important differences between the Windows 95 and NT 4.0 interfaces.

Chapter 4, "Networking Windows NT 4.0 Workstation," will help you understand the maze of issues involved in setting up your NT system on a Local Area Network (LAN). We'll also show you how to get started using the tools in Windows NT Remote Access to connect NT to the Internet, other NT servers or workstations, or another LAN, using your modem and phone line.

Chapter 5, "Installing and Running Applications," walks you through the procedures and issues you'll encounter when you add common business applications to Windows NT Workstation. We'll start with a general discussion of installation and security issues, and then we'll show you an example installation of the popular Microsoft Office 95 productivity suite. We'll also cover how to install shareware and freeware programs.

Chapter 6, "Windows NT Communications and the Internet," digs into the meat and potatoes of peer-to-peer LAN resource sharing, serial communications, Internet client/server communications, and group messaging and scheduling on NT. Here's the place to start if you already are comfortable with NT but want to get down to business configuring your workstation for general file-and-folder-level resource sharing all the way up to TCP/IP client/server and Internet communications. If you need assistance in using NT Remote Access Services, we'll get you up and running quickly as well.

Appendix A, "Installing Windows NT 4.0," guides you through the process of getting NT Workstation on your machine for the first time. Whether you're upgrading from NT 3.51, Windows 3.x, or MS-DOS, we'll show you all the tricks to make your installation quick and simple.

Appendix B, "Tips on Configuring Windows NT 4.0," is a great quick reference on security and Registry issues, memory management, and multitasking optimization, as well as drive management, boot options, and other ways to "tweak" the last bit of performance from NT Workstation.

Appendix C, "Tips on Running Legacy Applications," will help you with the major issues you'll encounter when operating MS-DOS, OS/2, and 16-bit Windows programs under NT Workstation.

Appendix D, "Tips on Performing System Maintenance," will help you understand normal product and system maintenance cycles, from installing NT Service Packs to backing up your hard drive.

Appendix E, "NT Information Sources," contains a wealth of different resources to help you grow in your knowledge of NT and related technologies. If you need serious technical information about NT, or if you just want to discuss NT topics with other users, this is a good place to start.

Appendix F, "Glossary," is a thorough listing of Windows NT, Internet, network, security, and other general desktop computing topics. Use this general reference in addition to the excellent Help system in NT itself.

Conventions Used in *The Essential Windows NT Book*

We've talked about the general content of our book, so now let's look at the basic structure of the presentation used throughout the edition. Each chapter or appendix follows the same plan, designed for consistency and ease of recognition as you move from area to area in your quest for NT Workstation mastery.

General Structure

Each chapter will begin with a brief introduction and a description of the topics covered. These topics will be clearly delineated by the use of various titles and subtitles, or heads, throughout the chapter. Tables, figures, and other illustration elements will be clearly marked and referenced in the text prior to their use. Since the primary topic of the book is a graphical-interface operating system, expect a few illustrations to help guide you visually through topics and procedures. We'll try our best not to clutter the pages with unnecessary pictures, but bear with us if a certain complex procedure requires a few carefully chosen illustrations (anyone that's ever spent more than five minutes on the phone with tech support, trying to visualize a technician's instructions, instantly realizes the truth in the worn adage about "a thousand words").

Special Styles and Elements

Throughout *The Essential Windows NT Book* you'll see various unique text elements designed to attract your attention in several ways. The most basic trick used is the application of different type effects to indicate special or unique content within the text itself.

For example, if you see type like this:

```
START EDIT C:\CONFIG.SYS
```

in a monospaced font, that means it's an instruction that we intend for you to enter (literally type it) in the context of the current program we're discussing (it's not part of the *description* of the process, application or procedure, it's part of an *action* we want you to take). Short instructions to be entered may also appear in **boldface** in the body of the text.

You'll also encounter numerous variations of numbered and bulleted lists for:

- Descriptions of procedures
- Sets of descriptions of program elements
- Other items of interest

throughout the book.

For example, if we write a sentence such as "Use File ➤ Open to select CONFIG.SYS," that's shorthand for:

1. Using the left mouse button, click on the File item in the Common User Access menu.

2. Select the Open menu item, which will in turn display a dialog box in which several files are listed.

3. Click on the file CONFIG.SYS once.

4. Click on the OK button once.

Numbered lists are great, but if we can save space by leaning upon your knowledge of general Windows menu concepts and conventions, we'll all be home right on time for dinner.

You'll also find other techniques for presenting special information to you in a visually arresting manner:

TIP: When you see text in a box like this, you know you've just received a *tip*. Tips are tidbits that will really make you more productive or save you major hassles.

CAUTION: The same goes for *cautions*. Watch out for these special warnings!

NOTE: *Notes* are a little less critical but still deserve your attention. After all, we put each one in a special box, didn't we?

The Importance of Reading Sidebars

Sidebars are where we'll share special information that is really too darned long to fit within the constraints of a *tip* or *note* or is simply not really that directly related to the material at hand but still pretty interesting. We may even share a recipe or two with you, so don't get in the habit of skipping those special text areas—your taste buds may suffer as well as your level of NT knowledge.

Onwards

We sincerely hope you enjoy *The Essential Windows NT Book* as much as we've enjoyed producing it. I've always thought new operating system releases are especially intriguing and fun—I hope this book shares that excitement in a way that gets your skin crawling with NT fever, too. Good luck, and happy computing!

Dick Cravens
Columbia, MO

CHAPTER 1

A BRIEF HISTORY OF WINDOWS NT

A very wise man once said, "You can't know where you're going if you don't know where you've been."

Before we dive into all the features, benefits, conveniences, and possibilities presented by Microsoft's Windows NT Workstation 4.0, let's take a little time to review the recent history of Windows computing. This chapter will bring you up to speed quickly on

- The general history of the Windows platform.

- What Windows NT is, and why it was developed.

- How Windows NT is different from other versions of Windows you may have used.

- The new features, benefits, and opportunities the capabilities of NT will give you.

If you're new to Windows or GUI computing, this is a great place to get "caught up" on the history of the Windows platform (this chapter certainly isn't intended as a totally comprehensive history of Windows computing, but it will provide a good general overview). If you're an old pro and want to get straight to work with the new stuff, feel free to leap ahead to Chapter 2.

If you're new to Windows or GUI computing, this is a great place to get "caught up" on the history of the Windows platform (this chapter certainly isn't intended as a totally comprehensive history of Windows computing, but it will provide a good general overview). If you're an old pro and want to get straight to work with the new stuff, feel free to leap ahead to Chapter 2.

Early Microsoft Windows: Basic Design, Benefits, and Limitations

The roots of Windows computing reach back to the origins of the PC and beyond. Xerox began research into the graphical user interface (GUI) late in the 1970s but was not successful in producing a commercial computing product from its efforts. The first company that bore commercial fruit based on the Xerox GUI research was Apple (with the ill-fated Lisa in 1982, and then more noticeably with the now-familiar Macintosh, first released in 1984). Apple produced these machines in an effort to differentiate its product line from the astoundingly successful IBM PC. The Intel-based PC (sporting the same traditional character-based terminal command line interface as the earlier Apple II) offered little real technological advantage over any of the Apple machines but had decades of IBM marketing clout behind it. Apple's response to the IBM threat polarized the PC market in ways that were unclear at the time but became crystalline in the years to follow.

Prior to the introduction of the IBM PC, a small Seattle company named Microsoft had already achieved limited success in publishing versions of the Basic language for a number of micro-computer designs. When approached by IBM with an offer to produce the first operating system for its PC, Microsoft responded with a variant of the then-prevalent CPM operating system, called MS-DOS (Microsoft Disk Operating System). The royalty stream from the IBM MS-DOS license fees funded additional Microsoft product development, most noticeably of a group of development language products and office productivity applications, all with character-based user interfaces.

When Apple approached Microsoft in late 1982 with requests for software for the forthcoming graphical Macintosh, it was not for a new operating system (Apple had its own team of crack engineers working on that, thank you) but for office productivity applications (word processors, spreadsheets) designed specifically for the new Apple GUI. Microsoft management immediately recognized the potential of the new graphical interface. Almost from that day forward, teams of Microsoft engineers worked to achieve the same GUI interface on the IBM PC platform, parallel with their success in producing applications for the Macintosh.

Their efforts have been continually thwarted by the memory and speed limitations of the Intel processors chosen by IBM for the first PCs (hopelessly anemic by today's standards, and hardly cutting edge at the time) and their own self-imposed limitations expressed in the MS-DOS operating system itself. Their salvation has been the continuing validity of Moore's Law, which states that processor power will double approximately every 18 months. Although Apple started with the technologically superior Motorola CPU (designed from the ground up for graphical computing), Microsoft and IBM lived through generations of Intel processors before realizing the promised horsepower of the modern 386, 486, and faster chips that have enabled Windows to achieve its present success.

Although Apple now maintains certain technological superiority in niche markets and continually nurtures a loyal installed base of customers, it has never recovered from the blow dealt by the combined competitive forces of the vast numbers of the PC market and the raw speed with which Intel has improved the CPU engine for the IBM-compatible PC. All of these trends have resulted in the virtual standardization of the Windows-Intel PC as the platform of choice for over 100 million personal computer users worldwide.

Great Ideas, with Great Room for Improvement

The earliest version of Windows to leave Microsoft was a pale imitation of the Macintosh interface, with no real applications beyond simple accessories such as a clock, a notepad, and a calculator. Users had to purchase special graphics-capable video display cards even to use it (the standard PC still came with a character-only display). Still, Windows 1.0 at least presented a graphical menu system for the IBM PC that was fairly tightly integrated with MS-DOS.

Advancement in hardware capabilities soon promised to give Windows more horsepower to work with. The advent of the Intel 80286 CPU formally erased the 640K memory bottleneck of the 8086 processor, but as Windows was really just a "shell" on top of MS-DOS, it didn't represent a drastic improvement in Windows performance (Windows couldn't work around the MS-DOS memory limitations due to design faults in the 80286 itself). There was no real ability to run more than one application at a time (called multitasking) in Windows 1.0, since MS-DOS 640K memory constraints prevented applications of any significant capability from running at the same time (early adopters remember many coffee breaks while waiting for the first Windows version of Adobe Pagemaker to load on their XT or AT). Graphics-capable video adapters soon became the norm, as the popularity of Lotus 1-2-3 grew and the demand for high-resolution displays grew with it. Color graphics capability soon followed as "clone" makers raced to produce new machines with features not yet found on True Blue IBM hardware.

So it wasn't until the introduction of the Intel 80386 that Microsoft had all the hardware goodies to make Windows dance and sing. The 386 CPU's advanced memory management capabilities opened many doors previously welded shut by the design and speed limitations of the older microprocessors. Microsoft engineers immediately proceeded to rewrite Windows for the new processor. Windows 3.0 was essentially new from the ground up, using many concepts developed in a joint operating system project with IBM (OS/2). The rest is one of the great product success stories of the century.

Windows 3.0

Windows 3.0, introduced in 1990, finally allowed the IBM PC and PC clones the ability to compete directly with the preeminent GUI computer, the Macintosh. Fueled by the ease of use promised by the new Windows and the fierce competition in the PC hardware market, the "Wintel" platform soon reached critical mass as relatively inexpensive graphical computing became a reality.

Windows 3.0 offered many improvements over previous attempts:

- A user-configurable Desktop and Program Manager (as shown in Figure 1-1)
- An enhanced File Manager (as shown in Figure 1-2)
- Greatly improved memory management (mostly due to the greater capabilities in the Intel 386 CPU) including virtual memory
- Fairly robust cooperative multitasking
- Multiple Virtual DOS Machines (allowing one Windows system to host many MS-DOS applications)
- A bundled suite of fairly useable productivity utilities (Write, Terminal, Paint, and other applets) allowing users to start using their graphical computing environment immediately

Microsoft followed the release of Windows 3.0 with new graphical versions of its major productivity applications. Microsoft Word and Excel transferred well from the Macintosh to the Windows PC and have dominated the market since. The previous champions (Lotus 1-2-3 and WordPerfect) were slow to produce Windows versions of their MS-DOS blockbusters and have never really recovered the market share lost in this critical transition period.

Figure 1-1.
Starting with Windows 3.0, Microsoft provided an integrated Desktop with the new Program Manager shell for organizing applications and other data.

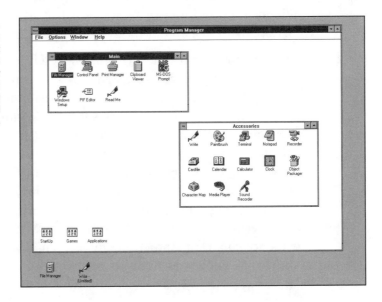

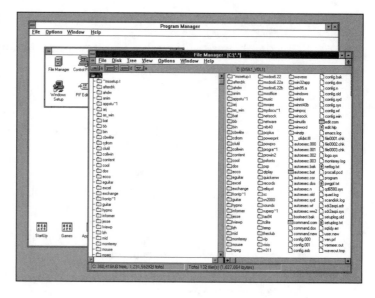

Figure 1-2
Combined with the Program Manager, the File Manager provided a powerful set of tools for customizing, configuring, and managing a Windows PC.

Advantages of the Windows GUI Interface

The sudden and enduring success of Windows 3.0, its children (Windows 3.1, Windows for Workgroups), and its relatives (Windows 95, Windows NT) is largely due to the improved interface introduced in version 3.0. Millions of users intimidated by the MS-DOS command line find the Windows interface to be extremely comfortable. The further refinements presented in Windows 95, and now in Windows NT Workstation 4.0, will only increase the popularity of the Windows platform.

The basic premise behind the Windows GUI (or others, for that matter) is that it's easier to recognize than it is to remember. MS-DOS or UNIX character-based terminal interfaces place most of the burden on the user in terms of understanding the available commands and services in the operating system; if you don't know what to do in the Windows GUI, on the other hand, you at least know where to find Help (and it's usually in the same place no matter what Windows application you're using, as shown in Figure 1-3). By taking another cue from the Macintosh and standardizing certain elements of the Windows interface, Microsoft has ensured that once you learn a procedure in one Windows program, it's likely you'll know how to do it in any other.

Microsoft didn't take away the MS-DOS command-line interface when it introduced Windows 3.0, it enhanced it. Recognizing that

Figure 1-3.
Microsoft established guidelines for the Common User Access (CUA) menu to help users know where to find common features in the widest possible variety of programs.

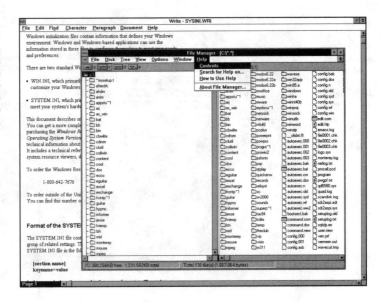

the two styles of computing are not mutually exclusive, Microsoft designed Windows 3.0 to present the strengths of both methods to the user by providing the ability to run MS-DOS sessions within the Windows 3.0 environment. The ability to manage multiple MS-DOS applications from within a GUI desktop has proved almost as attractive to many users as the GUI itself (see Figure 1-4). This "backward compatibility" with classic MS-DOS applications also ensured a smooth transition path to Windows for many MS-DOS users.

Increasing Productivity with Multitasking and Improved Memory Management

The single most revolutionary advance in Windows 3.0 after the GUI is the liberation of the PC from the restraints of single-application operation within the 640K MS-DOS memory model. The 80386 CPU implemented memory address schemes that allowed up to four gigabytes of RAM or other memory to be managed for computing tasks (as opposed to the 1MB limit of the 8086, with an effective 640K available to the operating system and applications). This meant that true Windows applications had access to virtually unlimited memory for their computing tasks. By additionally leveraging the 80386 CPU's ability to mimic or virtualize the 8086 processor in memory, Windows 3.0 gave users the tools to run as many virtual MS-DOS sessions as Windows memory allowed.

Figure 1-4.
Windows 3.0 and later versions took advantage of the new capabilities of the 386 processor to provide multitasking even for older MS-DOS applications.

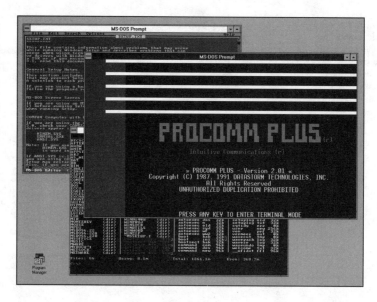

What Is Multitasking?

The earliest computer systems were designed for only one user at a time, performing only one application. When it became obvious that this was not the most cost-effective way to utilize extremely expensive computing equipment, engineers devised new operating systems that supported batch processing (for automation) and multiple terminals so that groups of users could time-share computing resources. Even though dozens of other users may have been using the mainframe at the same time, each individual user had fairly decent response at a terminal due to the technique of multitasking. In a multitasking system, processing time is shared among all jobs or applications. In a cooperative multitasking system (the kind used in Windows 3.x for Windows applications), all applications have essential the same rights to the processor, and it's generally up to the application to "let go" of the CPU when it's finished with it (this can lead to a sluggish performance or a hung system if the application doesn't play by the sharing rules or gets into trouble). In a preemptive multitasking OS (such as NT), the operating system controls which application gets the CPU, and for how long. Preemptive multitasking results in smoother, more reliable operation.

The effective result of all these new features was that users began to discover new and exciting ways to improve their productivity by combining the capabilities of different applications, in real time. Instead of running their spreadsheet, printing a table of figures, and then opening their word processor and reentering all the spreadsheet values into their document manually, users could keep both applications open and cut and paste between them. Beyond this, newer Windows applications offered DDE (Dynamic Data Exchange), which automated the exchange of information. Combining DDE with embedded macro or scripting languages in applications gave users previously unheard-of flexibility in customizing their Windows systems for almost any computing task. Suddenly Procomm Plus communications software could retrieve financial figures from an online service or other remote system and instantaneously send them to an Excel spreadsheet, which then automatically updated a Word report document and printed it for the boss's review over her first morning coffee.

Windows for Workgroups

As popular as Windows 3.0 proved to be, it hardly represented the culmination of Microsoft's plans for the Windows platform. User feedback revealed a number of problem areas in terms of overall stability and certain key product features. Most stability issues were addressed in a "maintenance" release, Windows 3.1. Other issues were addressed in what amounted to another incremental release (some dubbed it Windows 3.5) but was presented as a companion product: Windows for Workgroups 3.1.

Windows Meets the Network

Concurrent with the development of Windows, Microsoft and other companies had begun to address the need for shared resource and communications capabilities for groups of microcomputers in the form of the local area network (or LAN). Novell was the first vendor to produce a truly reliable network operating system (NOS), Novell Netware. Netware allowed desktop PC users to share applications, printers, file servers, modem pools, and other network resources, but it was fairly expensive to license and required very robust PCs for server duty.

Managing a Novell network was no small task, either; certification programs for network managers became de facto required, with minimal Certified Netware Engineer training costs in the thousands of dollars per person (the classic IS joke is that there's very good reason the Novell logo is blood red).

Microsoft attempted to compete with Novell directly with products such as Microsoft LAN Manager but met with extremely limited success. To counter the Novell dominance in this market, Microsoft once again followed Apple's marketing and technology lead by including networking capabilities with every copy of Windows for Workgroups (the Macintosh had network software and hardware in every machine). WFWG (affectionately known as "Woof-Woog" by computer geeks everywhere) included everything needed for file and printer sharing and simple messaging services right out of the box (except for the network card and cables, which you need no matter which network operating system you use).

Was this a Netware-killer? No, but this presented a 90 percent solution for most small businesses, just those folks that simply couldn't justify a Novell license and dedicated servers, much less the learning curve to administer a Netware LAN properly.

WFWG's Hidden Benefit: Greater Speed

Microsoft also began to sneak some new technology into WFWG that trickled out of the early development process that eventually led to NT and Windows 95. Although MS-DOS was a 16-bit operating system (and Windows had always been a 16-bit environment running above it), Microsoft found ways to allow certain parts of Windows to access the native 32-bit "protected mode" of the 386 CPU, allowing 32-bit device drivers and applications to be used alongside conventional 16-bit applications. The benefit? Faster access to drive subsystems and other input/output systems, resulting in dramatically enhanced Windows performance. The 32-bit file access and 32-bit drive access were reason enough for the upgrade from vanilla Windows 3.0 or 3.1 to WFWG 3.11 for many power users. Although Microsoft didn't exactly trumpet this development, the trade press made it clear that WFWG was the version of Windows to use for sheer performance, even if you didn't need any of its networking capabilities.

Easier Connectivity with Remote Access Services

The average user of WFWG probably never realized the low-level differences just mentioned, as they were not reflected in the top-level Windows interface. Other additional enhancements were more obvious. Remote Access Services (RAS) permitted a WFWG machine to connect to a Windows network over a serial connection as well as a direct network link. This allowed file sharing, printer sharing, and remote mail operation all over the phone line.

Windows Problems: Performance, Stability, Security

Despite the vast improvements Windows 3.x and WFWG represented over both previous Windows versions and MS-DOS, there was still great room for improvement. The customer concerns expressed after the release of Windows 3.x fell into three main areas:

- Memory management and multitasking performance
- General stability
- Workstation security

Memory and Multitasking Woes

Windows 3.0's memory management techniques, while breaking the 640K MS-DOS barrier, did suffer in performance due to the overhead required to perform the sleight of hand needed for the task. In essence, the HIMEM.SYS and EMM386.EXE memory managers slowed system performance considerably but were absolutely necessary due to the constraints of the MS-DOS memory address system legacy from 1981. In addition, Windows and Windows applications use "resource memory," a reserved memory area used to store Windows environment information. If this memory became full, Windows 3.x couldn't manage or allocate other available memory, no matter how much physical RAM the machine had!

A greater performance problem lay in the multitasking model used in Windows 3.x to allow backward compatibility with MS-DOS applications. Whereas true native Windows applications can be written from the ground up with CPU-sharing multitasking in mind, MS-DOS applications were not. Using single-tasking MS-DOS apps in the Windows environment required extensive overhead to keep the MS-DOS app from hogging all processor time (under MS-DOS, only one application typically uses the processor at a time, so this is the logical way for these apps to behave; the application has no means of knowing that it needs to yield to other applications so that they can have processor time).

Since MS-DOS apps are blind and power-hungry, Windows has to provide the multitasking logic for each MS-DOS app in use, as well as all Windows apps in use. To simplify the situation, Microsoft sacrificed some Windows application performance on the bet that Windows application developers would obey the rules and design their applications to yield the CPU on a regular basis (a bet they sometimes lost). This mix of "cooperative" multitasking for Windows apps and preemptive multitasking for MS-DOS apps resulted in downright sluggish performance under certain conditions and application combinations. The net effect of running an MS-DOS app under Windows 3.x is that each MS-DOS session gets as much processor time as all Windows and Windows applications combined.

Stability Worries: UAEs and GPFs

Another major issue with Windows 3.x and WFWG was error handling. In a multitasking system, if one application fails, it can affect the performance of all other running applications, as well as that of the operating system itself. Critics have compared the memory and multitasking structures of Windows 3.x architecture to an inverted house of cards, and not without reason. An errant Windows 3.x application can easily corrupt the memory used by other applications or even by MS-DOS itself; the resulting instability can bring down the entire Windows environment as well. The technical term first used to describe this type of error was "unrecoverable application error" (or UAE). The dreaded UAE message window would appear after a problem happened in Windows 3.0, and about the only recourse for the user was to reboot the machine, as Windows was predictably unstable after such a failure (users learned to save their files frequently).

This situation was improved somewhat in Windows 3.1 and WFWG with the introduction of the local reboot, which warned users with a big blue screen just prior to system failure and just maybe allowed them to close down the current application instead of the whole machine. Sometimes this worked, and sometimes it didn't (if you were too quick on the trigger or held down the Ctrl-Alt-Del keys a millisecond too long, all was lost). Other times you'd just get the "General Protection Fault" message dialog, which often could tell you which application had stomped around outside its own protected memory and what memory range had been nuked (a not-always-usable clue as to the victim application's identity). This was not always of use, and far less than always a comfort. The standard joke was that Microsoft simply renamed the UAE to the GPF. Although the remark was not technically true, the point was that Windows simply wasn't as robust as customers demanded.

Networking Exposure Equaled Security Risks

Another major area of customer concern was the lack of any real security for Windows systems, especially those on networks. This was a dual problem, in that the contents of the network (any servers, or other machines on the network) were wide open to whoever walked up to the Windows machine and booted it (WFWG uses password protection for network access, but it's simple to defeat); any single machine, although ostensibly secure from access from the network side, can be entered remotely using a variety of methods. To sum it up, if you can get physical access to a WFWG machine, you have access to all of its data, as well as the network it's on (if you're the least bit savvy about any of the Windows or network technology in use). This lack of security made Windows PCs literally unusable for many corporate, industrial, federal, and military customers, as secured data is absolutely required for much of the confidential work they do.

Window's Future: Major Progress

Microsoft's strategy in response to all these concerns has been twofold:

- Continue development of Windows 3.x to produce a more robust, better performing Windows for general use.
- Address the needs of corporate, industrial, and government users by developing a new version of Windows for "mission-critical" applications (those requiring substantial computing power, bulletproof stability, and near-absolute security) across a variety of hardware platforms.

This dual strategy has resulted in the development of two major products, Windows 95 and Windows NT (for New Technology). Some more specific goals for both these products included:

- Minimize or eliminate dependence upon MS-DOS as the primary operating system.
- Utilize the 32-bit capabilities of the 386 and later CPUs for better overall performance.
- Provide compatibility with a wider range of communication and networking technologies.
- Provide an enhanced user interface for substantially improved ease of use.
- Implement better interapplication communication and data sharing.
- Maintain backward compatibility with most Windows and MS-DOS "legacy" applications.
- Improve data storage systems, while maintaining backward compatibility.
- Work with the broadest variety of hardware, while minimizing configuration issues.

Microsoft's actual achievement of these goals has been incremental, but it has also been relatively swift and absolutely real. The result is the present state of Microsoft's operating system product line, centered on the double whammy of Windows 95 and Windows NT 4.0 (both Workstation and Server).

How exactly did Microsoft get here from Windows 3.x and WFWG 3.x?

Windows NT: Solutions and Opportunities

Microsoft foresaw the demand for a more professional version of Windows very shortly after real development of Windows 3.0 began and the architectural and performance compromises of that product's design became apparent. Microsoft also had an inside track on the future of the Intel CPU products; it didn't take a rocket scientist or a crystal ball to predict that the market would shortly demand more from Windows to match the capabilities of the 486 and 586 processors (the brand name "Pentium" was still cooking in Intel's marketing department at the time). In other words, Windows 3.0 was designed to meet the immediate needs of the market for a multitasking GUI interface for the PC, and Windows NT was designed for the future (remember, per Moore's Law, the future is usually only about 18 months away, in computing terms).

Microsoft staffed the NT development effort with personnel possessing years of experience in developing state-of-the-art operating systems for minicomputers and mainframes (for such companies as Digital Electronics Corporation). These experts brought with them the benefits of designing systems for enterprise-wide information services; coupled with the thorough expertise Microsoft already had in PC technology and the emerging horsepower of the Intel and other microcomputer CPUs, this combination was bound to produce a new operating system that promised to give the desktop PC capabilities to rival almost any current mainframe and all but the most recent supercomputers.

Microsoft Answers the Demand: Windows NT 3.1

The first version of NT released to the public was Windows NT 3.1 (named for the interface, which was essentially a mirror image of Windows 3.1's). This release was presented dually as Windows NT 3.1 and Windows NT 3.1 Advanced Server (also called NTAS for short). Although Microsoft did put substantial marketing forces into play for this release, it met with mixed success. NT 3.1 simply didn't offer the same general performance as the "consumer" version of Windows, on the same hardware. NT required almost double the RAM to support the same set of applications, due to its own considerable internal overhead for security and true preemptive multitasking. The price point was a bit higher for the desktop version and very pricey for the server. In essence, although the release didn't meet with any real success at retail and certainly didn't approach the popularity of Windows 3.1, it did establish a credibility toehold for Microsoft in the enterprise computing market.

NT 3.1 offered these improvement over Windows 3.1:

- True preemptive multitasking
- True 32-bit architecture
- Zero reliance upon MS-DOS
- The Windows NT File System (NTFS) with support for security and error correction
- C2-level security from both network and user console (with complete security-management applications)
- Support for OS/2 version 1.x applications
- An MS-DOS-style command prompt interface for Windows NT commands and batch operations, plus some MS-DOS, OS/2 1.x, and POSIX.1 commands and batch operations
- Greatly enhanced stability
- Compatibility with multiple processor platforms (DEC Alpha, MIPS R4000, Intel)
- Symmetrical MultiProcessing (SMP) support for systems with multiple CPUs
- Network support for IPX/SPX (Novell Netware), NetBEUI (Microsoft Network), and TCP/IP protocols (and other protocols by custom extension)
- OLE2 support for automation and information sharing between applications
- POSIX.1 support (for portable applications)

Windows NT Advanced Server: a Commitment to Enterprise Computing

Microsoft also released a version of NT 3.1 tuned for server tasks (file, printer, and application sharing). NT Advanced Server was basically a more beefy version of NT with less restrictions on scalability and connectivity. In addition to the features in NT 3.1, NTAS offered:

- Multitasking optimization for server and background tasks
- Support for 256 concurrent RAS connections (as opposed to 1)

- Unlimited client connections (as opposed to 10)
- Support for up to 32 SMP CPUs (as opposed to 2)
- Disk fault tolerance (RAID in software)

NT 3.5: the Breakthrough

As good as Windows NT 3.1 and NT Advanced Server were, they really didn't meet with much acceptance until the first real incremental release almost two years later. Windows NT 3.5 added considerable enhancements to 3.1's solid foundations:

- Much better performance relative to 3.1 on the same CPU and memory configuration
- Lower minimum memory requirements
- Better support for Netware
- Automatic recovery and restart options for troubleshooting
- Account lockout for multiple failed logon attempts
- High-performance TCP/IP protocol support

Concurrent support for TCP/IP, Novell, and Microsoft Network protocols via RAS connections

- Long filename support under both FAT and NTFS
- OpenGL support for 3-D graphics
- Greater reliability for 16-bit Windows applications via separate address space allocation
- Extended support for hardware and peripherals (especially graphics adapters)
- Improved compatibility with multimedia hardware and software (especially video)

NT 3.5's refinements brought many previously skeptical users into the fold. It certainly didn't hurt that the hardware ante had been upped in the interim between the NT 3.1 and 3.5 releases as well: most serious users now had 486 machines with a minimum of 16MB of RAM, and NT 3.5 fairly purred under that hood. If you had a Pentium with more than 16MB RAM, you were probably experiencing true bliss with the combination of stability, speed, and security on your desktop.

What more could the PC world want?

NT 3.51: Further Refinements

Well, for starts, NT users and NT network administrators wanted a few other tweaks to the "old" NT:

- Support for the PowerPC processor
- Lower memory requirements
- Better performance for 16-bit Windows applications, especially on RISC processors
- A fix for Pentium floating-point problems
- Support for PC Card (PCMCIA) peripherals
- Better online documentation
- A more configurable command-line interface
- Compression for NTFS drives
- Support for individual user profiles
- Support for uninterruptible power supplies (UPSs)

Microsoft delivered all of this with the NT 3.51 release in the summer of 1995, just weeks before the media-blitz computing-hype marketing-overkill-featuring-soundtrack-by-Rolling-Stones event of the 90s: the release of Windows 95, the successor to both Windows 3.11 and Windows for Workgroups for the consumer-level Windows public.

Windows 95: New Face, New Capabilities, Pretty Much the Same Old Underwear

About the same time one Microsoft team began work on NT, other minds in Redmond began brewing the next successor to Windows 3.x and WFWG. Originally titled Windows 4.0, this product was to sport a completely new interface, faster performance, improved multitasking, greater stability, 32-bit application support, a far easier installation (with automatic detection and configuration of most peripherals), and better networking. Microsoft succeeded beyond expectations on most counts.

As Windows 4.0 release slipped later and later into 1994, Microsoft's marketing troops fought the negativity in the trade press by renaming the product Windows 95 (shortened to Win95 by almost everyone who had to say its name more than twice a day). Finally, in August, Win95 rolled out, to more than moderate (but not truly overwhelming) success. Microsoft's rumored internal target for conversion of the installed base of existing Windows 3.x users to Win95 was 25 percent, which by all indications was achieved. Most new machines shipped with Windows 95, so most new growth in the PC market represented Win95 licenses. But that still left many, many millions of users that haven't made the jump from 16-bit to 32-bit Windows. Although the trade press has all but boycotted coverage of 16-bit Windows computing, a large conservative element still run their machines with Windows 3.x.

A Better Learning Curve and Faster Adoption through Better Design

Even if Win95 didn't win all previous Windows users as converts, it did point the way towards the future of Windows very, very clearly. The new Win95 interface (as shown in Figure 1-5) eliminates some of the user confusion regarding the distinction between Program Manager and File Manager, and it is more clear regarding the status of running applications. Microsoft has quoted many studies that indicate users can learn Win95 more quickly than Windows 3.x.

The biggest technological step forward in Win95 is the 32-bit architecture, which provides enhanced preemptive multitasking, better overall performance potential, and better theoretical stability. Win95 is more stable and a better performer than Windows 3.x in some areas but not as bulletproof and rocket-fast as Microsoft might have you believe from its advertising. Many compromises were made in the 32-bit design of Win95 to accommodate the need for backward compatibility with older 16-bit Windows MS-DOS applications, all of which make their own hit on speed and stability. If you run all new 32-bit applications under Win95, odds are you'll really see the performance difference. If you're running mostly 16-bit applications written for Windows 3.x, it's quite possible that Windows for Workgroups will outperform

Win95 on the same machine (a lot depends on the specific machine and the exact mix of applications). Another way to say it is: if you want Win95 to run as well as WFWG, try adding 50 percent more RAM. Still, Win95 doesn't require the same RAM as NT.

Figure 1-5.
Windows 95's new interface combines the best of Program Manager and File Manager into one harmonious whole.

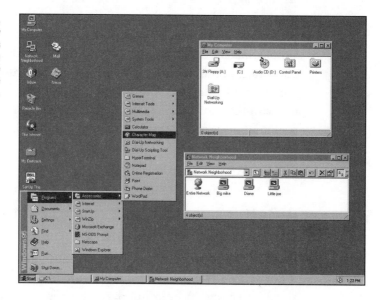

Welcome to the Future: Windows NT Workstation 4.0

So what this all means is that, even though Microsoft has a brave new operating system with a great new interface for the masses (Windows 95) and a very stable operating system with a familiar face for professionals, it doesn't have one perfect solution for everyone. To summarize, Windows 95 has these main problems:

- It compromises performance for legacy 16-bit Windows and MS-DOS support.
- It runs only on Intel CPUs.
- It still isn't very stable or secure compare to NT.
- It really needs more memory than Windows 3.x.

Windows NT 3.51, by contrast, has these main problems:

- It really needs more memory than either Windows 3.x or Win95.
- It doesn't have the Windows 95 interface.

So you have to ask yourself: if you were Microsoft, what would you do?

Windows 95, Windows NT 4.0, and Microsoft's Strategy for the Future

Microsoft has made it clear that it intends to keep on producing two complementary operating systems for the foreseeable future. It acknowledges publicly the desire for a single operating system but is adamant that while the company knows how to build it, the installed base of computers really doesn't have the hardware to support it (bear in mind that no one really expected MS-DOS to hang in there this long, but millions of PC users still work on XT- or AT-level machines running character-based applications). Microsoft will continue to attempt to blanket the market with solutions for all parts of the spectrum, while quietly pushing the envelope toward the higher performance expected from the newer hardware.

Windows 95 is positioned as the operating system that protects your investment in hardware and software. Windows NT is presented as the operating system for the future, more than ready to use the new horsepower in the most current machines. The largest single complaint Microsoft has faced regarding NT since the release of Windows 95 is that companies using both have to train users to use both, and they have to learn how to maintain both. The solution, of course, is to produce a version of NT with the Win95 interface: Windows NT 4.0, Workstation and Server. After many months of preparation, anticipation, and testing, that product is now here.

Both Windows 95 and Windows NT 4.0 deliver ease of use, power, and simple connectivity. Both use the same 32-bit Windows applications. Whereas Windows 95 is targeted for laptops and entry-level machines with lower RAM capability, Windows NT 4.0 is aimed at the enterprise where hardware resources are essentially allocated as needed to accomplish the task at hand.

Never before in the history of desktop personal computing have users been faced with such excellent choices. In the rest of this book, we'll look at what you can do with the premier member of the new Microsoft operating system family.

CHAPTER 2

WELCOME TO WINDOWS NT 4.0 WORKSTATION

Now that we've covered the history of Windows computing and the origins of Windows NT, let's look a bit closer at Windows NT Workstation and take a brief introductory overview of specific new features in the NT 4.0 Workstation.

This chapter covers:

- Windows NT Workstation and how it differs from NT Server

- Major changes and improvements in Windows NT 4.0 Workstation

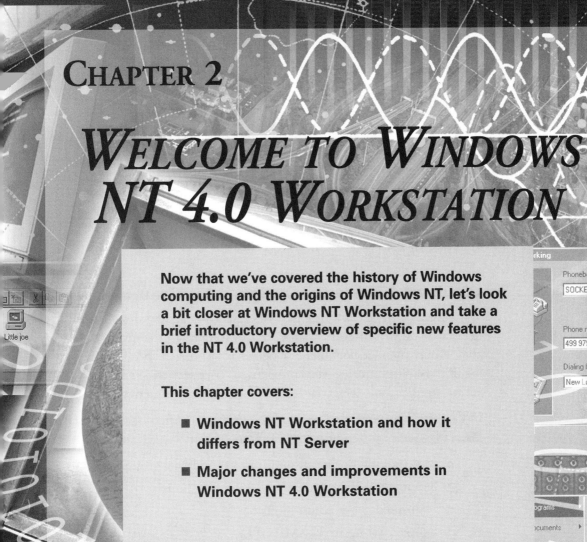

Why Windows NT Workstation?

In Chapter 1, we covered the general history of Windows computing and the basic market needs that drove the development of Windows NT. Just as there were distinctions between a set of user needs for consumer-level Windows and the demands for an enterprise-computing-strength Windows NT, there are different needs driving the dual, complementary products of NT Workstation and NT Server. Although this book concentrates on NT Workstation, it's vital that you understand these differences so that you may better evaluate which serves your individual needs best.

Windows NT Server: Designed for Groups

Windows NT Server is a true network operating system designed to provide network resources and services to users in the most reliable, robust manner possible. NT Server is optimized specifically for this task, and it offers the connectivity, user services, and administrative tools to service a distributed computer network.

In Chapter 1, we outlined some of the primary distinctions that make NT Server different from NT Workstation:

- Multitasking optimization for server and background tasks
- Support for 256 concurrent RAS connections
- Unlimited client connections
- Support for up to 32 SMP CPUs
- Disk fault tolerance (RAID in software)

In addition, Microsoft has minimized support for certain features of NT that really won't be used much on the server (for example, the Win16 subsystem that supports older Windows 3.x applications isn't loaded automatically). NT Server's disk and memory caching are optimized for larger data sets. NT Server also has higher default priorities for remote users, and it includes spooling task threads.

Windows NT Server is designed to host Microsoft BackOffice applications such as Exchange Server and SQL Server, in addition to acting as a gateway to other network and messaging systems (many NT Servers are hosts for SMTP gateways for Microsoft Mail/Internet Mail communications). NT Server also makes an excellent platform for Internet/intranet services; Netscape and most other Internet server technology providers offer Web server versions for NT. Microsoft even includes its own Web server design, the Internet Information Server (IIS), with every copy of NT Server and Workstation.

Windows NT Workstation: Tailored to the Single User

Although it's certainly possible to use NT Server as a desktop operating system, it's something like driving a Greyhound bus three blocks to work; there are simply better-optimized solutions. NT Workstation is that solution for the PC desktop, designed for the interactive, multitasking environment of today's business applications. NT Workstation brings the power and performance of high-end UNIX engineering workstation systems to the user for thousands of dollars less in hardware (and gives the user more choice in hardware platforms: Intel, PowerPC, MIPS R4000, and DEC Alpha versions of NT Workstation are all shipping today).

NT Workstation 4.0 offers the highest level of security and protection for sensitive data on the desktop. NT's stability prevents users from having to reboot their desktop systems when applications

What Is Microsoft BackOffice?

BackOffice is a family of client/server applications and services designed to work in a tightly integrated manner with Windows NT Server. The Microsoft Exchange Server, the SQL Server, the SNA Server, and the Systems Management Server are some of the early BackOffice products available for this platform. For more information, visit the Microsoft Web site at

```
http:// www.microsoft.com/TechNet/bkoffice.htm
```

or

```
http://www.microsoft.com/TechNet/boes/bo/bosi/te
chnote/bf103.htm
```

for detailed information.

fail, resulting in less data loss, as well as less loss of productivity and revenue when system resets eat critical work hours. The slight additional expense for NT's hardware overhead is minor compared with the clear practical advantages of a more stable desktop computing platform.

What's New in Windows NT 4.0 Workstation?

Now we come to the really fun part: looking at all the new goodies that are in the newest release of NT Workstation. We'll cover the basic changes here, and we'll tell you where to find additional information later in this book as well.

The Windows 95 Interface: a New Look for NT Workstation

Microsoft has received quite a bit of feedback from the Windows 95 release, and a lot of it wasn't criticism but demands that the same interface be made available for NT as well. Corporate and institutional users simply don't want to train users on two GUIs. Although Microsoft always had plans to migrate NT to the new design, the transition was definitely accelerated due to user demand. The first version of this new "shell" was presented in the form of an unsupported update for NT 3.51 that was available on the Microsoft FTP server (ftp.microsoft.com) as a free download. This update worked so well that many NT users adopted it imme- diately for their everyday work, even though most underlying interface elements (Control Panels, other system dialogs) hadn't been updated. Now we have the new interface in a more complete form, and it's as close a match as you can expect to its sister product, Windows 95 (see Figure 2-1). The NT Workstation 4.0 interface even makes some minor improvements to the Win95 Desktop, providing a glimpse of the next iteration of Win95.

Figure 2-1.
The new Windows NT Workstation interface builds on the strengths of the Windows 95 Desktop by adding NT-specific details.

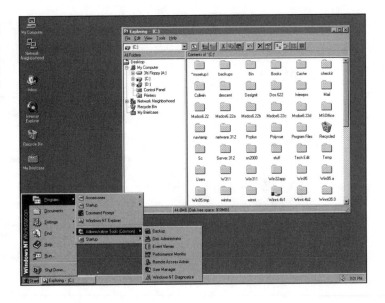

For more detailed information on the Windows NT Workstation user interface, see Chapter 3.

NT 4.0's Improved Security Management

Windows NT is designed from the ground up for secure operation, both from the user console and via any other means of access to the system. In addition to the Level C2 security that NT users have enjoyed from version 3.1, version 4.0 brings additional administrative tools for user management. Figure 2-2 illustrates one way that the revised NT interface makes security management simpler for drive-level sharing.

You can find a great deal of additional information on NT Workstation security features and procedures in Appendix B.

New Configuration Tools

NT 4.0 benefits from the move to the Win95 interface beneath the hood as well as at the Desktop. Figure 2-3 shows the new Control Panel design that combines most of the system configuration in one handy location.

Figure 2-2.
A simple right-mouse click on drive C: leads to the Sharing Properties management tools for that drive.

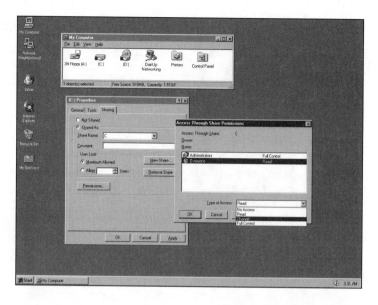

Figure 2-3.
NT 4.0's Control Panel contains most of the configuration utilities you'll need for daily use.

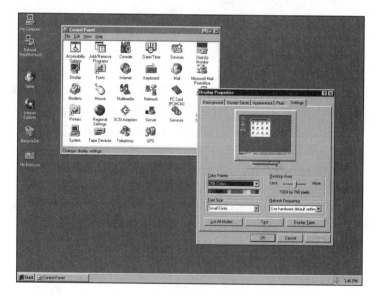

NT 4.0 also supports both User and Hardware Profiles. User Profiles allow multiple users to have completely different Desktops and other configuration options linked to their own unique NT logon information. Figure 2-4 shows the Properties sheet for User Profiles management.

What Is C2 Security?

The advent of computing and network communications technology has caused much revision to the business, government, and industrial communities' thought processes regarding security issues. Prior to the implementation of data processing, you usually had to steal an *object* to perform a theft (and the theft was obvious due to the absence of that object). Since computer systems and information management have become a modern reality, it's now obvious that it's quite possible to steal *time* on a computer system as well as *data* without the loss of either being noticed, unless you're watching your computer and information resources very closely. Since time and data now have clear and great value as resources, this has become a major concern in all areas of computing.

The government has provided some very clear guidelines and definitions for the policies, procedures, and standards that apply to computing done within its own structures and by vendors wanting to provide goods or services to the government. Developed initially for the Department of Defense, the *Trusted Computer Standards Evaluation Criteria* (or "Orange Book") is the last word for anyone working under, or with, these systems. This set of security standards describes multiple levels of security for hardware, software, and information. Each level defines types of physical security, user authentication, operating system security guidelines, and user application design, in addition to setting limits on what other types of systems may connect to the secured system.

Level C2 security defines a controlled-access environment in which not only is physical, user, OS, application, and communications security maintained, but administrator access is tracked, logged, and audited. In a C2 system, no one person may alter the system without leaving a trail for others to follow.

Is C2 the most secure type of system? No. The Orange Book describes levels that deliver much higher security, but C2 is the level most suitable for most of the tasks required by everyday users. For example, higher Orange Book Levels (B1 through A) require additional physical procedures, such as labeling every object in the computer system, including all removable media down to the last floppy, that have no real productive or security merit in most work environments.

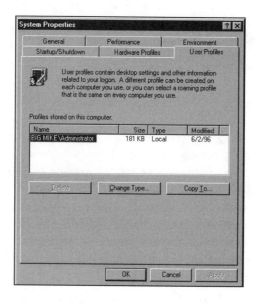

Figure 2-4.
User Profiles are
easily managed via
the System Properties
dialog accessed from
the My Computer
right-mouse menu.

Another excellent addition is Hardware Profile support, as shown
in Figure 2-5, also available from the My Computer Properties
dialog. You can create multiple configurations that enable or
disable certain hardware for particular operating conditions; you
then select the profile at system startup.

Windows NT 4.0 also adopts the "Wizard" approach to assisting
users with new configurations (as shown in Figures 2-6 and 2-7).

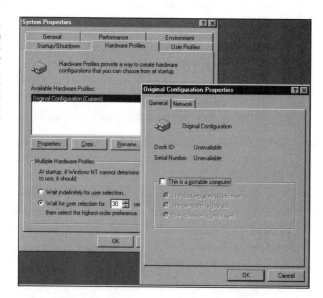

Figure 2-5.
Hardware Profiles
support lets you fine-
tune your computer
hardware configuration
depending upon the
location you're
operating from
(a great boon for
laptop users).

By answering a few simple questions, you'll be guided through most new configuration processes fairly painlessly.

We'll cover each of these individual configuration areas in greater detail later in the book.

Figure 2-6.
The New PhoneBook Entry Wizard makes setting up a new dial-up networking connection quick and easy.

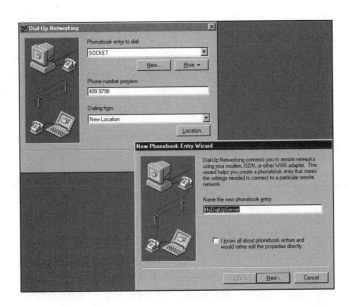

Figure 2-7.
The Add Printer Wizard makes connecting to even a network printer a breeze.

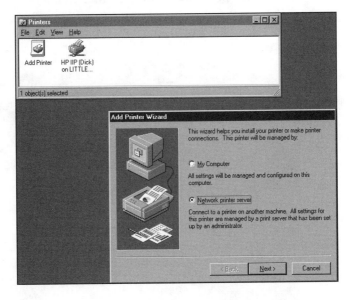

Enhanced Networking and Communications

Microsoft has continually improved its networking and communications features with each release of Windows. Here's a brief overview of what's new and improved in Windows NT 4.0 Workstation.

A Better Networking Interface

Windows NT 4.0 builds upon version 3.51's excellent support for networking and communications by consolidating the configuration for each area in a more consistent manner, again following the overall design of Windows 95's Dial-Up Networking and Network Control Panel configuration systems. Figure 2-8 shows the new design of the Network Properties dialogs.

See Chapter 4 for more information on specific procedures to get your installation of NT Workstation working on your network.

HyperTerminal

Windows NT 4.0 also gains the HyperTerminal application from Windows 95. HyperTerminal offers simple terminal emulation and file transfer features that will cover most users' needs in connecting to bulletin-board systems and other character-based asynchronous serial communications sessions (see Figure 2-9).

Figure 2-8.
NT 4.0 visually integrates network configuration dialogs using the Windows 95 Properties interface to excellent advantage.

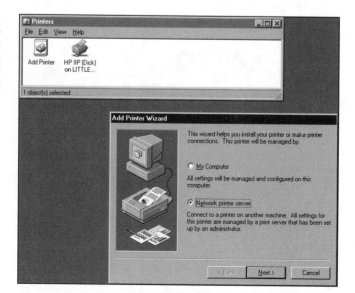

Figure 2-9.
The HyperTerminal
communications
program, while less
than impressive,
supports basic ANSI
and VT terminal
emulations, as well
as most popular file
transfer protocols.

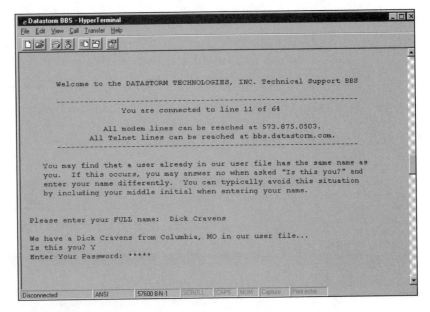

Remote Access Services

Remote Access Services have undergone a bit of a face-lift in NT 4.0 and are now referred to as Dial-Up Networking, another move to make 4.0 "Win95ish" (see Figure 2-10). Incoming call support (RAS Server) is still configured via the Remote Access Admin interface, but outgoing calls are made using the Dial-Up Networking icon in the My Computer folder. There's also a Dial-Up Monitor that runs in

Figure 2-10.
Windows NT 4.0
offers separate
interfaces for RAS
management, one for
outgoing calls and
one for incoming.

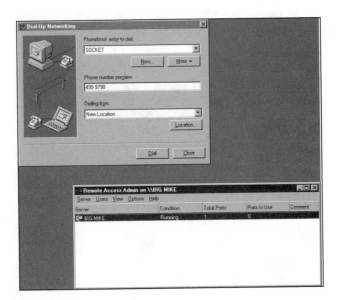

Messaging and Internet Communications

Perhaps the biggest change in NT communications in version 4.0 is the addition of Microsoft Exchange and Internet Explorer (as shown in Figures 2-11 and 2-12 respectively).

Exchange is the client half of a new messaging platform designed to run on NT Server. The Exchange client offers fax, Microsoft Mail,

Figure 2-11.
Microsoft Exchange comes with NT 4.0 and provides Microsoft Mail, fax, and Internet Mail services in one user interface.

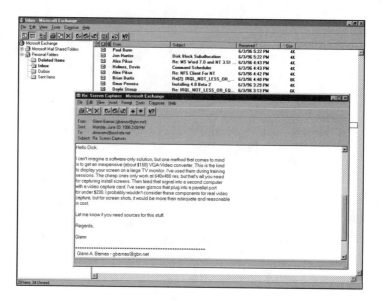

Figure 2-12.
Internet Explorer is an excellent Web browser that is well-integrated with the Windows NT operating system.

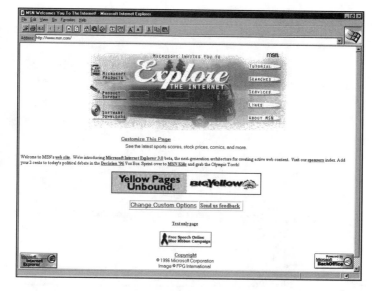

and Internet Mail services out of the box, and it can be extended to support almost any type of messaging or document type. Internet Explorer is Microsoft's answer to other World Wide Web browsers; it offers the same basic set of functions as Netscape and other such software but has additional enhancements that are the result of tight integration with the Windows NT Desktop and file system. For more information on Exchange and Internet Explorer, see Chapter 6.

Improved Bundled Applications

Microsoft has always provided enough basic productivity applications with Windows to make your computer useable for simple tasks immediately. This release is consistent in that respect; be ready for some pleasant surprises in regard to the quality of some of the bundled applications.

Windows Explorer

It's critical that every computer user have a good file management utility. In Windows NT 4.0, Microsoft has migrated the Windows 95 Explorer application, here known as Windows NT Explorer (as shown in Figure 2-13).

For more information on using Windows NT Explorer, see Chapter 3.

Figure 2-13.
NT inherits the Win95 Explorer application for file management. You can open multiple Explorer windows, browse the network, and even customize the Explorer interface to suit your personal work habits.

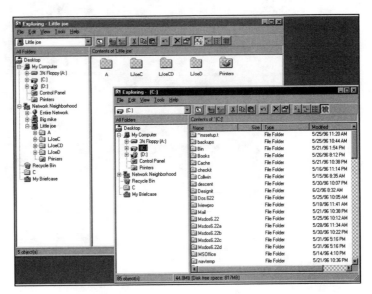

Paint

Windows NT 4.0 has also benefited from the much-improved version of the original Windows Paintbrush, now simply called Paint in Win95 and NT 4.0. Paint offers conspicuously better editing tools and is very much faster than its 16-bit ancestor. Figure 2-14 illustrates Paint's new interface and toolset.

For more information on using Windows NT Paint, see Chapter 3.

WordPad

Microsoft has also replaced the venerable Write word-processing program with a new application called WordPad (as opposed to NotePad, the simple text editor). WordPad (shown in Figure 2-15) has essentially the same feature set as the original Word for Windows 1.0, which makes it pretty darned useable for basic word-processing tasks. WordPad reads and writes .DOC, .TXT, and .RTF file formats in addition to the .WRI files used by its predecessor.

For more information on using Windows NT WordPad, see Chapter 3.

Figure 2-14.
Windows NT 4.0
Paint is downright
awesome, dude.

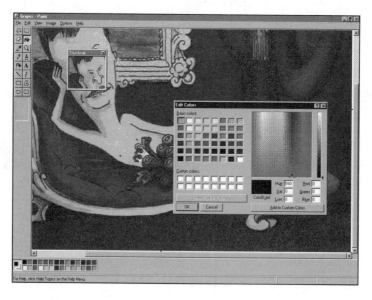

Figure 2-15.
WordPad provides
everything you need
for basic word-
processing tasks, and
it supports most of
the major Windows
document formats.

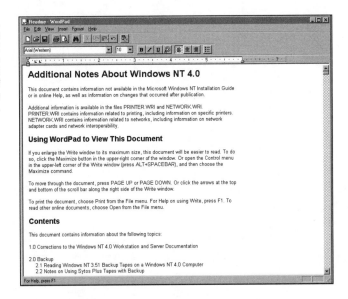

Onward

That's a brief overview of the new features and capabilities in Windows NT 4.0 Workstation. In the next chapters, we'll go into much greater detail on how to use NT 4.0 so that you can realize its benefits quickly. Here's to a great NT voyage!

CHAPTER 3

INTRODUCING THE NT 4.0 DESKTOP

Now that you have a basic understanding of the evolution of Windows computing and the place Windows NT Workstation holds in it, we can look at the largest new part of Windows NT Workstation 4.0: the Windows NT Desktop, and all of its new features and tools. We'll also look at the most basic procedures for using Windows NT, to get you off to a true running start.

In this chapter, we'll look at how to

- **Start Windows NT Workstation**

- **Log on to Windows NT, log out, and shut down your workstation safely**

- **Use the NT Help system**

- **Manage files and folders and how to create Shortcuts**

- **Print with Windows NT Workstation**

We cover all of the basics of operating and configuring the new Windows NT Workstation Desktop allowing you to quickly master and customize it to fit your needs.

Starting and Stopping Windows NT

Running Windows NT Workstation is really as simple as turning on your computer. Once NT is installed, it handles the complete boot process from start to finish (other than those parts handled exclusively by the system hardware).

It's OK not to know every phrase or acronym we use in this book (no one human can know them all, which is why people write and buy computer books). Don't forget there's a handy glossary of Windows NT and other general computing terms in Appendix F.

The Windows NT Boot-Up Process

What steps does NT go through in starting up your machine? If you're used to MS-DOS and earlier versions of Windows 3.*x*, you will notice some differences almost immediately. The biggest is: *there is no MS-DOS.* NT controls the machine from the outset.

When you start an Intel PC with Windows NT installed, you'll see the following:

1. The hardware Power On Self Test (POST) messages, displaying information about the display adapter, mother-board BIOS version, and primary peripheral device profiles (COM and LPT ports, hard drives, floppy drives, and so on). At this point there's usually a message on screen about what key to press to enter the hardware setup utility, or to make CMOS settings.

2. Next, NT will load the OS Loader. This boot-management module allows you to select from the choices of loading NT in the current video mode, NT in VGA mode, or from your last version of NT (or 16-bit Windows, if it was installed).

3. NT will check your hardware with a program called NTDETECT and then load the NT operating system kernel (indicated by the famous NT blue boot screen displaying what version of NT you're running and how

many processors your machine has). A period-character "gas gauge" shows you the status of the NT kernel loading process. This step may take more than a few seconds depending upon your machine's speed.

4. At this point, the NT Desktop background appears (by default in Microsoft turquoise blue-green) with the Microsoft Windows NT Workstation logo bitmap in the center of the screen. Immediately following this, NT will display the Begin Logon dialog. Press the Ctrl, Alt, and Delete keys simultaneously to bring up the Logon Information dialog, which you will use to actually log on to your NT system.

NOTE: See Appendix A, "Installing Windows NT 4.0," for additional information on how NT Workstation is installed.

Logging On to Windows NT

Depending upon how your system was installed, the Logon Information dialog may show your own user name or "Administrator" as the default in the User Name field. If you're the administrator, you should know your own password. If you're not the administrator (and someone set the machine up for you), you should have been provided with your correct user name and password. It's vital that you have this information before you proceed, as NT simply won't let you use the machine without the proper authentication.

Once you've logged on, Windows NT will display the Desktop as shown in Figure 3-1.

NOTE: See Appendix B, "Managing NT Security," for more information about system logon and user authentication.

Figure 3-1.
The Windows NT
Workstation Desktop
in all its glory

Shutting Down: a Brief Introduction to Windows NT Security Basics

One of the Microsoft's primary goals in designing NT Workstation was to provide you with a more secure desktop operating system. Therefore it's critical that we cover the most absolutely basic security features before we proceed with any other discussion of your new system. As you've already seen, security is built in from system boot on up, and this is just as true when you shut down or log off your NT Workstation. You have several choices as to how much of NT to shut down or secure. Before we try out any of the new Desktop features, we'll cover the major procedures in this section.

Logging Off

To shut down all applications and log off NT Workstation (but leave the computer running):

1. Enter [Ctrl]+[Alt]+[Del] at the keyboard, just as you did when you first logged on. This will cause Windows NT to display the Windows NT Security dialog.

2. Click on the Logoff button. Windows NT will display a dialog warning you that proceeding will end your NT session.

3. Click on the OK button. Windows NT will close all applications and return to the same state you saw immediately following system bootup (the Begin Logon dialog will be displayed over the Microsoft Windows NT Workstation 4.0 screen).

You can repeat the logon procedure we described earlier to reenter Windows NT at this point. For more information about the Windows NT Security dialog, see Appendix B.

Why Not Just Use the Power Switch?

Modern operating systems are complex, and Windows NT is certainly no exception. At any given time, the operating system alone may have dozens of files open, a full disk cache, several live network connections, and various application data files all in memory. Shutting off the power to such an intricate and dynamic system is literally the same as sweeping the contents of your real desktop to the floor or trash can when you leave work each evening (sure, it'll all be there somewhere, but putting it back together may be quite the undertaking). Do yourself and your data a favor: use the Windows NT Shutdown feature before you turn off your computer power.

Turning off the power to your computer without using Shutdown is like turning off your car engine while you're on the interstate. Sure the car will stop somehow, but isn't it better first to get off the freeway while there's still power to the brakes, steering, and turn signals, and while you've got some engine power to make it up the exit ramp?<None>

Shutting Down Windows NT

Logging off is just one of the options you have when you leave your machine. Windows NT allows you to

- Leave your machine secured but running (allowing background operations to continue)
- Leave your machine secured but running and ready for another user (saving them rebooting)
- Shut the machine down totally

You can access all of these options from two main locations, but not all of them from each (that will make more sense in a moment). You saw the first location (the Windows NT Security dialog) in the previous example. The other main area is the Shutdown option under the Start menu. To use it, follow these steps:

1. Click once on the Start menu button at the lower-left of the Desktop, at the left of the Taskbar. Windows will display the Start menu as shown in Figure 3-2.

Figure 3-02.
Click once on the Start button to see the menu.

1. Move your mouse cursor over the Shutdown entry and click once. Windows NT will display the Shut Down Windows dialog, giving you three main choices:
   - Shut down the computer
   - Restart the computer
   - Close all programs and log on as a different user

2. Choose the first item, and click on Yes to continue. Windows NT will display a dialog saying that it is saving all system data, which will be followed by the Shutdown Computer dialog, which says "It is now safe to turn off your computer."

3. From here you can hit the power switch or click on the Restart button to reboot the PC.

Changing Users without Rebooting

You can also use the Shutdown feature to shift from one user to another without rebooting the PC. If you choose the third option in the Shut Down Windows dialog just described, NT Workstation will close all running programs and put the system back in the awaiting-logon state as if you had just booted from a cold start. The advantage is that this lets another user get into the system very quickly (even on a very fast machine, NT can take over a minute to boot).

> **NOTE:** See Appendix B, "Managing NT Security" for more information about system logoff, user authentication, and support for multiple users.

Securing Your System While It's Running

Here's where we learn how to secure your NT Workstation while you leave everything on it running. To lock NT Workstation:

1. Enter Ctrl+Alt+Del at the keyboard, just as you did when you first logged on. This will cause Windows NT to display the Windows NT Security dialog. NOTE: Windows NT will *not* warn you before enacting the next step—it will perform it immediately.

> **CAUTION:** *Only* administrators or those with administrator status should lock a Windows NT Workstation. Don't lock a Windows NT system unless you know how to unlock it or are acting on the instructions of someone who does. If you can't unlock the system, the only way to reenter it is to reset it from the hardware level, which can result in data loss since the system is not shut down before NT locks it (a locked NT Workstation is still operational except for the user console; other users may be connected to it and be exchanging data, or you or others may have applications, servers, or services running on the system).

2. Click on the Lock Workstation button. NT will display the Workstation Locked dialog, which states:

   • This workstation is in use and has been locked.

   • The workstation can only be unlocked by [Domain/Administrator] or an administrator.

   • Press Ctrl+Alt+Del to unlock this workstation.

Your system is now locked and secured, and only an administrator-level user may open it.

3. Windows NT will leave all applications and connections running while it's in a locked state. To return to the running system, repeat the logon procedure we described earlier to reenter Windows NT.

For more information about the Windows NT Security dialog, see Appendix B.

Windows NT Workstation 4.0's New Face: Desktop Basics

Windows NT is primarily a graphical user environment. To use Windows NT Workstation to its fullest potential, you'll need a thorough understanding of the components of the basic interface elements used throughout the operating system. Figure 3-3 shows a typical Windows NT Workstation 4.0 Desktop with two applications in use. Let's use this example to look at the controls, menus, and tools available there.

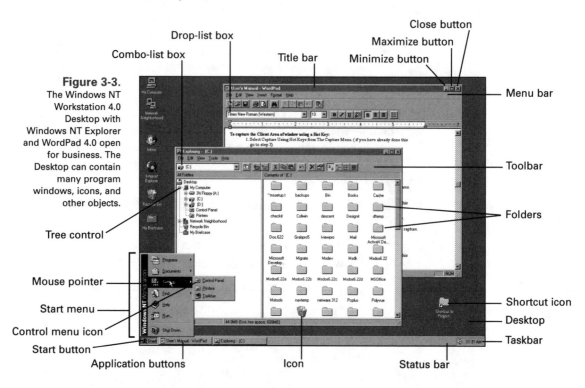

Figure 3-3.
The Windows NT Workstation 4.0 Desktop with Windows NT Explorer and WordPad 4.0 open for business. The Desktop can contain many program windows, icons, and other objects.

Now let's take a little closer look at each of the items in the Windows NT 4.0 interface. If you're thoroughly familiar with Windows 95, you may want to skip ahead quite a bit, as Microsoft has stayed very nearly completely true to its promise to make Windows NT 4.0 a twin of Win95.

Primary Windows Interface Components

Each of the objects itemized in Figure 3-3 is either part of the Windows NT Workstation Desktop or part of the standard application window interface design used in NT 4.0. First let's take a look at the function of each of the Windows NT Desktop parts:

- **Mouse pointer:** This is the cursor used to indicate what object will be activated or selected when you double-click or single-click with the left mouse button (you can also use the right mouse button in Windows NT; more on that later).

- **Start button:** When you move the mouse pointer over the Start button and click on it with the left mouse button, Windows will display the Start menu (described next).

- **Start menu:** This is the main hierarchical menu (essentially replacing Program Manager groups, if you're familiar with that program from earlier versions of Windows). You can find just about every control for Windows NT from this menu. This type of menu is also called a *cascading* menu.

- **Taskbar:** This is the main display area for the Start button (and buttons or other controls for most running applications and utilities).

- **Icons:** Used to represent data, programs, or other system components. Icons have a slightly different meaning and power in Windows 95 and NT than in previous versions of Windows, so treat them gently (don't move any unnecessarily) until you're sure how they work (more on that later, too).

- **Desktop:** This is the area where you begin and finish your Windows NT sessions, and where all application and other windows are displayed. The Desktop is a highly configurable workspace that you can use to store icons, run programs, and display graphics (in earlier versions of Windows, the functions of the Desktop were split between

Program Manager, File Manager, and a less-capable version of the Desktop).

- **System tray:** The area to the far right of the Taskbar is used for the Clock display, the system audio Volume Control, the Dial-Up Networking Monitor, and other status and information tools.

- **Application buttons:** These are used to switch between applications, change how an application is displayed, or close a program.

- **Folders:** The basic container for program files or other data (equivalent to an MS-DOS directory), under Windows NT, folders may be arranged hierarchically and nested, just as directories may in MS-DOS, and folders may reside on the Desktop if the user desires.

- **Shortcuts:** Icons that represent or point to an object, yet behave like that object when you act upon them, these "aliases" allow you to visually organize your Desktop and menus without altering the data structure of your system or duplicating data across that system.

- **Foreground application:** The only program that currently has the system console "focus" (active keyboard input) as opposed to background applications, the foreground application usually also enjoys priority over other programs for processor resources.

- **Background application(s):** One or more programs that, while still running, are not currently accepting input from the keyboard or mouse, background programs usually have lower priority than foreground programs.

Common Application Interface Components

Now let's look at the items that are part of the standard Windows NT 4.0 application window interface:

- **Title bar:** Use this area of the program window to move the window. It also displays the program title, and the name of the current document or contents in the program if appropriate. The Title bar also houses other interface tools (described next).

- **Control Menu icon:** This icon is used to access the application window Control menu for resizing, moving, or closing the application.

- **Minimize button:** Clicking on this shrinks the current window into an application button on the Taskbar.

- **Maximize button:** Clicking on this button while a window is less than full screen makes it full screen. Clicking on it when the program is full screen restores the window to its previous size.

- **Close button:** Clicking on this button shuts the application down completely.

- **Menu bar:** This area contains the Common User Access (CUA) menu, which can be used via the mouse or keyboard. Underlined characters in the menu denote "hotkeys" that are to be used with the [a] key to provide keyboard shortcuts for those preferring not to use the mouse.

- **Tool bar:** This area sports mostly icons but can also offer combo and list boxes. Most of the tools here duplicate other menu items, but they are faster to use, or most frequently used.

- **Tree control:** This type of display allows you to review and manipulate hierarchical storage structures (such as the contents of your hard drive or network server) with the mouse or keyboard cursor controls. You'll see this control in more Windows applications and dialogs in the future as it offers a very flexible means of navigating complex information structures.

- **Drop-list box:** This is another type of control that you'll see in most Windows applications. A list box allows you to choose from a set of items but doesn't take up a ton of space (click on the arrow at the right to display the contents). Some list boxes allow you to enter input directly as well.

- **Combo-list box:** This variation on the drop-list box adds the ability to navigate using other control types, such as a tree control. You'll see this type of control in many dialogs used for file management in Windows NT 4.0.

- **Status bar:** This area at the bottom of an application window is used to display different messages about menus or other aspects of program operation.

Other Common Interface Components

We won't bore you with the full gamut of different interface goodies in Windows NT 4.0, but there are a few more that you are guaranteed to encounter and certain to need. Figure 3-4 shows a very common component, the right mouse button context menu, with the Properties item for that object selected.

Figure 3-4.
Right-click on almost any object in Windows NT 4.0 and you'll get the context menu for that item. As the name implies, the menu will change according to the context of the object and when the menu is used.

This context menu is for the My Computer object on the Desktop. Click once on the Properties item in that menu, and Windows NT will display the System Properties dialog for the My Computer object icon as seen in Figure 3-5.

Figure 3-5.
The System Properties dialog has several tabbed panes allowing you access to a wide variety of settings for your system.

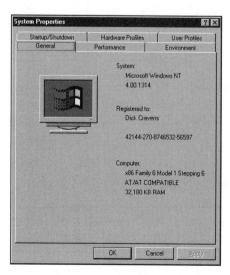

You'll notice almost immediately that this dialog has various panes topped by tabs. Click on the Performance tab and another set of configuration options are displayed, as shown in Figure 3-6.

Figure 3-6.
Click on a tab to reveal the contents of another pane. Notice further controls on this tabbed pane.

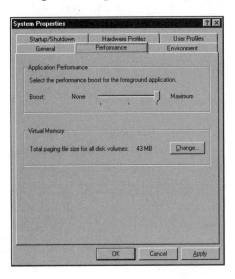

Property dialog tabbed panes can also contain other controls and dialogs. Clicking on the Change button in the Virtual Memory section of the pane shown in Figure 3-6 reveals another "child" dialog where you can adjust virtual memory settings for your system (don't touch them for now, just look at Figure 3-7).

Figure 3-7.
Property dialog panes can lead to other settings dialogs.

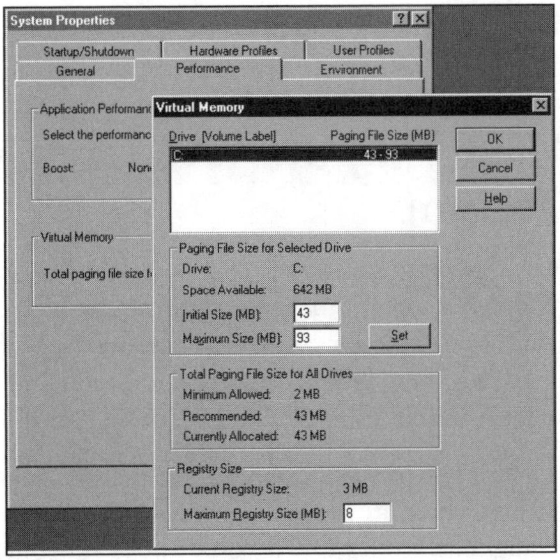

Further new items in the Windows NT 4.0 interface are the new common dialogs for File Open and File Save functions. These dialogs are shared by most 32-bit applications designed for Windows NT 4.0. Figure 3-8 shows the File Open dialog as it appears when called from WordPad.

Figure 3-8.
Windows NT 4.0's new File Open dialog supports long filenames and is generally easier to navigate than its predecessor. For example, by clicking on the combo-list control at the top of the dialog, you can open a document on the Desktop or another drive quickly.

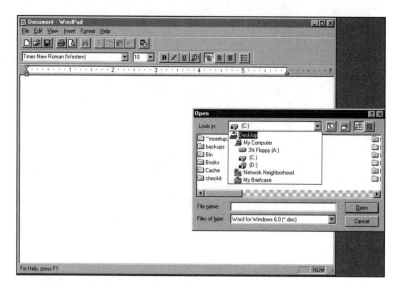

If you're comfortable with all the interface controls we've shown you here, then you're 90 percent of the way home learning how to navigate Windows NT 4.0's new interface. The rest is mostly simply exploration and practice.

Mastering the Windows NT 4.0 Desktop

Now that you've made the overview of NT's new interface, we can get down to the business of exploring the new Desktop in more detail. In this section, we'll make an overview of the general design of the Windows NT Workstation 4.0 Desktop; in the next section we'll get started using the new Desktop and show you all the ropes.

Again, if you're a Windows 95 "old-timer," *most* of this will be familiar (there are some NT-specific items under the skin throughout), so it's OK if you want to skip ahead. If you're new to Windows computing, your time here will be well spent.

Presenting the Start Menu

OK, so the logical place for us to start is, well, Start (sorry, I've been wanting to say that for about three books now). One of Microsoft's goals in the design overhaul in the Windows 95 interface (now inherited by Windows NT 4.0) was to simplify the operation of a Windows computer for the novice. The Start button is a pretty good step in that direction, but there's still some room for explanation in its use.

Figure 3-9 shows the initial section of the Start menu that results when you click on the Start button with the left mouse button.

Figure 3-9.
The initial section of the Start menu reveals the major categories of Windows NT 4.0's menu system.

Let's take it from the top down, shall we?

The Programs Group

If you'll click once on the Start button and then again on the Programs item, you'll see the first-level cascade of that menu as shown in Figure 3-10.

There are six main items under the Programs group on a pristine NT 4.0 Workstation installation:

- The Accessories group
- The Startup group

- The Command Prompt icon
- The Windows NT Explorer icon
- The Administrative Tools (Common) group icon
- The Startup group icon (for Common user startup items)

Let's take a brief look at them each before we cover the other areas of the main Start menu.

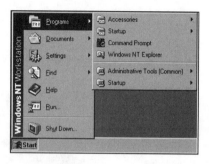

Figure 3-10.
The Programs Group menu reveals other levels to explore. Unique to NT are the Administrative Tools submenu and the second Startup group.

The Accessories Group

Click on the Accessories group icon under the Programs menu, and NT will display the cascade menu shown in Figure 3-11:

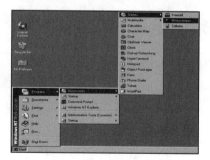

Figure 3-11.
The Accessories group menu leads you to a wide variety of useful "applets," and some fun stuff, too.

The Accessories group contains a variety of useful smaller applications ("applets") that Microsoft has included with Windows since early versions. You'll probably use some of these daily, so it's good to get acquainted with them early. This group includes

- **Games group:** The venerable Freecell, Minesweeper, and Solitaire (remember, don't get caught!)
- **Multimedia group:** CD Player (for controlling analog audio playback from your CD-ROM drive), Media Player

(for digital media: audio, video, and animation files), Sound Recorder (for recording and playing digital sounds), and Volume Control (for adjusting playback volume and relative volume among audio devices)

NOTE: See Appendix B, "Control Panels."

- **Calculator:** The classic, basic ten-key calculator with scientific functions as well

- **Character Map:** A graphic view of the complete PC character set for each installed font (see Figure 3-12). You can use this utility to insert characters or symbols not found on the PC keyboard (for example, the trademark symbol, ™).

Figure 3-12.
NT Character Map adds support for Unicode for extended character sets using that standard.

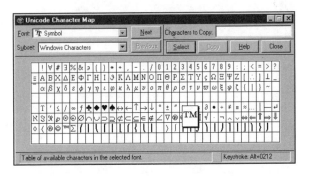

- **Chat:** A utility to allow text-based communications with any other computer on your Microsoft Network.

- **Clipbook Viewer:** This utility allows you to store information from the Windows Clipboard in a file (called a Clipbook) that can be reused and shared, even across the network.

- **Clock:** This is yet another screen clock (in addition to the one in the Taskbar tray). Try setting this one to Analog, No Title: it has a true round shape, not round within a rectangle like earlier versions!

- **Dial-Up Networking:** This is the client side of Windows NT Remote Access Service (RAS). You can start a predefined connection from here or define a new one.

NOTE: For more information on Dial-Up Networking, see Chapter 6, "Connecting to the Internet Using Dial-Up Networking."

- **HyperTerminal**: A fairly complete terminal emulation package (see Figure 3-13) for character-based serial communications with BBS systems, online services, and various other systems plus support for ZMODEM, a very popular and user-friendly file transfer protocol.

Figure 3-13.
HyperTerminal walks you through creating settings for your terminal connections.

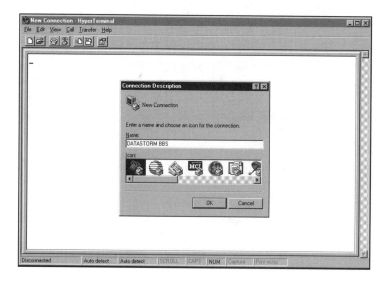

NOTE: See Chapter 6, "Connecting With HyperTerminal," for more information.

- **Notepad**: A simple text editor
- **Object Packager**: A tool for creating embedded and linked information (of one data type) for insertion in a document of another data type (for instance, for inserting an spreadsheet range into a word processing document)
- **Paint**: A bitmap editing program for creating or altering graphics files

- **Phone Dialer:** This tool (seen in Figure 3-14) lets you store and dial phone numbers using your modem. If offers support for phone cards and speed dialing, and it can be used with other applications, too.

Figure 3-14.
You're only a single mouse-click away from reaching your favorite folks via automated dialing with Phone Dialer.

- **Telnet:** A VT52/VT100/ANSI terminal emulator for Internet and other TCP/IP communications sessions with various host systems
- **WordPad:** A true word-processor application (successor to Windows Write) that handles simple document tasks and is compatible with Microsoft Word documents (it's essentially an older version, Word 1.0)

The Startup Group

The next entry in the Programs group is a little-used feature called the Startup group. Very simply explained, the Startup group is used to automate application execution at boot time. By placing a program icon, document icon, or shortcut in this group, you're telling Windows to run it as soon as Windows starts.

> **NOTE:** See "Customizing the Start Menu," later in this chapter.

The Command Prompt

The Command Prompt is a character-based interface to Windows NT; it is NOT simply an MS-DOS emulation, as many new NT users assume. You can run any command or application that will run under NT from the Command Prompt, plus you can perform batch operations, administer networks, and control data exchange between applications and NT subsystems.

> **NOTE:** For more information on the Command Prompt, see "Mastering the NT Command Prompt," later in this chapter.

Figure 3-15 details the Windows NT Command Prompt as it appears when run from the Start menu. You can also run a Command Prompt session full-screen by using the (Alt)+(Enter) key sequence when it's the foreground application.

Figure 3-15.
Although the Windows NT Command Prompt looks much like an MS-DOS window, it actually supports five operating systems (Windows NT, Windows 3.*x*, MS-DOS, MS OS/2 1.*x*, and POSIX).

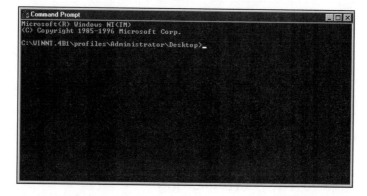

> **NOTE:** See " Mastering Windows NT Explorer," later in this chapter.

Windows NT Explorer

Windows NT Explorer is the successor to the File Manager program familiar to Windows 3.*x* and NT 3.*x* users. Figure 3-16 shows the basic Explorer interface.

You can navigate local and network storage systems with Explorer. You can launch programs, copy files, and perform almost any other management task from this interface.

Figure 3-16.
Windows Explorer offers a variety of ways to view, manage, and manipulate the contents of your Windows NT system.

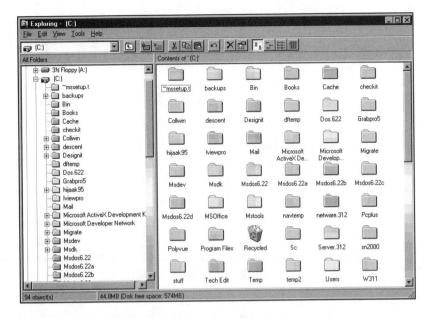

Administrative Tools (Common)

Windows NT comes with a serious set of system management tools for security, media management, system backup, diagnostics and performance evaluation, and remote network communications. These programs are used via the icons shown in Figure 3-17.

Figure 3-17.
You can manage almost every aspect of your NT Workstation from the Administrative Tools menu.

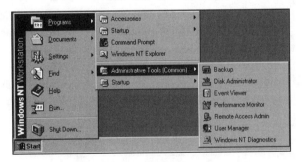

Here's a summary of the capabilities of these system utilities:

- **Backup:** A utility for making copies of your critical data, to protect it from accidental erasure or catastrophic system failure. You can back up to a wide variety of tape systems, from both NTFS and FAT storage media, and from both local and remote drives.

What Is Explorer?

Answer #1: The Windows NT Explorer utility is the heir apparent to File Manager, the venerable Windows utility for file and network connectivity management.

Answer #2: Explorer is a Windows NT control subsystem that provides windowing and presentation services to a variety of Windows objects or programs (My Computer, Network Neighborhood, Exchange).

When you're using Windows NT Explorer, you're in a Windows application designed for file management. When you click on My Computer, you're opening an object that Windows will display using the same interface elements and other controls as Explorer (it's referred to as an Explorer window, in a generic sense).

Think of it this way: Windows NT Explorer is the topmost, visible part of a set of Windows services organized specifically for easy file management, with roots that go deep into Windows itself. Other parts of Windows use these roots as well to organize and display information (drives, mail messages). This is just one way Microsoft has made NT more efficient, by reusing parts of one program in another when needed.

Internet Explorer is similar but tailored for navigating and presenting data types prevalent on the World Wide Web. In future versions of Windows (as we all get more "connected"), the distinction between Internet and local systems will diminish; Microsoft has already announced plans to merge Internet Explorer, Windows Explorer, and the Desktop into one basic information and data management system.

NOTE: See Appendix D, "Securing Your Data: Backing Up Windows NT," for more information.

- **Disk Administrator:** This tool (shown in Figure 3-18) lets you create and delete partitions, format and label volumes, view disk information, create and manage different types of drive volumes, and create and manage disk stripe sets.

Figure 3-18.
Disk Administrator
is command central
for all media-level
drive management
tasks. Do your
homework before
you venture here.

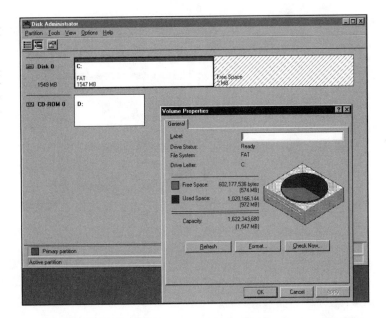

NOTE: See Appendix D, "Tips on Performing System
Maintenance."

- **Event Viewer:** Windows NT security calls for a complete audit trail for all system events. Event Viewer allows you to log security, system, and application events for review or documentation (as shown in Figure 3-19).

- **Performance Monitor:** This tool allows you to measure your local system performance, or the performance of any other system on your network to which you have rights. You can view, chart, and export the logged performance data for reports.

- **Remote Access Admin:** This is the management tool for the server side of Dial-Up Networking. Use this utility to manage RAS servers or user rights on those servers.

- **User Manager:** Used to create and manage user accounts, user groups, and policies. Figure 3-20 shows the User Manager window, from which you can view and manipulate all user information for your workstation.

Figure 3-19.
Event Viewer provides you with elaborate levels of detail regarding NT Workstation's performance. You can even view the logs on other computers on the network if you have the appropriate rights.

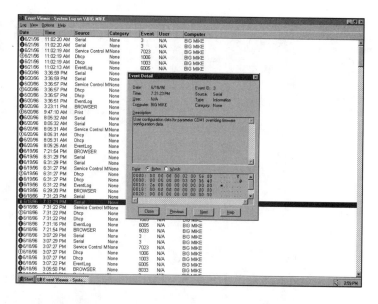

 NOTE: See Appendix B, "Managing NT Security," for more information.

Figure 3-20.
User Manager provides all the tools for manipulating user accounts, user groups, and policies for your NT Workstation.

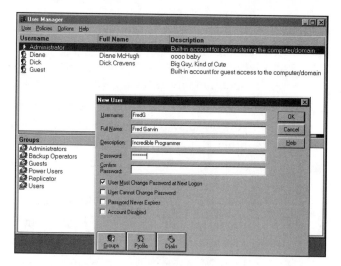

- **Windows NT Diagnostics:** you can view details on memory, services, environment, network, resources, and the NT Workstation version, plus run other system utilities, all from this utility shown in Figure 3-21.

Figure 3-21.
The Windows NT
Diagnostics window
offers you information
in close to real time
about your NT
Workstation system.

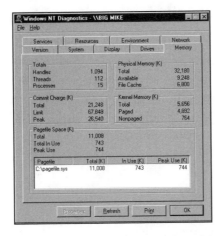

Other Programs Group Entries

Why a second Startup group in the bottom Administrator section
of the Programs group? This one is controlled by the administrator
only, for the benevolent benefit of all users on the workstation.

What else is the Program group used for? Anytime a new application is installed on your system, odds are very good its install
program will create an icon or nested group here for it. You can
also customize the menu as well. Figure 3-22 shows a fairly fully
populated Programs Group menu, after the installation of
Microsoft Office 95 Professional.

Figure 3-22.
Most applications
installed under
Windows NT
automatically add
their icons to the
Programs Group
menu. You can also
customize the menu
after installation to
suit your personal
tastes.

NOTE: See "Customizing the Start Menu," later in this
chapter for more information.

Opening Files from the Documents Menu

You can open documents with a simple double-click in Windows NT Workstation. What if you don't remember where the file was when you last opened it? Maybe it's on another computer on the network, and you didn't think to make a Shortcut to it before you closed it. No worry! Windows NT keeps a list handy for you. Just open the Documents section of the Start menu for a list of the last files you opened from any folders on your Desktop (as shown in Figure 3-23).

Figure 3-23.
Any file you've opened from the Desktop will appear in the Documents menu. Windows NT requires an application association for each file data type to provide this feature, but most installed applications will create the association automatically when they're installed.

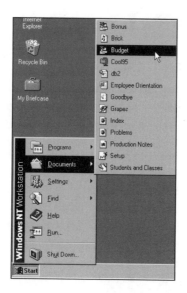

It's nice that Windows NT provides this service for you, but what happens after weeks of using NT Workstation when you fill up the document menu? You can clear the whole menu fairly easily by following these steps:

1. Click once with your right mouse button on the Taskbar. A context menu will appear. Select Properties, and Windows NT will display the Taskbar Properties dialog.

2. Click once on the Start Menu Programs tab, and the Properties pane shown in Figure 3-24 will appear.

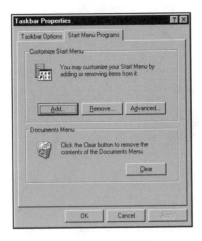

Figure 3-24.
You can clear the entire Documents menu from the Taskbar Properties dialog window.

1. Click once on the Clear button in the Documents Menu section of the Properties pane.

2. Click once on the OK button to close the window. Windows NT has cleared the Documents menu, as shown in Figure 3-25.

Figure 3-25.
Although Windows NT lets you clear the entire Documents menu, you can't choose which icons to lose and which to keep. Don't depend on keeping icons here long-term.

TIP: You can create permanent icons for frequently accessed files using Shortcuts. See "Mastering Shortcuts" later in this chapter.

The Settings Menu

The Windows NT Start menu also provides a simple way to get to all the day-to-day configuration items for your system via the Settings menu (seen in Figure 3-26).

Figure 3-26.
You can use the same familiar Start menu to get to all the Windows NT Workstation configuration controls.

From here you can access the Control Panels, Printers, and Taskbar properties for Windows NT.

TIP: How can you tell where to go to configure NT Workstation? Here's a rough but still useful rule of thumb: if you're configuring your workstation, go to the Start menu Settings group. If you're configuring *others'* access *to* your system, use the Start menu Programs group Administrative Tools.

The Control Panel Group

This set of wizards, dialogs, and other controls (shown in Figure 3-27) is where you go to alter major configuration items on your workstation system.

Figure 3-27.
Most configuration options not related to security are available from the Control Panel Group window.

If you're a salty old Windows NT user, there's not a ton of new material here. We'll cover each of these items in greater detail as needed throughout the rest of the book, and in Appendix B, "Control Panels."

The Printers Group

Use this icon to open the Printers Control Panel directly (seen in Figure 3-28) without opening the major Control Panel group first.

Figure 3-28.
You can view installed printers, alter their configuration, or install a new printer from the Printers Control Panel.

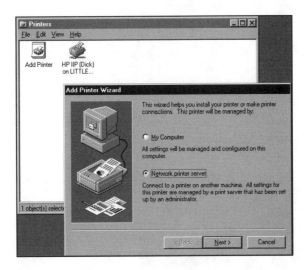

Check out "Control Panels" in Appendix B for details on using these tools.

The Taskbar Properties Dialog

Another way to get to the Properties dialog for the Taskbar (seen again in Figure 3-29) is through the Settings menu. This is the same dialog we opened using the right mouse button earlier in the chapter, just preset to a different Properties pane, the Taskbar tab.

> **NOTE:** See "Customizing the Start Menu," later in this chapter for more information.

The Find Menu

Having a large drive system or a networked computer can be a curse as well as a blessing, especially if you have a lot of different applications or data, and a lot of computers on your network. If you're getting that lost feeling, Windows NT can help with the Find menu (shown in Figure 3-30).

Figure 3-29.
The Taskbar
Properties dialog is
also for adjusting
the behavior of the
Taskbar itself, in
addition to the
Programs and
Documents menus.

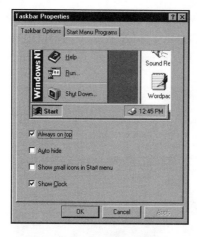

Figure 3-29.
The Taskbar
Properties dialog is
also for adjusting
the behavior of the
Taskbar itself, in
addition to the
Programs and
Documents menus.

Figure 3-30.
You can locate files,
folders, or computers
using the Find features
in the Start menu.

NOTE: See Chapter 4, "Locating Computers Using Find,"
for more information.

The Windows NT Help System

Another major area of improvement over previous versions of NT
Workstation is the Windows Help version 4.0 inherited from
Windows 95. Help on Windows NT itself is available from the
Start menu Help command. This new version of the Help engine
supports full-text and indexed searches as well as a much more
attractive appearance (seen in Figure 3-31).

Most new Help files written for this format will come with decent
if not excellent indexes (like the one shown in Figure 3-32).

If the topic you're seeking isn't in the index, Help 4.0 offers full-text
search functions as well. The first time you access the Find tab on a
Windows NT 4.0 Help file, you'll see the dialog seen in Figure 3-33
asking you just how detailed a search you intend to make.

Figure 3-31.
The Windows NT Help system uses the familiar tabbed-dialog design seen in the rest of Windows' property dialogs. A tree control shows you the structure of the entire Help file on each topic to speed your search as well.

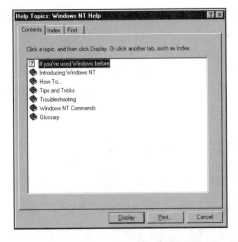

Figure 3-32.
Most applications are providing better indexes for their Help systems to take advantage of Help 4.0's new index search and display features.

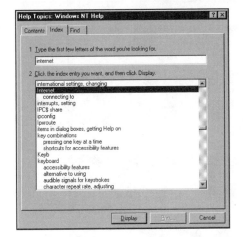

Figure 3-33.
Windows NT 4.0 Help will let you customize the level of detail available to you in full-text searches. If drive space is no issue, choose Maximize for the most thorough performance.

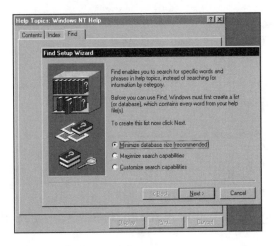

Follow the prompts to complete the search index, and then enter the term for which you desire information in the top field of the Find tab (as shown in Figure 3-34). As you type, you'll notice that the progressive resolution search engine eliminates topics until it's narrowed them to those that match or include your request (see Figure 3-35).

Figure 3-34.
Start typing the term you're searching for . . .

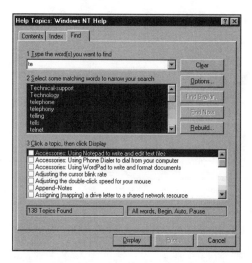

Figure 3-35.
. . . and the Help engine will narrow the results to show only the appropriate matches.

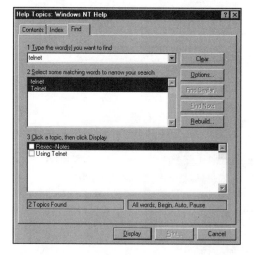

Click on the topic of choice, and Help will display the text you seek. You can print the Help information or copy it to the Clipboard if you wish to use it elsewhere or share it.

A major section of the Windows NT Help system has been dedicated to acclimating those users coming to NT from the Windows 3.*x* interface. To see this section:

1. Start the NT Help system from the Start menu using the Help command.
2. Click on the Contents tab. Windows Help will display the Contents tab as seen in Figure 3-31.
3. Double-click on the entry "If you've used Windows before." Help will display the window shown in Figure 3-36.

Figure 3-36.
Answers to common questions about the changes in the Windows NT 4.0 interface are available from the main Help Contents tab. Just click on a topic for additional information.

The Run Command

Sometimes you need to use a program just once, without installing it on your system permanently, or you want to use a program you know is on your system but not in your menu. Users of Program Manager and File Manager in earlier versions of Windows will undoubtedly remember the Run command available from their File menus. Since both these programs are now gone (or sunk into the Desktop, to be more precise), there's an improved Run command in the Start menu (see Figure 3-37).

The Windows NT 4.0 Run command dialog offers some really useful options. There's a really keen drop-down list for repeating commands, and a nifty Browse button.

Figure 3-37.
You can still start
programs with the
Run command. You'll
need to know the
name and location of
the program (or you
may Browse to find it).

NOTE: See Appendix C, "Tips on Running Legacy Applications," for more information.

Shutdown

We've probably already beaten the Shutdown issue to death (get it?). See the section earlier in this chapter ("Shutting Down: A Brief Introduction . . . ") if you need to review the main options on how to stop your system in an orderly manner.

The Windows NT Desktop Proper: the Main Icons

In the quest for a simpler interface, Microsoft has arranged the Desktop to follow simple and logical visual guidelines related to system functions. The Start menu is one response to usability research showing that novice computer users really didn't understand the basics of interacting with their computer (literally not understanding "where to start" in the Windows interface). The other elements of the Desktop are designed to fulfill similar needs and solve similar problems, while balancing the needs of both power users and novices.

Now that we've toured the Start menu, let's see what the other elements of the NT Desktop have to offer us. In this section we'll briefly cover:

- The Taskbar
- My Computer
- Network Neighborhood
- Inbox
- Recycle Bin
- Internet Explorer
- My Briefcase

The Taskbar

Although we've already discussed, manipulated, used, abused, and otherwise studied the Taskbar as we've investigated other parts of the new Windows NT interface, there are still some items we can mention, and more information to point you to.

One problem with the Windows 3.x Program Manager/Desktop interface was that it was very easy to "lose" programs because they were covered by other applications. Ask any support technician at a major software company, or any Help Desk veteran, about major areas of Windows confusion during the introduction of Windows 3.0, and they'll tell you horror stories of users with fifteen MS-DOS sessions running behind Program Manager. Bear in mind that multitasking was a new concept to most PC users at that time.

The Taskbar solves this problem by taking a small area of screen real estate and using it to display and control running programs. In addition to the Start menu, the Taskbar hosts application buttons for each open program (shown in Figures 3-38 and 3-39). By clicking on a button, you bring a program from the background to the foreground (giving it the system "focus").

You can also use the Taskbar application buttons to resize and close programs. A right-click on an application button displays the context menu for that button (the same menu used on a mini-mized application icon on the Windows 3.x Desktop). Figure 3-40 shows the application button context menu.

Figure 3-38.
The Taskbar application buttons show two running applications, but only Excel is visible (note that the Excel button has a depressed appearance).

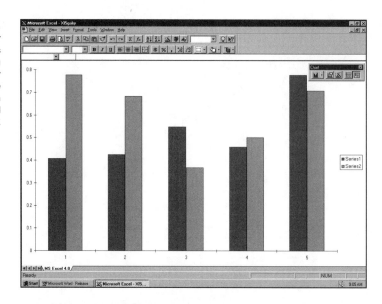

Figure 3-39.
Clicking on the Microsoft Word application button brings it to the foreground, making it the active application.

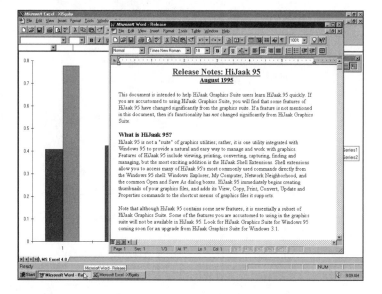

You can also move the Taskbar about the Desktop (as demonstrated in Figure 3-41). Just click on the Taskbar with the left mouse button and drag it to any side of the Desktop.

For more detailed information on configuring the Taskbar, see "Customizing the Taskbar," later in this chapter.

Figure 3-40.
You can Restore, Move, Size, Minimize, Maximize, and Close applications from the Taskbar using the right mouse button.

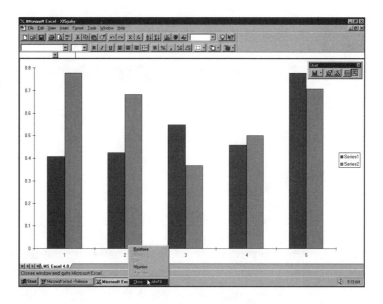

Figure 3-41.
If the need strikes you, you can change the Desktop fairly drastically and almost make NT look like one of "those" computers (you know, the ones with the fruity name).

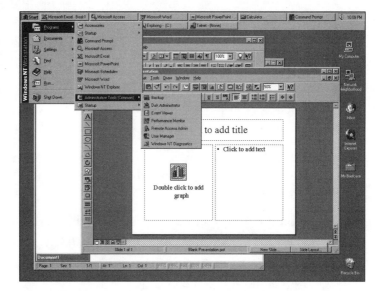

My Computer

Another problem addressed in the new Windows NT Desktop design is the lack of distinction between local and network systems. Research has shown that the average user can't distinguish between the two worlds without a little guidance, so Microsoft has designed the new interface in a way that makes such distinctions more clear. The first part of this solution is seen in Figure 3-42.

Figure 3-42.
A typical My Computer folder (yours may look slightly different depending upon your hardware and software installation options).

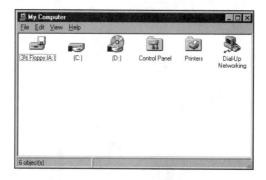

As you can see, this folder displays all local drive subsystems (on this system, A:, C:, and D: drives) plus the major configuration tools for the local system (Control Panel, Printers, Dial-Up Networking). Although this folder looks just like any other folder on your system, you'll find that it's special in that it's protected (you can't drag items to or from it, as you can on the Desktop or most of the rest of the system). This arrangement assures that you'll always have access to these devices and utilities, and it prevents casual user mistakes from interfering with the normal operation of the NT Desktop. (Admit it, sometimes you delete stuff accidentally, right?)

Double-clicking on any of these items will open them in a new folder. Figure 3-43 shows the result of double-clicking on the icon for the C: drive.

You can also right-click on items in this folder. Figure 3-43 also shows the context menu for the C: drive.

Click on the Properties entry to see information on drive C: (as shown in Figure 3-44).

The My Computer folder window has other controls and functions, which we'll cover along with other similar window controls in "Mastering Windows NT Explorer," later in this chapter.

NOTE: Also see the "What Is Explorer" sidebar, earlier in this chapter (pp. 60) for more information on how folder windows work.

Figure 3-43.
The contents of the C: drive on this machine. Note that directories are displayed as folder icons, and files, with the icon for their respective data types, or with a generic file icon.

Figure 3-44.
Just about every object in Windows NT 4.0 has a context menu Properties dialog. Note that Properties dialogs don't appear in the Taskbar as an icon, since they're considered part of a running window, not a separate window.

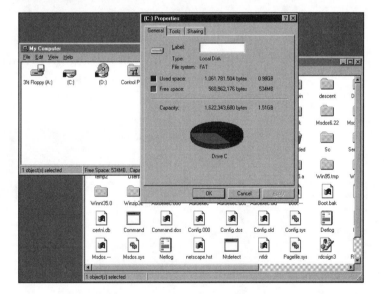

You guessed it: the Control Panel, Printers, and Dial-Up Networking icons behave identically to the other entries by those names we've looked at in the Start menu. They're just here in the My Computer folder for easy access.

The My Computer icon has its own context menu, as well. Figure 3-45 shows the options available from a right-mouse click on this icon.

Figure 3-45.
The context menu for
the My Computer icon
has the standard
functions plus some
unique to this folder.

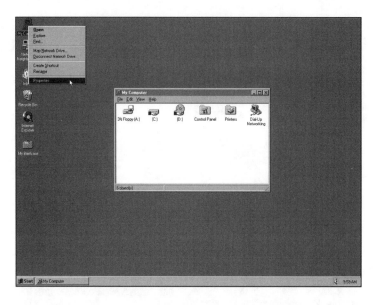

Click on Properties to display the System Properties dialog for the
My Computer icon (shown in Figure 3-46). You'll see tabs for a
variety of configuration items for your system. This is the same
dialog that is used by the Control Panel group System icon.

Figure 3-46.
The System
Properties dialog
contains multiple tabs
for configuring your
system. Be sure you
understand the issues
involved before you
alter any settings here
(see Appendix B for
specific information).

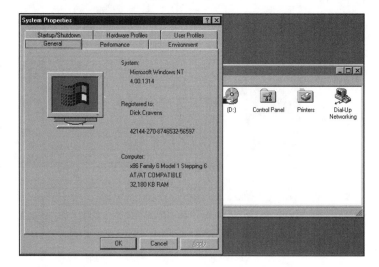

Network Neighborhood

Following the design theme of grouping items by function, Windows
NT uses the Network Neighborhood icon to contain the tools for
network management. Double-click on the Network Neighborhood
icon to open its folder window (shown in Figure 3-47).

Figure 3-47.
Large or small, your
network will be visible
in the Network
Neighborhood folder
window. Windows
Network machines in
your domain will be
visible at the top level
of this folder, as will be
any other networks or
computers via the
Entire Network icon.

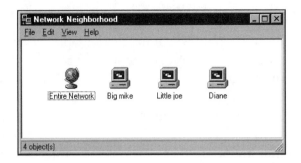

 NOTE: See Chapter 4, "Getting Your NT Workstation
on the Network," for specifics on installing and
configuring network access on your workstation.

If your network drivers are already installed and you've got rights
to other computers on the network, you'll see icons for other
machines in this window. To view resources on other computers,
just double-click on the computer icon and Windows will open a
new folder window for that machine (see Figure 3-48).

Figure 3-48.
Once your network
configurations are
ready, resources on
other systems are
just a few clicks away.

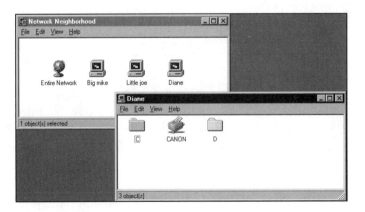

Just like the My Computer folder window, the Network
Neighborhood icon and folder window have other controls, prop-
erties, and functions, which we'll cover in "Mastering Windows
NT Explorer," (later in this chapter), and Chapter 4, "Getting
Your NT Workstation on the Network".

The Inbox

Depending upon which installation options you chose (or which were chosen for you), you probably have an icon called Inbox on your Desktop, right below the Network Neighborhood icon. Double-click on it and a program called Microsoft Exchange will start. If no one configured Exchange for you, you may see the Exchange Wizard, but if it is already set up by a wonderful system administrator or other generous soul, you'll see the Exchange application looking something like Figure 3-49.

Figure 3-49.
Exchange is a great mail application that comes free with Windows NT. You can use it with Microsoft Mail, Internet mail, and any other customized messaging functions and transports that you install.

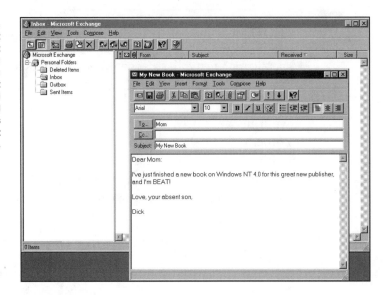

The Recycle Bin

One of the simplest but handiest new features of the NT Desktop is the data dumpster, Recycle Bin. This tool is designed to help the user that's prone to deleting files accidentally, and it helps manage the mess by holding on to "trashed" items just in case. As the MS-DOS mavens among you know, files really aren't truly deleted when you delete them, only renamed. Recycle Bin takes advantage of this fact to allow you a safety buffer so that you can change your mind after you've tossed something and get it back quickly and easily. It works like this:

1. You open a folder and see an item you despise or don't really need. You click on it with the right mouse button, and the context menu for the item appears (as seen in Figure 3-50).

Figure 3-50.
Click an item once with the right mouse button to select and display its context menu. Move the mouse pointer to the Delete entry, and the file's final journey begins.

2. Select Delete from the context menu. Windows NT, in its mercy, will ask if you are truly sure this item should be "sent to the shredder" (see Figures 3-51 and 3-52). Click the Yes button if you are sure your decision is just.

Figure 3-51.
There's no excuse for remorse; Windows has given you a chance to change your mind . . .

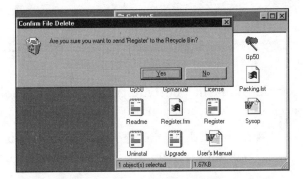

Figure 3-52.
. . . before the file is No More.

Windows will take care of the rest, disposing of the body without any muss or fuss. Should you regret your decision, you do have one last chance to redeem the data, though:

1. Double-click on the Recycle Bin icon to open it, and you'll see the doomed file awaiting final execution.

2. Click once on it to select it and then go to the File menu and choose Restore (as shown in Figure 3-53).

Figure 3-53.
There is yet hope for doomed data. Restore puts the file right back where it was before you became so judgmental.

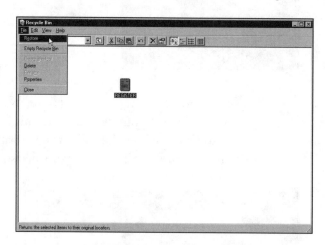

Should you be in a hurry to get rid of the offending material, or need the drive space, you can hasten the destruction of data thus:

1. Right-click on the Recycle Bin icon. Windows will display the context menu for it as shown in Figure 3-54.

Figure 3-54.
Take back your drive space quickly with the Empty Recycle Bin command.

1. Windows again asks you to reconsider with a Confirm File Delete dialog. Click on Yes to proceed, and your drive will be cleansed. Notice that your Recycle Bin icon is now empty.

You can adjust the amount of drive space Recycle Bin can allocate for deleted files awaiting final destruction by using the Properties settings for Recycle Bin. Just right-click, select Properties, and stand back for the Recycle Bin Properties dialog to appear (seen in Figures 3-55 and 3-56).

Figure 3-55.
You can set the amount of recycle buffer space using the Recycle Bin Properties dialog. Set the amount globally for all drives . . .

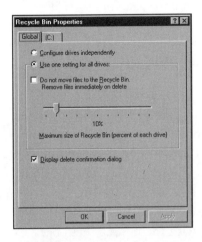

Figure 3-56.
. . . or for each drive independently (if you have more than one).

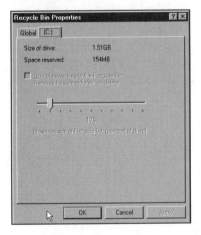

You may also instruct Windows to skip the whole recycling process completely, or just not bother you with the pesky confirmation dialog, by setting different options here.

Internet Explorer

This is the Windows NT version of Microsoft's Web browser. We'll cover it in Chapter 6, so jump ahead to there if you need information immediately (see "Surfing the World Wide Web with Internet Explorer".

My Briefcase

Microsoft's usability testing also turned up another big area for improvement: helping users keep data synchronized when they move from machine to machine. Briefcase allows you to move files to a portable computer and then back to your main system without having to compare them in any way (Windows handles all the messy stuff for you).

Using Briefcase is pretty simple:

1. Select and drag files you wish to "travel" with you from shared folders on the network or your main computer to the Briefcase icon on the Desktop of your portable computer (your computers must be networked).

2. Drag the files from your Briefcase and use them on your portable machine as you normally would. When you're finished with them, drag them back to the Briefcase.

3. When you're back from your trip, reconnect to your network, right-click the Briefcase icon on your portable machine, and select Update All from the context menu (shown in Figure 3-57). Briefcase will update all files automatically.

Figure 3-57.
Briefcase makes it simple to synchronize files when you return from your journey.

You can even use Briefcase with floppy disks, if you're not fortunate enough to have a network connection. To do this, follow these steps:

1. Put a blank formatted floppy in your main computer's floppy drive.

2. Select and drag files you wish to "travel" with you from folders on your main computer to the Briefcase icon on the Desktop of your main computer.

3. Drag the Briefcase icon from your main computer desktop to the floppy drive icon.

4. Take the floppy to your portable computer, and drag the Briefcase icon from the floppy to the Desktop on that machine. Open it and edit the files as necessary.

5. When you're ready to synchronize the files, close the Briefcase on the Desktop of your portable, drag it to the floppy on that machine, and remove the floppy from that drive when it's finished moving.

6. Insert the floppy in the drive of your main computer, open the floppy drive icon, and select Update All from the context menu for the Briefcase icon.

You can also selectively update files individually from within the Briefcase by using the Update Selection command from the Briefcase menu (you'll need to open the Briefcase icon fully to use this feature).

The Basics of Windows NT 4.0 Operation for Daily Use

Now that you've completed the overview of the design changes in the new NT interface, we can get down to business and cover some of the purely functional aspects of using the new interface.

The Basic Windows NT Techniques

There are several operations that are so fundamental to successful Windows NT operation that we'll cover them here again at risk of repetition. You've already used several of these if you've followed the examples in this chapter, but it can't hurt to make sure we've covered them clearly and completely.

Mastering the Two-Button Mouse

Microsoft and other companies have marketed multibutton mice for many years, but it's only recently that software for the PC really began to take advantage of the second (right) mouse button as a matter of course. Some forward-looking application vendors (two notable examples are DATASTORM's Procomm Plus for Windows and NetManage's ECCO) made excellent use of the right button early in their Windows 3.*x* production cycles, as did Microsoft with its Office applications (Word, Excel, PowerPoint, Access), but in general the "wrong" button was ignored.

> **NOTE:** See Appendix B, "Control Panels," for more information.

The Right Mouse Button

All that's changed with Windows 95 and Windows NT 4.0. These versions of Windows make such thorough use of both mouse buttons that you'd better plan on buying a new rodent if it's got any problems at all. As we've demonstrated many times earlier in this chapter, the right mouse button context menu is, by obvious design, critical to the operation of the new interface. Almost every object in a Windows NT 4.0 system has a context menu associated with it (per the examples shown in Figures 3-58 and 3-59).

Figure 3-58.
The right-mouse context menu is prevalent in the new Windows NT 4.0 interface.

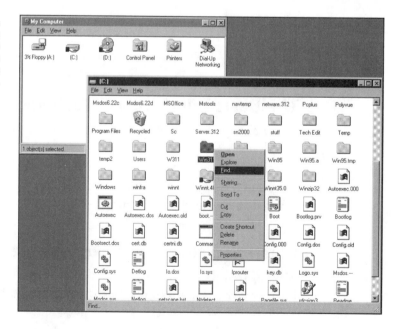

Figure 3-59.
It's called a context menu because it changes according to the object it's called from and the state of that object when it's used. Note how the top entry in this object's menu is really an indication that Windows needs more user input to perform the Open function (the ellipsis indicates that another dialog will appear, asking you to identify the application you wish to open the file for).

The right mouse button is also used for drag-and-drop functions. Try this:

1. Open a folder with some files in it (be sure you can see the Desktop around the folder; if not, reduce the size of the folder window).

2. Click on one of the files with the right mouse button, holding the button down.

3. Drag the file to the Desktop and let it go. Windows will display the drop-context menu as shown in Figure 3-60.

Figure 3-60.
When you drop a file on the Desktop (or in a folder) using the right mouse button, you get the menu shown here.

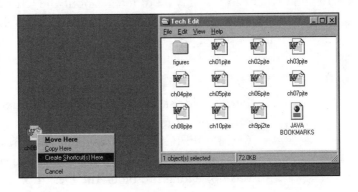

1. Move the mouse cursor over the Create Shortcut item and click once. Windows will create the icon for the Shortcut (as shown in Figure 3-61).

Figure 3-61.
The new Shortcut on your Desktop. Note the icon name, and the arrow on the lower-left corner of the icon (both dead giveaways that it's a Shortcut, eh?).

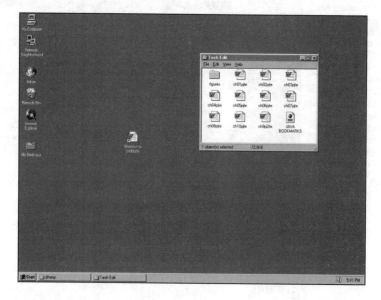

NOTE: See "Mastering Shortcuts" later in this chapter for more information.

The Left Mouse Button

You've used Windows for years, and you've used a mouse for years. So what can possibly be different about the left mouse button? Of course, the button itself hasn't changed (Microsoft doesn't have *that* much power *yet*), but how Windows uses it has changed subtly. In short, your mouse is now a bit smarter than before. Try this to demonstrate:

1. Find a folder that contains both documents and an application program (for example, we'll use C:\MSOFFICE\EXCEL, where our spreadsheet program is installed). Open the folder enough to see the contents, but not enough to block the Desktop.

2. Left-click on a data file and hold it.(for example, XLREADME has the text file icon type). Drag it to the Desktop as shown in Figure 3-62 and drop it.

Figure 3-62.
Use the left mouse button to click-hold-drag-drop it on the Desktop.

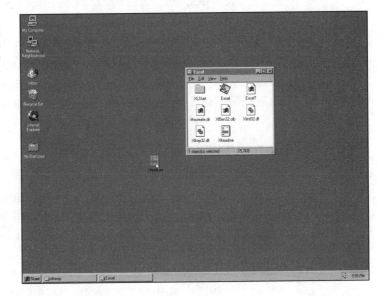

3. Left-click on the Excel program (you can tell by the icon that it's a program file) and drag it to the Desktop and drop it just like you did the XLREADME file. You'll get the result shown in Figure 3-63.

Figure 3-63.
Windows NT 4.0 knows better than to move a program file without express instructions to do so, so it creates a Shortcut to the program file automatically as a safety feature. Everybody's happy . . . unless you really need to move the file.

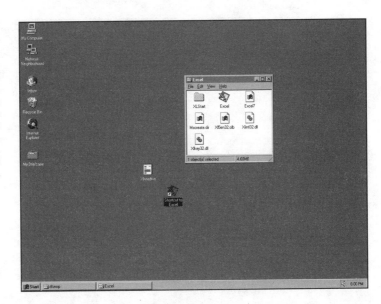

Now why did Windows NT not let you move the Excel program file, although it was perfectly happy letting you move the text file? Remember, Windows knows what type each file is (for most common file types, and certainly for executable or program files) and knows that moving application files can cripple programs. Moving a text or other data file may be a hassle, but it usually won't cripple the program, so you can do that without any interference.

So how to move a program or application file when you really, really mean it? Use the right mouse button, as we showed you earlier.

Mastering New Windows NT Common Dialogs

Another major change in the interface of Windows is less than obvious and is just a little bit beneath the hood. Still, you'll run into it fairly quickly, so we want to prepare you for it. Just about every program you open in Windows will use the same common dialogs for common functions (File Open, File Save, File Save As, Print, and so forth). It may not seem such a major deal that these have changed in Windows NT, until you start to use one and get a little lost. Figure 3-64 shows the basic File Open dialog used in WordPad as an example.

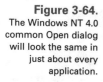

Figure 3-64.
The Windows NT 4.0 common Open dialog will look the same in just about every application.

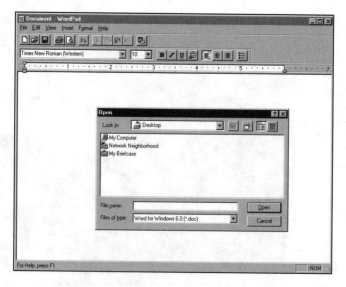

There are several really excellent new parts to this "boring old everyday Open dialog" that will make your life *much* easier if you'll use them to your benefit. Right off the top:

- It supports long filenames (more on that in a few paragraphs).
- You can jump directly to the Desktop or to other machines without leaving the dialog.
- You can change the display of the files to get more information about files without leaving the dialog.
- You can create new folders without leaving the dialog.
- There's Help right there without leaving the dialog.

You may have noticed I like not having to leave the dialog to do things. :-)

Figure 3-65.
Navigating the network to load a file is cake with the new dialog design.

Figure 3-65 shows the biggest advantage to the new design, the tree-control-combo-drop-list-navigation-tool at the top. You can bop all over the ol' network in no time with this baby.

You can adjust the dialog display easily to suit your needs. For example, Figure 3-66 shows the Details view of the folder I'm keeping the illustrations for this chapter in. I'm using the mouse to adjust the size of the Name field so that I can see the time and date of each file more clearly. All I had to do was click on the Details button and then click on the field header to adjust my view.

Figure 3-66.
You can adjust the
display of the File
Open list much as
you can change a
folder window.

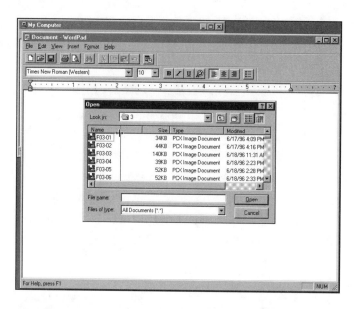

If I'm feeling especially groggy, I can use the built-in context-sensitive Help (the What's This? button) to figure everything out. Figure 3-67 shows me clicking on part of the Open dialog after I've clicked on the What's This? button, and Figure 3-68 shows what happens next.

File Save and File Save As dialogs are essentially the same as the Open dialog in most applications.

Using Long Filenames

One of the really nice touches in the new interface (and underlying file system) is support for long filenames (known to true computer geeks as LFN support; feel free, amaze your friends with a new obscure acronym, it's on me). Using long filenames is really pretty easy, but there are some distinct guidelines you'll need to follow:

- Keep them reasonable (don't get silly, or you will be despised by coworkers).
- Use only the allowed characters.
- Use fewer than 256 characters.
- Expect to be confused when using them on a mixed-computing environment (specifically mixed 16-bit and 32-bit systems).

Figure 3-67.
Click on the What's
This button, and
then on part of the
Open dialog . . .

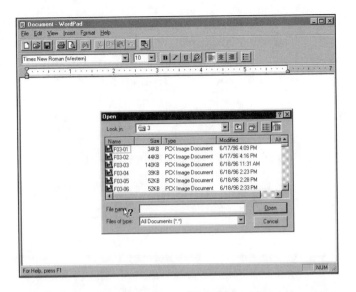

Figure 3-68.
. . . and here's the
resulting information.
(Wish I had one of
these on my
checkbook!)

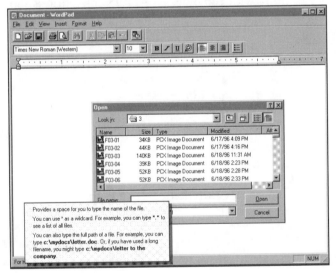

The first item in the preceding list is simply common sense. The whole idea behind long filenames is to make computing more human-friendly, but such a thing can be taken *way* too far. "PM Status Report 8-15-96" is very much better than the old MS-DOS 8.3 filename limitation that would force you to use something hideously cryptic, like "PMR81596.DOC," but "Product Manager's Status Report to Uppermost Management for August 15 1996" is pushing the limits of common etiquette (plus it won't fit most dialogs). Save everyone around you some hassle, and be reasonable.

Despite the real progress made in this area, there are still some characters you can't use in a filename. Figure 3-69 demonstrates how Windows will snatch you straight out of long-filename-reverie to remind you what's legal and what's not.

Figure 3-69.
Be aware of the reserved characters that are improper in filenames (serves you right for making one that dumb and long, anyway).

The real issue here is that these characters are still needed by the file system for various reasons, not least of which is backward compatibility with the older MS-DOS conventions. So stay away from:

forward and backslashes	/ \
the colon	:
the asterisk	*
the question mark	?
quotation marks	"
angle brackets	< >
the pipe symbol	|

Repeat to yourself: I can live without these in my filenames—and you'll be OK.

The last item in my warning list is a bit harder to explain, so I'll use some illustrations (I haven't been shy before, have I?). If you're dealing with a mixed computing environment (16-bit Windows, MS-DOS, and 32-bit Windows all on the same machine or multiple machines on the network) then you'll encounter "long filename truncation." Basically, older systems can't deal with long filenames, so 32-bit Windows systems (NT, Win95) have extra smarts built in to do it for them. Let's take a very simple example, a Microsoft Word file named "In Progress" created on a 32-bit machine with long filename support (like, say, Windows NT

Workstation 4.0, perhaps?). Here's how the file will look on different systems on a theoretical network:

Windows NT 4.0:	In Progress
Windows 95:	In Progress
Windows NT 3.51:	In Progress
Windows NT 3.x:	INPROGR~.DOC
Windows 3.x:	INPROGR~.DOC
MS-DOS:	INPROGR~.DOC

In this case, Windows knows to get rid of the offending space in the middle of the filename and inserts a tilde character to denote that there's more to the name than meets the eye (don't worry, through the magic of LFN, you get the full name back when you next use the file on a machine with LFN support— unless you save the file on the "older" system, in which case you're stuck with the truncated name until you rename it).

Another example: what happens when you have two similar long filenames, like "In Progress to Bombay, India" and "In Progress to North Hackensack, New Jersey"? Get ready for this one:

Windows NT 4.0:	[as written previously]
Windows 95:	[as written previously]
Windows NT 3.51:	[as written previously]
Windows NT 3.x:	INPROG~1.DOC, INPROG~2.DOC
Windows 3.x:	INPROG~1.DOC, INPROG~2.DOC
MS-DOS:	INPROG~1.DOC, INPROG~2.DOC

In other words, if you have two files that end similarly within the eight-character limit of the MS-DOS filename, the system will shorten the name further to make room for a number! So, without entering into a formal discussion of Long Filename Truncation Algorithm Theory and Practice, you can see that you're going to have to possess a little smarts about this topic yourself to keep track of your files in a mixed environment.

Mastering Shortcuts

Another absolutely basic technique in Windows NT 4.0 is that of creating and controlling Shortcuts. The Shortcut is arguably one of the top three usability enhancements in the new interface, and you'll be well-served by time invested in learning how to manipulate Shortcuts effectively.

Creating Shortcuts

A Shortcut is basically an icon that represents or points to an object and yet behaves like that object when you act upon it. These "aliases" allow you to visually organize your Desktop and menus without altering the data structure of your system or duplicating data. Here's the Official Version of how to create a Shortcut:

1. Right-click anywhere on the Desktop (or in a folder). Select New ➤ Shortcut (as shown in Figure 3-70) and click once.

Figure 3-70.
You can create a shortcut from any folder or the Desktop via the right mouse button context menu.

1. Windows will display the Create Shortcut wizard shown in Figure 3-71. If you don't know the drive, path, and filename you want to create the Shortcut for, you can select the Browse button and identify it, as shown in Figure 3-72. When you've identified the desired object, click on the Next button to continue.

Figure 3-71.
Enter the name of the file or program you want the Shortcut to be based on . . .

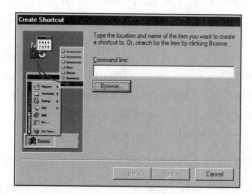

Figure 3-72.
. . . or navigate to it
and select it using
the Browse dialog.

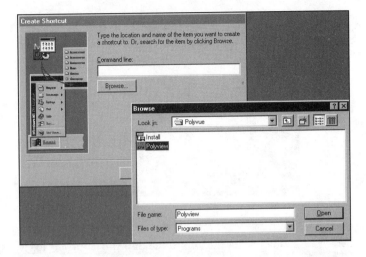

1. The Create Shortcut wizard will next display the dialog shown in Figure 3-73. Change the name in the edit field, or click on Finish to accept the one provided.

Figure 3-73.
You may customize
the Shortcut name,
or click on Finish
to accept the
suggested one.

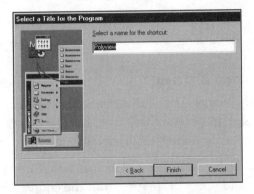

You may find it's just as easy to use a more direct method to make up Shortcuts on the fly. Try this procedure:

1. Open the folder for the program containing the program or data file for which you want to create the Shortcut.

2. Right-click the file and drag it to the Desktop (or the other location where you want the Shortcut to reside).

3. Release the right mouse button to drop the icon, and click once on the Create Shortcut Here entry as shown in Figure 3-74.

Figure 3-74.
Windows will make
the Shortcut where
you drop the icon.

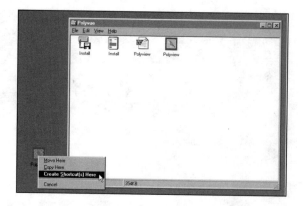

 TIP: If the file you're making the Shortcut for is a program,
you can simply left-click-drag it to the desired Shortcut
location, and Windows will create the Shortcut
automatically.

You can still rename the Shortcut by right-clicking on it and selecting
Rename, or clicking twice on the Shortcut name to edit it directly.

Configuring Shortcuts

Creating a Shortcut was so simple that there can't be much more
to it, right? In general that's true, but there may be times you need
to update, reconfigure, or otherwise manage it. For example:

1. Right-click on the Shortcut we created in the last exercise,
   and select Properties from the context menu. Windows
   will display the Properties dialog for the Shortcut (our
   example being seen in Figure 3-75).

2. Click on the Shortcut tab to see the meat and potatoes
   (shown in Figure 3-76). In this tab you can change the
   target file specification, specify the default directory for
   the program when run, assign a shortcut key for the
   Shortcut, and tell Windows to run the program in a
   normal window, as an icon on the Taskbar (minimized),
   or full screen (maximized). You can also use the Find
   Target or Change Icon buttons.

Figure 3-75.
The Polyvue Shortcut Properties dialog allows you to tune the Shortcut's properties after you've created it. The General tab displays information about the Shortcut.

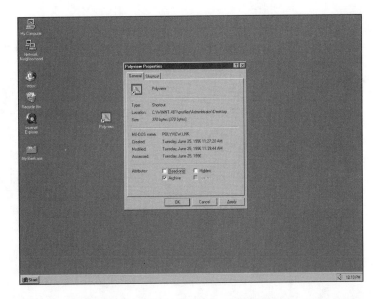

Figure 3-76.
The Shortcut tab is where you can actually alter the Shortcut settings.

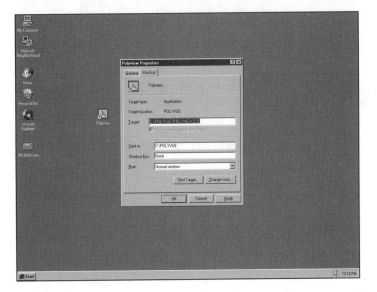

3. For example, let's say (mostly for the sake of making a dull exercise mildly amusing) that I really, really *hate* parrots. Click on the Change Icon button, and Windows will reveal the Change Icon dialog shown in Figure 3-77. Here I have browsed to another file and selected a more seemly icon for a graphics file viewer, one sure not to offend parrot-haters like myself. Next, I click on the OK button to return to the Properties dialog for the Shortcut.

Figure 3-77.
You can use icons
from any file on
your system for
any Shortcut on
your system.

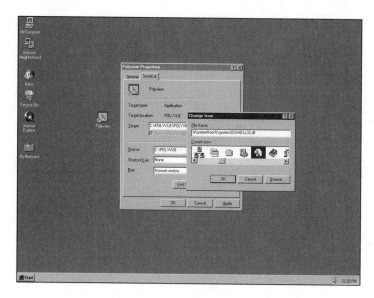

4. Now I click on the Apply button to see how majestic the new icon is on my Desktop. Figure 3-77 demonstrates that I have chosen well, and that I may click OK to close the Properties dialog, knowing that my Desktop is now safe from images of mad tropical birds.

Configuring the NT 4.0 Desktop

Now that you know your way around the NT Desktop, let's look at how you can personalize that personal computer using the tools provided by the Desktop itself. Remember, the Desktop is a program in itself and has configuration options very much like other objects in NT.

Managing Desktop Properties

To view the option settings for the appearance and other functions of the Desktop, follow these steps:

1. Right-click on the Desktop itself, and choose Properties from the context menu. Windows will open the Display Properties dialog as shown in Figure 3-78.

Figure 3-78.
You can preview
the effects of your
settings before you
apply them to the
Desktop.

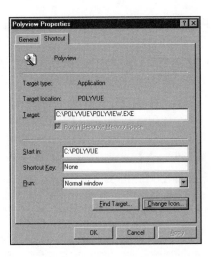

1. Click on the desired tab to view the settings for the functions of the Desktop.

Pretty simple, eh? No big hocus-pocus, just another Properties dialog (you can also reach this one via the Display icon in the Control Panel folder from the Start menu). From here you can change settings for the

- Desktop background
- Screen saver
- Desktop appearance
- Plus! features
- Display settings

We'll take a brief look at each of these areas now. For more information, see Appendix B, "Control Panels".

TIP: Don't forget you can use the What's This? tool in Windows NT Properties dialogs for context-sensitive Help.

The Display Background

Windows NT 4.0 comes with a nice but plain background, a blue-green (actually cyan) with no texture. You can change this to suit your individual tastes from the Background tab of the Display

Properties dialog (seen in Figure 3-78). You can choose from available patterns, edit a pattern, or skip patterns and use a bitmap, tile the bitmap, or use a bitmap big enough to fill your whole Desktop, or have a small bitmap centered in the Desktop and a pattern all around it. In short, you have enough tools and flexibility here to create something either truly ugly or sublime.

> **CAUTION:** Desktop bitmaps use memory. If you're low on RAM already, stick with that plain background, and you'll have a faster machine.

Patterns and bitmaps must be in .BMP format, but they no longer have to be in the Windows directory (you can browse to select them as well). Experiment!

The Screen Saver

First off, I have to burst a big bubble: screen savers don't save screens (well, not unless you have really old equipment). You see, modern monitors don't suffer from the persistent-phosphor problems that led to screen burn-in when the same image sat in one place for hours and days on end (in fact this was mostly a problem on monochrome systems; will both of you using NT on monochrome displays raise your hands, please?). So the terrible secret is not that screen savers don't work, but that *most people don't really need one.* They're purely for fun. OK, you can say they're for security, I guess, but most screen savers added password-protection as an afterthought. Besides, NT is secure anyway, right?

Seriously, the advantage to a screen saver for security on an NT system is the automatic timeout feature (the screen saver will kick in after a preset length of time and can be set to require a password to let you back to the Desktop). On most non-NT systems, a password-protected screen saver means you rebooted the machine to get in, and you should know by now that won't work with NT.

Figures 3-79 and 3-80 show the Screen Saver Display Properties panel and the settings dialog for one of the NT Screen Savers.

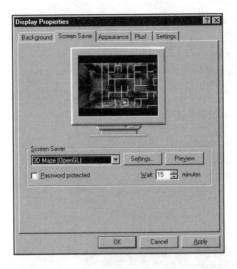

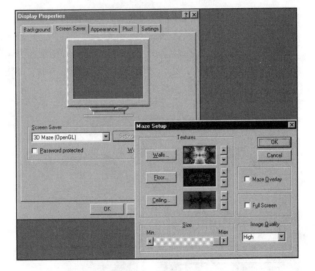

Configuring the Display Appearance

The Appearance tab provides you with an almost unlimited set of
options for customizing the look of your Windows NT
Workstation and the programs you run on it. There's a control for
almost every interface component on your system right here in this
panel. Figure 3-81 shows the Appearance dialog with the Scheme
list selected.

Figure 3-81.
Windows NT
Workstation comes
with a wide variety of
schemes for almost
every occasion,
need, or whim.

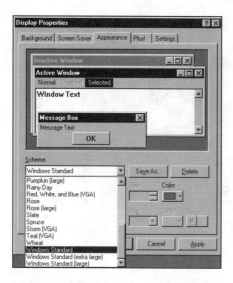

Schemes are actually sets of options saved under a name. You can create a new set or rename an existing one to suit your tastes. Figure 3-82 shows the Item list used to select specific parts of the interface for alteration.

Figure 3-82.
You can individually
adjust almost every
part of the interface
for size and color
and then save those
settings as a new
scheme.

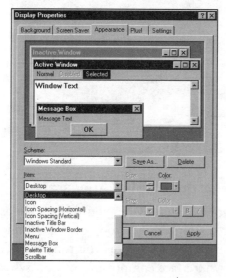

A more direct method of manipulating these settings is simply to click on the part of the interface you wish to edit in the preview window and change the settings directly. Figure 3-83 shows the result of clicking on the Active Window scrollbar and then clicking on the Size spin control to increase the scrollbar width.

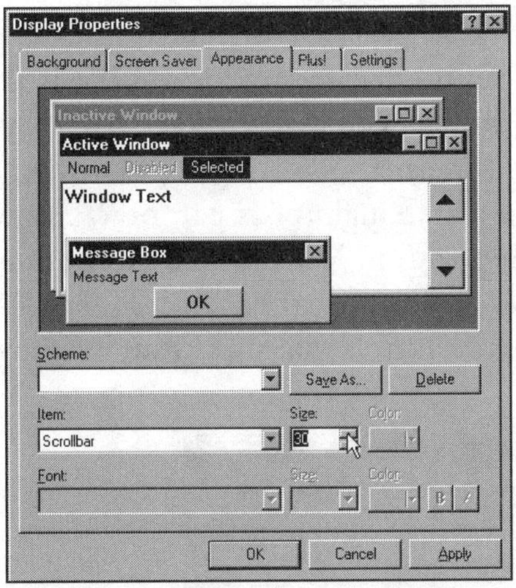

Figure 3-83.
You can adjust interface values directly from this panel (no, I really don't like them my scrollbars this wide, just my ties).

This can get silly pretty quickly also, but it does provide a very real solution to those with vision problems. Figure 3-84 demonstrates how you can alter the interface to make parts of it more legible if necessary.

Figure 3-84.
You can try different font sizes out in the preview window before you save the scheme or apply the change to the Desktop.

Again, don't be afraid to experiment: you can always select Windows Standard from the Scheme list to get back to the installation defaults.

The Plus! Display Features

When Microsoft introduced Windows 95, it also released a companion product called Microsoft Plus! that contained several components (Internet tools, Desktop schemes, display features) that are generally thought of as part of Windows 95, even though they don't ship with it. Much of the Plus! product is now part of Windows NT 4.0 at no extra charge. Figure 3-85 shows the additional interface controls that these features provide.

Figure 3-85.
You can customize the protected Desktop icons, change icon sizes, and further enhance your Desktop using the Plus! features.

If your display system has more than 256 colors and offers a very high resolution, try these display options (just click the check box to select the ones you desire). You may have to restart your system, depending upon your hardware.

The Display Settings

This dialog (Figure 3-86) is essentially the same as the one in Windows 95 and Windows NT 3.51, and it still represents a *drastic* improvement over Windows 3.x video-driver-hell. You can adjust almost every display hardware and software variable from this panel: resolution, color depth, default font size, and the refresh frequency of your video display adapter. You can even test your new settings before you start using them.

NOTE: For more information, see Appendix B, "Control Panels".

Figure 3-86.
Although Windows NT gives you a lot of power over your display hardware adjustments, be cautious in making changes. It's possible to harm your vision and your monitor if you use the wrong setup.

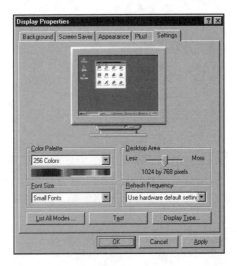

In general, if your display looks right and you don't have any specific need to change it, then leave it alone. If you do need to alter the settings, write down the current set in case you need to return to it (the one big thing missing in this dialog is a Scheme feature like in the Appearance panel).

Customizing the Start Menu

The next area that most of you will want to alter on the Desktop is the Start menu itself. Microsoft has anticipated this and has built in some goodies to help you. To personalize your Start menu, follow these steps:

1. Right-click on the Taskbar and select Properties from the context menu. When the Taskbar Properties dialog appears, click on the Start Menu Programs tab to see the panel shown in Figure 3-87.

Figure 3-87.
Windows has tools
built-in to make
customizing your
Start menu simple.

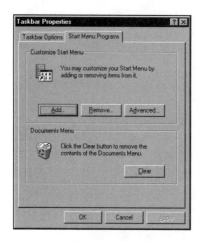

1. To add a program icon to the Start menu, click once on the Add . . . button. The Create Shortcut wizard will appear (as in Figure 3-88).

Figure 3-88.
We're back in wizard
territory, creating
Shortcuts for the
Program menu. Fill in
the blank or browse
to find your
desired program.

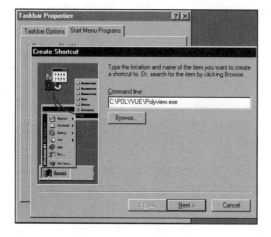

1. After you've provided the name of the program you want to add to the Start menu, click on the Next button and the Create Shortcut wizard will show the dialog seen in Figure 3-89.

Figure 3-89.
There are still a few tricks up this wizard's sleeves. Select which Start menu folder you want your application Shortcut to appear in, and click on the Next button to continue.

1. You can select from among the existing folders, or create a new folder for the Start menu, before you click on Next to continue.

2. Windows will display a dialog asking you to name your menu entry. Edit the name, or simply click on Finish to complete the process. You'll need to close the Taskbar Properties dialog, or continue to add other Start menu icons if you desire to.

Removing icons from the Start menu is a similar process:

1. Right-click on the Taskbar and select Properties from the context menu. When the Taskbar Properties dialog appears, click on the Start Menu Programs tab to see the panel shown in Figure 3-87.

2. To remove a program icon to the Start menu, click once on the Remove . . . button. The Remove Shortcut/Folders window will appear (as in Figure 3-90).

Figure 3-90.
Ooooops! I put my icon in the wrong place. I'll click on the icon, and then on Remove, to nuke it.

1. Select the offending icon and click once on Remove to get rid of the darned thing. Windows will offer you a chance to reconsider via the Confirm File Delete dialog. You know what's best.

2. When you're finished deleting icons, click once on the Close button to vanquish the Remove Shortcut/Folders window.

If you're truly brave you can move to the Advanced level of Start menu customization:

1. Right-click on the Taskbar and select Properties from the context menu. When the Taskbar Properties dialog appears, click on the Start Menu Programs tab to see the panel shown in Figure 3-87.

2. Click once on the Advanced . . . button. The Exploring - Start Menu window will appear (as in Figure 3-91).

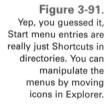

Figure 3-91. Yep, you guessed it, Start menu entries are really just Shortcuts in directories. You can manipulate the menus by moving icons in Explorer.

1. Navigate through the Explorer controls to find the icons you want to add, move, or remove. Simply drag them into or out of the Start menu folders in the Explorer window to manipulate them.

There's another method of editing the Start menu directly; you can skip the Taskbar Properties dialog by right-clicking directly on the Start button as shown in Figure 3-92.

NOTE: See "Mastering Windows NT Explorer," later in this chapter for more information.

Figure 3-92.
A right click on the Start button will bring up a context menu that leads to an Explorer view of the Start menu directories as well.

Customizing the Taskbar

You've already seen the level of flexibility allowed in adjusting other parts of the Windows interface. Windows also allows you to alter the size, position, and behavior of the Taskbar. To adjust the Taskbar, right-click on the Taskbar and select Properties from the context menu. The Taskbar Properties dialog box appears as shown in Figure 3-93.

Figure 3-93.
The Taskbar Options panel doesn't have many adjustments, but the options are all useful ones.

The preview window in this dialog will respond according to the settings you choose. You can Apply the settings before you close the dialog to see how the new settings work for you.

As we demonstrated early in this chapter, you can simply grab the Taskbar with the left mouse and drag it to the side of the Desktop you prefer. You can also control the size of the Taskbar by clicking on the edge of it and dragging when the cursor changes to the double-arrow that denotes window adjustment mode for the cursor (see Figure 3-94).

Figure 3-94.
You may click-drag
the edge of the
Taskbar window to
resize it just like
most other windows.

Managing Files and Folders

Now that we've looked at the Desktop components and the basic techniques you'll need to work in Windows NT Workstation, we can go into more detail about the primary application you'll use as you navigate the Desktop and the storage media on your system.

NOTE: See the sidebar "What Is Explorer," pp. 60 earlier in this chapter for more information.

Windows NT Explorer is the basic file and folder management application for Windows NT. It's also a set of capabilities and features that are presented in other applications and objects throughout NT. As we examine Explorer, you'll see how this is true, and how to turn your understanding of the Explorer application and interface into an advantage in using the rest of the Windows NT interface.

Mastering Windows NT Explorer

I've always been a firm believer that the best way to learn anything is to just start doing it. Let's start our study of Explorer by navigating about your computer.

1. Click on the Start button. When the Start menu appears, select Programs, Windows NT Explorer with a single click. Windows will run Explorer and display the Explorer window shown in Figure 3-95 (your display may look

slightly different, depending upon what hardware and software you have installed; I sincerely hope, for your sake, your system is more tidy than mine).

TIP: You can also start Explorer quickly from the Start button right mouse button context menu.

What's a File? What Is a Folder?

Computer software designers have often borrowed metaphors from other human environments, such as the everyday office. Windows computing is rife with terms like *desktop, file, folder,* and *mailbox.* The goal in borrowing these names is to help the user be more comfortable with the conceptual side of the computing environment, if not the technical.

Humans need to organize things in their work, and so do computers. Files and folders are just names for logical means of organizing data in a computing system. File and folder icons are used to visually represent that data and allow the user to manipulate the data in a graphical user environment.

The term *file* is used both to refer to any discrete structured bit of information in a computing system and, more commonly, to data used as a document when translated to hard-copy printout (such as a written work, a spreadsheet, or a database report). A file can technically be a executable program (such as Microsoft Word) or a document created and manipulated by that program (such as CH3.DOC, the Word document file I'm editing now as I write this chapter), but the common nontechnical usage now usually refers to the document, not the program.

A *folder* is a place to store one or more files. In older file systems (such as MS-DOS) these were called directories (old-timers, remember the DIR command?). You can store folders within folders *hierarchically* to create complex filing systems for storing your data. Windows NT Workstation 4.0 gives you almost unlimited flexibility in manipulating folder structures to manage data to meet your work needs.

Figure 3-95.
The components of
the main Windows
NT Explorer window.

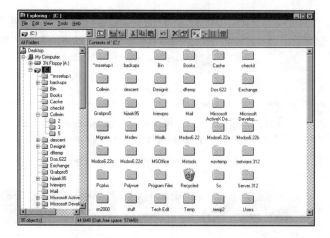

1. Click on a folder icon in the tree control in the left pane
    (for example, the MSOffice folder under the C: branch of
    the folder tree). You may need to scroll down in the left
    Explorer pane to see the folder you desire. Explorer will
    display the contents of the folder in the right pane
    (as shown in Figure 3-96).

Figure 3-96.
You can display the
contents of a folder
simply by clicking on it
in the left pane.

1. Notice the small plus symbol box on the tree to the left of
    the MSOffice folder and many of the other folders. Click
    once on the plus symbol box, and Explorer will expand
    the tree to show subfolders in the MSOffice folder (as
    shown in Figure 3-97).

Figure 3-97.
You can expand or contract the folder tree in the left Explorer pane with a single click on the Expand/Contract box. Notice that some folders don't have this box (this indicates there are no subfolders nested within them). Also note that expanded folders have a minus symbol instead of the plus (click on the minus to contract the folder display).

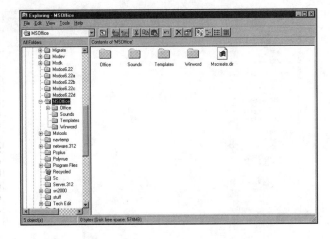

1. Notice that expanding the display in the left pane didn't change the view in the right pane. You can scroll up and down the left pane and expand/contract its branches at will, but until you actually click on another folder, the right pane will remain the same. Test this by clicking once to expand the Program Files folder in the left Explorer pane (don't click on the folder, just the plus sign to the left of it). Explorer will expand the Program Files folder without altering the right pane, as shown in Figure 3-98.

Figure 3-98.
You can investigate the contents of other left pane branches without changing the contents displayed in the right.

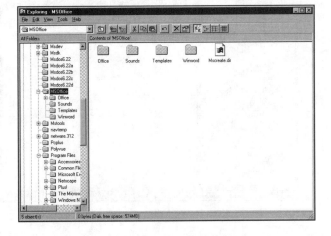

1. Now click once on the Program Files folder icon in the left pane. Explorer will now display the contents of that folder in the right pane (see Figure 3-99).

Figure 3-99.
Clicking once on a
folder in the left
pane causes Explorer
to display its contents
in the right.

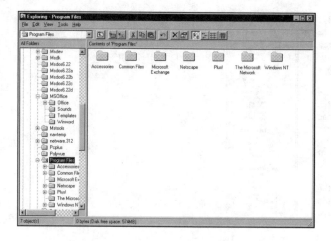

1. Expand the left pane Program Files Accessories folder by
   clicking once on the plus sign directly to left of the
   Accessories folder icon. Notice that it's hard to read the left
   pane tree since we've expanded it so much. Move the mouse
   cursor to the border between the left pane scrollbar and the
   right pane display area, and when the cursor changes to the
   double arrow, click and drag it until you can see the entire
   left pane tree width (as shown in Figure 3-100).

Figure 3-100.
You can easily adjust
the left/right pane
width for a better
display of your
drive's contents.

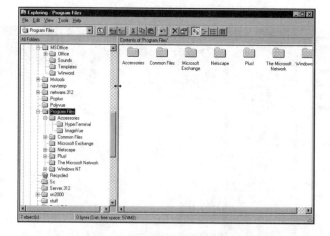

1. Don't worry that a folder has been partially hidden at the
   far right of the right pane. Go to the View menu, and
   select Arrange Icons, Auto Arrange to correct the display.

2. Use the scrollbar on the left pane and move to the top of
   the left pane tree. Look for the My Computer icon, and
   click once on the contract tool to the left of it (the minus
   sign in the small box). Explorer will display the tree as
   shown in Figure 3-101.

Figure 3-101.
The top level of
Explorer's view of
your system. When
you jump up a level
above a drive
subsystem, Explorer
will automatically
display the contents
of the selected item.

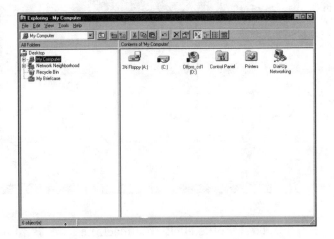

That's a quick overview of how to use Explorer to view the contents
of your system. Now let's use Explorer to check out the contents of
another machine on a network.

> **NOTE:** For more information on setting up Windows
> NT Workstation 4.0 on a LAN, see Chapter 4 "Getting
> Your NT Workstation on the Network".

Exploring Network Computers

In Figure 3-101 you saw how the topmost level of the Explorer
view is of your Desktop, not just the drive we started on. We left
the Explorer window with My Computer highlighted in the left
pane tree control, with the right pane showing the contents of the
local system. Now let's try looking at the contents of another
computer on a local area network (LAN):

1. Click once on the Network Neighborhood icon in the left
   Explorer pane. Explorer will display the contents of
   Network Neighborhood in the right pane.

2. In the right pane, double-click on one of the computer icons (for this example, I'll use my own network, seen in all its glory in Figure 3-102).

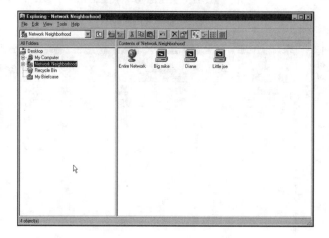

1. Double-click on a machine icon. Explorer will reveal the contents of that system (any contents that are shared, that is). Figure 3-103 shows the shared contents of the machine "Diane" (who's owner is especially cute, and brews a really mean cup of Java).

1. Double-click on any folders in the right pane to view their contents. Explorer will display the folder contents in the right pane as you navigate (see Figure 3-104).

Figure 3-104.
Notice that Explorer
updates the left pane
view as you browse in
the right pane (looks
like Diane's been a
busy girl between
cups of coffee;
some of this stuff
wasn't there
yesterday!).

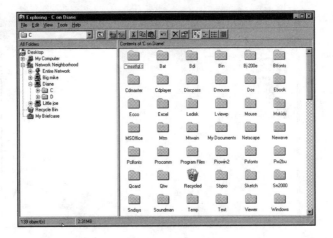

TIP: You can also jump directly to another machine or
folder by using the left pane tree control.

1. By now you may be as curious as I am about what exactly
   is up on this machine (where did Diane get the money for
   a new printer and software? Did the garage sale do *that*
   well?). Let's look at the other drive on "Diane." Go to the
   Toolbar (right underneath the menu) and click on the
   icon of the little folder with the up arrow. This will take
   us up a level, back to the display we saw in Figure 3-103.

2. Double-click on the other right-pane drive icon on the
   remote computer (in this case, the icon is labeled D).
   Explorer will display the contents of that drive (see
   Figure 3-105).

NOTE: For more information on sharing network
resources, see "Sharing Folders," later in this chapter.

So there's an overview of how you can use Explorer to view files
and folders (and other resources, such as printers) on your local
system and the network. You probably notice that I sneaked in
some exercises on using both the left and right panes to navigate,
as well as some other tools in Explorer. They'll come in handy as
we continue to learn about this program.

Figure 3-105.
You can move between
drives on remote
systems just as if they
were on your local
computer using either
the right pane folder
view or the left pane
tree control.

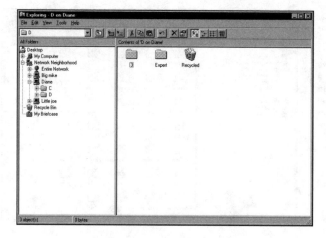

Other Explorer Views

Let's look at some other options within Explorer that you'll surely
want to know about. First off, be sure that you know you can use
Explorer in a full-screen view by maximizing it. Simply click on
the Maximize button (in the middle of the group of three at the
top-right of any Windows NT program window). Second, you can
control the display of information in the right pane quickly by
using the Toolbar. There are four main styles of view available:

- Large icons
- Small icons
- List
- Details

Each of these views is available by clicking on the appropriate
icon at the right end of the Explorer Toolbar, or from the View
menu. We'll use each of these views in the next few exercises, so I
won't take up time, space, or petroleum products by talking about
them now.

The Explorer View Menu

Before we go further, let's look at some other options that can
affect the content of what's displayed in Explorer, not just the style
of the display. To view these options, select View ➤ Options from
the main Explorer menu. Windows NT Explorer will display the
Options dialog shown in Figure 3-106.

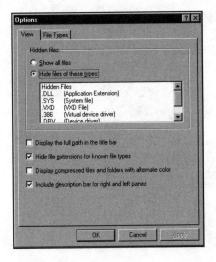

From this dialog you can:

- Reveal or continue to hide "hidden" files
- Tell Windows NT to always display the complete file path in all Explorer windows (not just the current folder name)
- Reveal or continue to hide filename extensions for all registered file types
- Display compressed data with different icon colors
- Hide or display the description bars for Explorer panes

If you need additional information on any of these options, be sure to use the "What's This?" Help icon button in the top right of the dialog to get additional information.

Clicking on the File Types tab in the Explorer Options dialog reveals the pane shown in Figure 3-107. This dialog displays registered file types and allows you to edit the settings for each or add additional types. This set of controls determines what happens when you double-click on a file that's not a program, by telling Windows NT what application you want to use to open, play, or otherwise use the file.

Figure 3-107.
You can manage file
associations from the
File Types dialog.
Know whereof you
adjust before you go
messin' round here.

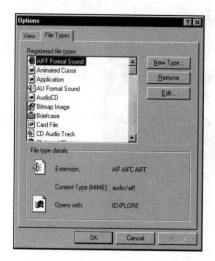

TIP: Remember to review the icons in the View ➢ Options ➢ File Types dialog whenever you have trouble identifying a file from its icon.

Other Explorer Menus

Now that we've peeked at the View menu, let's take a moment to view the other menus in Explorer. Click on drive C: in the Explorer left pane and then select the File menu; you'll see the drop-menu shown in Figure 3-108.

Figure 3-108.
The File menu is
minimal if you have
no objects other
than a drive selected.

Select Properties from the File menu, and you'll get the Properties dialog for drive C: (as to be expected, we've selected drive C: in the left pane). Select File ➢ New, and you'll see the menu cascade shown in Figure 3-109.

Figure 3-109.
This menu is essentially the same as the right mouse button context menu for the Desktop and folders (you may have other items here depending upon your installed software).

Now click on any old item in the right pane and select the File menu again. Figure 3-110 shows the difference.

Figure 3-110.
Your File menu options depend upon the object selected. Selecting a folder results in more options than selecting a drive of a single file, since there are other features for folders (such as sharing).

Essentially, the File menu in Explorer behaves the same as the right mouse button context menu anywhere else in Windows NT. There are three other menus in Explorer that we haven't looked at:

- Edit
- Tools
- Help

Each of these will be critical in the exercises that follow in the next sections of this chapter, so carry on and I'll give you details on each of them when the time comes.

Other Views of Explorer

I'll digress slightly for a moment to show you one of the more beautiful features of the overall Windows NT 4.0 interface technology design: reusable components. Follow me on another little exercise:

1. Using the left pane tree control in Explorer, select My Computer (so that the right pane of Explorer shows the contents of My Computer).

2. Resize Explorer on your desktop so that you can see the My Computer icon on the Desktop. Double-click on Desktop My Computer to open it, and arrange your Desktop to look something like Figure 3-111.

Figure 3-111.
Why do you need two views of the same stuff? Hang with me, we're almost there.

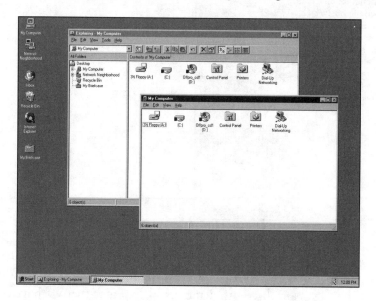

3. Now select the View menu in the My Computer window (the one opened from the Desktop icon, not the Explorer window). Select Toolbar so that it's checked, and your screen looks like Figure 3-112.

So rather than having to sit through two boring tutorials, one on My Computer, and this one, you should now realize just how much you can leverage your investment in Explorer knowledge as you use the rest of Windows NT Workstation 4.0. Here's further proof:

Figure 3-112.
The resemblance is striking. Except for the left pane, the My Computer Window is almost precisely the same as the Explorer one. You'll find that all other controls are nearly identical as well.

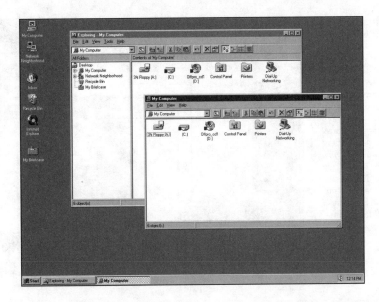

1. Select View ➢ Options from the My Computer window main menu. Windows NT will display the Options dialog. Click on the View tab and then the File Types tab (you'll see they look almost identical to the Explorer ones you saw earlier in this chapter).

TIP: Remember to review the icons in the View ➢ Options ➢ File Types dialog whenever you have trouble identifying a file from its icon.

2. Click on the Folder tab to return to it so that your screen looks like the one pictured in Figure 3-113.

3. Close the Options tab by clicking on OK when you're finished.

This is another example of the ultimate flexibility the designers of Windows NT 4.0 have brought to the user: you can choose the very interface you want to use to navigate the file system and control how the interface behaves. The underlying file and display services are essentially the same, regardless of how you use them.

Figure 3-113.
This is the main difference in the My Computer view of NT vs. the Explorer two-pane view. From the My Computer view, you can open multiple windows or always have the same window that changes to display new content as you navigate. The menus have minor differences, but you can perform the same basic tasks from either.

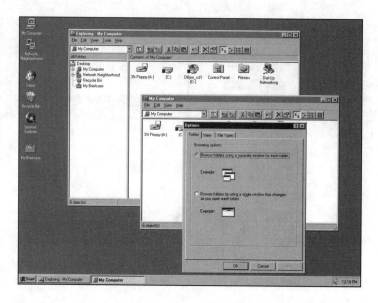

Managing Files and Folders with Explorer

Now that you're familiar with the Explorer interface and navigation procedures, we can try some of Explorer's everyday procedures. In this section, we'll:

- Copy files
- Move files
- Delete files

all from the Explorer interface.

Copying Files with Explorer

Copying files with Explorer couldn't be much simpler, except that you have to choose which of the easy ways you want to use to do it with:

- Using drag-and-drop
- Using the Edit menu

I know, life is hard sometimes. To copy files via drag-and-drop:

1. Open the Explorer window to the folder where the files you want to copy are (for example, as shown in Figure 3-114).

Figure 3-114.
Lasso-selecting files is
pretty darned fast if
they're all in a
contiguous group.
Just click on the
background and
drag the cursor to
contain the icons
you want to select.

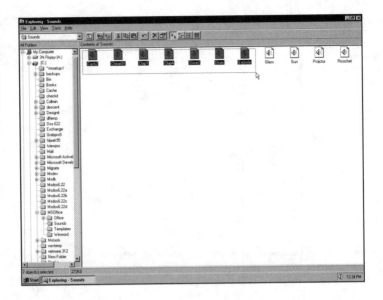

2. Select the files using one of these methods:

    • Click on one file.

    • Ctrl-click on multiple files.

    • Lasso-select multiple files by drawing around the files with the left mouse button.

    • Combine the preceding steps.

3. When the files are all selected, locate the target folder in the left Explorer pane. Don't click on the folder yet, just adjust the left pane so that it's visible.

4. Return to the right pane and click/hold on the selected group with the right mouse button. Drag the group to the target folder and release it. Explorer will display the context menu shown in Figure 3-115. Select Copy here and let 'er rip.

Alternatively, you may want to go the really easy route, using the Edit menu. Try this procedure:

1. Select a bunch of files (review the exercise immediately preceding this one if you're lost).

2. Select Edit ➤ Copy.

Figure 3-115.
Drop the selected
files on the target
folder and tell
Windows you want
to copy them.

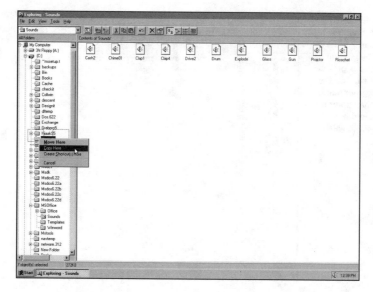

3. Here's the different part: click on the target folder in the
   left pane to open it so that it is displayed in the right
   pane.

4. Select Edit ➤ Paste. Explorer will put the copied file in
   the folder currently open in the right pane.

That's really all there is to it. About the worst case is that you'll
already have a file by that name in the target directory, in which case
you'll see a warning dialog such as the one shown in Figure 3-116.

Figure 3-116.
Windows won't take
the responsibility for
overwriting files of the
same name, so you
may have to resolve
conflicts such as this
one. Know your data!

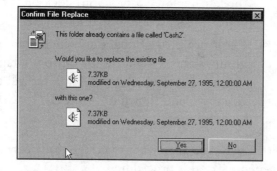

Remember, Copy and Paste are available from the right mouse
button context menu as well, so you can select them there instead
of the Edit menu if you choose.

TIP: You can also copy files by selecting them and dragging them with the left mouse button. If you're dragging them to a folder on a *different* drive or computer, simply select and drag them and they'll be copied, not moved. If you want to copy files to a folder on the same drive using the left mouse button, select them and then depress and hold the Ctrl key while dragging and dropping them to the target folder.

Moving Files with Explorer

You've already seen a couple of procedures for copying files. Moving files is essentially the same procedure, except you delete the source files when you're done (or rather, you tell Windows to do it for you). To move files with the right mouse button menu:

1. Open the Explorer window to the folder where the files you want to move are located.

2. Select the files.

3. When the files are all selected, locate the target folder in the left Explorer pane. Don't click on the folder yet, just adjust the left pane so that it's visible.

4. Return to the right pane and click/hold on the selected group with the right mouse button. Drag the group to the target folder and release it. Explorer will display the context menu shown in Figure 3-115. Select Move.

To move files using the Edit menu:

1. Select a bunch of files (you really should know how by now).

2. Select Edit ➤ Cut.

3. Click on the target folder in the left pane to open it so it is displayed in the right pane.

4. Select Edit ➤ Paste. Explorer will put the moved files in the folder currently open in the right pane.

Remember, Cut and Paste are available from the right mouse button context menu as well, so you can select them there instead of the Edit menu if you choose.

TIP: You can also move files by selecting them and dragging them with the left mouse button. If you're dragging them to a folder on the *same* drive, they'll be moved, not copied (unless they're program files; use the right mouse button for program files).

Deleting Files with Explorer

Just as there are many ways to copy and move files in Explorer, there are several ways and means to delete files as well:

- Drag them to the Recycle Bin (left or right mouse button drag and drop).
- The File menu Delete command
- The [Delete] key (the old-fashioned way)
- The right mouse button Delete command

I'm going to trust you to try these out all by yourself. The basic procedure is this:

1. Select the file.
2. Pick a way to delete it (see the preceding list for guidance).
3. Delete it.

Remember, if you screw up, review the section on the Recycle Bin earlier in this chapter.

NOTE: See "The Recycle Bin," pp. 80 earlier in this chapter for more information.

Managing Folders with Explorer

There's basically one thing to remember as we discuss managing or manipulating folders in Explorer: treat them just like files. All the procedures we've just covered regarding file management apply equally well to moving folders or groups of folders. Selecting, copying, moving, and deleting folders all involve pretty much the same procedures as doing those things to individual files, so just get out there and go for it (how does it feel to be an expert?).

OK, so there is one big difference. . . .

Sharing Folders with Explorer

You can control sharing rights at the drive, folder, and file level in Windows NT Workstation 4.0 (only down to the folder level on FAT file systems, however), so be aware that you have other options for controlling folders in Explorer. We'll discuss those specifics again in Chapter 4, "Getting Your NT Workstation on the Network", and in Appendix B, "Managing NT Security". Stay tuned, or go ahead, *touch that dial.*

Spicy Smoked Ginger Ribs (Missouri Style)

OK, I promised the faithful sidebar readers among you a really great recipe somewhere in the book. This section is just a wee bit dry (how exciting can Windows NT Explorer be?), so I thought this would be just the place to sneak in the food part. Perhaps the editors won't catch it (or maybe they're hungry too).

First, start with your basic cheap water smoker (I use the three-foot-tall black kind that looks a lot like the cousin of a certain cute robot from a famous science-fiction movie trilogy). If you have the recipe or instruction book for the smoker, read it first so that you can ignore the manufacturer's recommendations more efficiently later.

Start with about ten pounds of good quality charcoal in the bottom pan of the smoker, which will be brought to a white-hotness (be sure to let any starter burn completely off). Leave the water pot out of the smoker until later (cover the inside of it with aluminum foil).

After the fire is lit and is burning down, go into your kitchen, get a large pot, and start boiling the hickory and apple wood chips (about three quarts of chips to 1.5 gallons of water). While the chips start boiling, turn them off and let them soak uncovered. Start preparing the pork ribs (buy the kind that in Missouri are called "country style," which means they are mostly meat, not 85 percent fat and bone like most spare ribs). Salt the ribs liberally, as they will be sitting in a fairly low-heat smoker for some time and thingies-you-don't-want-to-eat can grow during the first hour or so of cooking (the saline environment provides protection against such culinary atrocities).

Spicy Smoked Ginger Ribs (Missouri Style) cont...

When the ribs are salted, place them in a container to keep the cats off them while you prep the smoker. Drink a (*insert favorite beverage*) while the wood chips boil and the fire burns down some more.

Take three apples, cut them in half, and put them in a small bowl. Find your pound box of black pepper, the fresh ginger root, the stick of real butter, the pint of honey, the four cloves of garlic, and the bottle of single-malt scotch. And a two-quart saucepan.

Get another big pot and a large colander. Slowly pour the wood chips into the colander, carefully saving every drop of the precious wood-water. Find a volunteer, and carry the pot of wood-water, the colander of steaming hot wood-chips, the bowl of apple halves, the pound box of black pepper, and the container of ribs to the smoker. Be careful not to burn yourself on the chips or wood-water, and be careful not to spill any, because you'll need every chip and drop for what's next.

If the charcoal is ready (it should be), *very carefully* pour the wood-chips over the fire (don't lean too far over the charcoal when you pour the chips in or you'll get a real faceful of steam). Immediately after that, put the water pot in position. Quickly pour in the wood-water, being careful not to spill any on the fire (save any extra for topping off the water pot later). Quickly pour in the apples and one half of the pound box of black pepper. Place the grill over the water pot, and start arranging the ribs. When all the ribs are in place, close the smoker. Do not peek at it!

Go back to the kitchen, add the stick of real butter into the saucepan, and heat it slooooooowly over a very low heat, as it can scorch quite easily. When the butter is melted, pour in the honey, the rest of the black pepper, and about a half cup of the scotch. Start chopping up, or grinding up, a few ounces of the fresh ginger and all the garlic. Add them to the mix and keep it cooking until it's a fragrant goo. Set it aside, but don't let it cool too much. You may want to keep it in a larger pan of hot water to keep it heated but not in danger of burning.

Check the smoker in about an hour. Be sure to keep the water pot near full by topping it off through the little side door of the smoker. *Don't open the top of the smoker.* If you used enough

> ## Spicy Smoked Ginger Ribs (Missouri Style) cont...
>
> charcoal, this is about all you'll need to do for another three hours. Have another (*insert favorite beverage*).
>
> After the first four hours, top off the water pot again, and gently stir the charcoal through the little side door you used for watering (you may add more charcoal through this door if you're careful, but start it outside the smoker in another container first, and be sure to let it burn all starter off as well or your ribs will taste like so much jet fuel). Reheat the butter-ginger-honey-garlic-scotch-pepper stuff until it pours easily. Open the smoker top, and quickly pour it all over each and every rib. Close the smoker lid *immediately*. Do not peek for another three hours, except to check the water. After three hours, start checking the ribs.
>
> When the ribs are so soft you can tear them with your bare fingers, they're ready (usually seven to eight hours in summer, longer in winter).
>
> Try not to eat them all at once.

Printing in Windows NT Workstation 4.0

We've shown you how to start your computer, get around the Desktop, open files, start applications, customize the menus, open documents, copy, delete, move and otherwise puree your data—so how do you print something? Glad you asked.

For the sake of keeping this section simple, we're going to assume that you've been fortunate and whoever set up and installed your system, including Windows NT Workstation 4.0, has taken care of connecting and testing your printer hardware and NT printer drivers. If not, proceed to Go, which is located in Appendix B, "Configuring Printers" (where we actually cover configuring, installing, troubleshooting, and whatever else you might need to know about NT printing). If your system *is* already set up, you're in luck, because this is really pretty short and sweet.

Printing from Files

You don't need to open an application to print a data file, you just need to have that application installed. Just as in earlier versions of Windows, the operating system will take care of all the dirty work if you have all the tools in place for the job. To print from a data file:

1. Select the file with the right mouse button. When the context menu appears, select Print.

2. Stand back.

Windows will call the application, and the application will load the file and print it. On a fast machine, this is fairly quick depending upon the application.

What if the Print command doesn't appear in the context menu for the file? Then Windows can't help you, because it has no way of knowing how to handle the file. All of this depends upon file associations, just like several other functions that you may take for granted within Windows.

> **NOTE:** See Appendix B, "Managing File Associations," for more information.

Printing from Applications

Although printing files from the right mouse button menu is quick simple and easy, printing from within applications gives you more control. The procedure is like this:

1. Open the application (for instance, WordPad) and open the file, or find the file and double-click on it to start the application with the file loaded (your choice).

2. When you're ready to print the file, select the Print command from the File menu. The application will display a dialog much like the one in Figure 3-117.

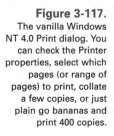
Figure 3-117.
The vanilla Windows
NT 4.0 Print dialog. You
can check the Printer
properties, select which
pages (or range of
pages) to print, collate
a few copies, or just
plain go bananas and
print 400 copies.

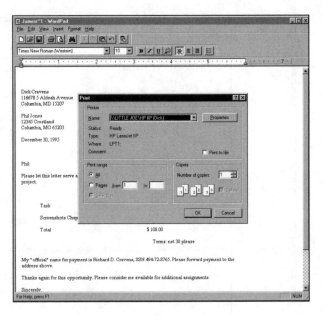

1. When you've set all the options you desire, click on OK and Windows NT 4.0 will send the job to the printer.

Print Preview

You may also wish to take advantage of some application's print preview features. WordPad, for example, allows you to look at a miniature preview of your document before you send it to the printer. To use print preview:

1. Open the application (for instance, WordPad) and open the file, or find the file and double-click on it to start the application with the file loaded (your choice).

2. When you're ready to preview the file, select the Print Preview command from the File menu (it may be in a slightly different location depending upon the application). The application will display a window much like the one in Figure 3-118.

Figure 3-118.
Some applications offer a Print Preview feature, in which you can make adjustments to margins, zoom in to view the document, adjust the printer settings, and the like before you commit the job to the printer.

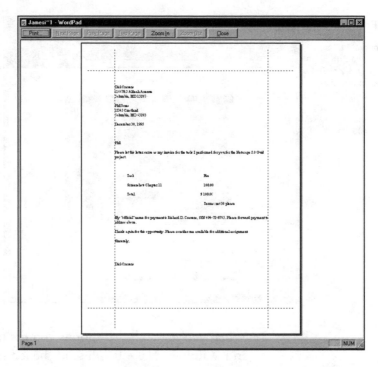

1. When you've set all the options you desire, click on Print and the application will display the Print dialog (or click on Close if you need to return to the document for further editing).

2. When the Print dialog appears, make any further adjustments as necessary, and then click on OK to send the job to the printer.

Express Printing in Applications

Most Windows applications now have a "express" printing button (as seen in Figure 3-119) on their Toolbar. Pressing this sends the current document to the printer immediately, using the current printer settings in the Print dialog seen in Figure 3-117. If you're using the same printer and printer settings again and again, this may be just the ticket for you.

Figure 3-119.
Most newer Windows
applications will let you
send a job straight to
the printer without any
intermediate dialogs.

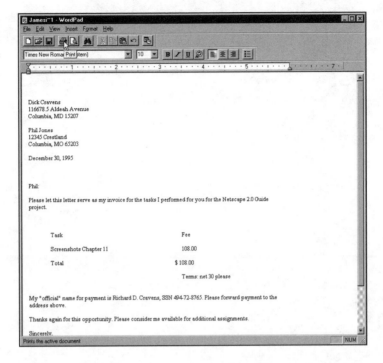

Onwards

In our next chapter, we'll look at how to get your Windows NT
Workstation on the network and talking to other systems. Then,
in Chapter 6, we'll take a look at connecting to other computers,
networks, and the Internet over the phone lines.

CHAPTER 4

NETWORKING WINDOWS NT 4.0 WORKSTATION

Just as no man is an island, no computer can function totally disconnected from other information systems. The history of modern electronic computing is largely the story of various models for connectivity between users, computer systems, and the outside world of information. In keeping with this rich tradition, Windows NT Workstation 4.0 is designed from the ground up to provide the latest, most robust and flexible set of tools for interconnectivity and communications in the history of desktop computing, on any platform. In this chapter, we'll introduce you to

- **Basic networking concepts**

- **Simple procedures for configuring Windows NT for network access**

- **Basic network protocol choices and configurations**

- **Remote networking services**

This chapter's "sister" in describing Windows NT Workstation 4.0's connectivity features is Chapter 6, "Windows NT Communications and the Internet." You may want to skip ahead to that chapter if your system is already on the network and you need basic assistance in using the communications applications in NT 4.0.

Basic Network Concepts

It's outside of the scope of this tome to provide a complete reference to modern PC networking technology, but we can touch on a few basic principles just in case you're new to this area of computing.

TIP: See Appendix F, "Glossary," for definitions of any new networking or computing terms.

Here are a few primary concepts that you need under your belt before we begin:

- **Network:** Two or more computers normally connected for the interchange of information or services
- **Network connection:** The physical or logical means by which one computer is linked to the network and therefore to other computers
- **Network interface card (NIC):** The adapter that provides physical and logical interfaces for network connections
- **Drivers:** Code that allows the operating system and applications access to a device. A network driver allows access to a network interface card.
- **Client:** An application, computer, or other entity that issues requests and receives service
- **Server:** An application, computer, or other entity that receives requests and issues service in response
- **Host:** A computer on a network (also referred to as a *workstation* or *node*)
- **Domain:** A group of computers on a network (also referred to as workgroup)
- **Protocol:** Any set of rules or procedures for exchange of information
- **User:** You (or anyone else with access to the network)
- **Logon/logoff:** The processes used to start a network session and end it (also interchangeably referred to as login/logout)

There, that wasn't that scary, was it? Don't be intimidated by computer networking terminology; it's really no harder than most stereo instructions, or plumbing (and it's definitely easier than tax forms). You just need to get your feet wet to feel comfy. Most people use networked systems all day long and simply don't realize it, since the devices on those networks aren't typically thought of in the same way as computers. The telephone system is one large network, as are the newest cable TV systems. If you use an automatic teller machine, you're on a true computer network (it just doesn't run Windows—yet). By the time you're finished with this chapter, you'll see how networking with Windows NT is really simpler than getting cable service (at least in my town).

If you haven't yet networked your PCs, you need to seriously consider the benefits of doing so. Even having two home PCs constitutes justification for networking for many people (hey, you can be the first on your block with an NT domain!). The free fall of network interface card prices and the inclusion of networking capabilities in the operating system have eliminated the most obvious objections to networking for most users. Here are some of the basic advantages to networking your PCs, for either home or business:

- **Sharing of resources:** Files, applications, printers, storage, backup devices
- **Speed of access:** No more "floppynet"
- **Lack of media restrictions:** Now you can move that 4MB database file without large-capacity removable media—the network doesn't care how large the file is, it just moves it or shares it.
- **Enhanced automation:** The easier it is to share information, the simpler it is to tell the computer how to do complex repetitive work for you.
- **Enhanced communications:** The easier it is to share information, the more people will do it.

Plus, as every employee at a software development firm knows, the number one reason to network computers:

- **Playing multiuser games:** Doom, Descent, Duke Nukem, and so on, otherwise known as *network performance testing*

So now that you're sold on the networking idea, let's get down to showing you how easy it is to do it.

Getting Your NT Workstation on the Network

There are several steps to networking an NT Workstation. The steps are all really pretty simple; there are just quite a few (depending upon how many network *types* you need access to, perhaps more than quite a few). At the highest level, the tasks can be broken down into the following:

- Establishing the physical connections (interface card and cables)
- Configuring the hardware
- Installing support drivers
- Configuring the software (protocol and host settings)
- Installing network client software (network services)
- Confirming the connections

That's pretty much it, and pretty much the order you have to attack it in. If you've already done part of the sequence, feel free to skip ahead (Windows NT Setup may also have done part of the work when your system was installed). Here we go!

Installing Network Hardware

There are two parts to every computer process or operation, the logical and the physical. Networking is no different. If you don't have a network adapter in your PC already, it's pretty simple to add one.

NOTE: NT Setup generally will automatically detect and install the *first* network card it finds on a machine. If you have more than one, you'll need to begin the installation process manually. NT will still help you, but you'll need to tell it to start.

Configuring the Network Adapter

Your network adapter card needs a unique set of system resources to function correctly, just like every other adapter card in your system: a base I/O address and an IRQ setting. You'll probably not need to know or adjust the actual values for these settings with most major late-model network cards. If you do need to adjust these values, there are generally two ways to do so: via hardware jumpers or via software settings. Please consult your hardware documentation for details (there are simply too many types of adapter cards to even begin to discuss the procedures here). Odds are pretty good that NT can work with the default settings for your card.

> **TIP:** You can save yourself some trouble before purchasing or installing a network card by checking the Windows NT Hardware Compatibility List to see if the brand and model of card are supported. See Appendix A, "Installing Windows NT 4.0," for more details.

Installing Network Drivers

Once your card is physically in the machine, you'll need to tell NT what type of card it is:

1. From the Start menu, open the Control Panel group and double-click on the Network icon. Windows NT will display the Network Control Panel. Click on the Adapter tab and then on the Add button. Windows NT will display the Select Network Adapter dialog as shown in Figure 4-1.

2. Select your adapter card from the list and click on the OK button. A Network Card Setup dialog will appear as shown in Figure 4-2. Select the appropriate settings for your card and click on the OK button.

3. If your system contains more than one hardware bus (most Pentiums do), you'll need to tell NT which bus the network adapter card is on (see Figure 4-3). Confirm the information and click on OK to continue.

Figure 4-1.
NT 4.0 comes with
drivers for a very wide
variety of network
interface cards.

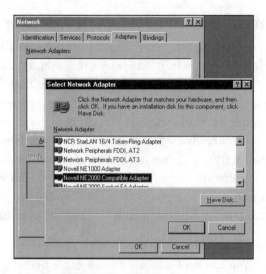

Figure 4-2.
You'll need to confirm
your network card
settings.

Figure 4-3.
You may need to
confirm which adapter
bus the network card is
on. Consult your PC
documentation if you
need assistance.

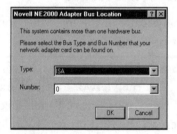

4. Windows NT Setup may need to copy some files from
   your installation media. If a dialog appears asking for the
   location of the installation files, provide it and select
   Continue to finish installing your network adapter drivers.
   Windows NT will copy the files, and the name of your
   adapter will appear in the Network dialog Adapters tab
   pane as shown in Figure 4-4.

Figure 4-4.
When the drivers are
installed, NT will
display your adapter
in the Network
Control Panel.

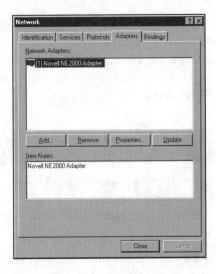

Windows NT will prompt you to restart your system to invoke the new drivers. That's all there is to installing your network card. Now let's tell it what networking languages we want it to speak.

Installing Protocols

There are a wide variety of network protocol types. Windows NT Workstation comes equipped to handle the most common ones and can be configured to handle any future ones that are yet to be written. All networking protocols and services used with NT are true 32-bit in design for the highest performance (16-bit applications will work fine with them, however). Protocols supported in the basic NT 4.0 Workstation package are

- NetBEUI (Microsoft Networks)
- TCP/IP (Internet, intranet, UNIX client/server)
- NWLink IPX/SPX (Novell Netware)
- IBM DLC (AS400, other mainframes)
- AppleTalk (Macintosh)

As mentioned above, other protocol types can be supported via third-party drivers (Banyan Vines and UNIX NFS are the most obvious examples). See your network administrator or vendor for information on other protocols.

Windows NT Workstation 4.0 can support all these different protocol and network types simultaneously—and over multiple network adapters, or some even via the serial port and a modem. RAS (Remote Access Services) allows network connectivity using NetBEUI, TCP/IP, and IPX/SPX.

Choosing a Network Protocol

How do you know which protocol to use? If you're on a corporate network, the choices are usually made for you—use the protocols everyone else is using (see your friend the network administrator for details).

If you're setting up a home or small business system, and you're the administrator, choose the protocol that is simplest and meets your needs. Microsoft has made the Microsoft Network protocol (NetBEUI) incredibly simple to use, and it meets the needs of most users quite well. If you're planning on connecting your network to the global Internet, TCP/IP is a logical choice.

In any case, don't forget that Windows NT supports multiple simultaneous network types for truly flexible connectivity. Adding another network protocol as your expertise and needs grow is no problem at all in most systems.

To add a network protocol to your system:

1. From the Network Control Panel, click on the Protocols tab and select the Add button. Windows NT will display the Select Network Protocol dialog as shown in Figure 4-5.

2. Select the protocol you want to install (for this example, NetBEUI) and click on OK. Setup will need to copy some files, so tell it where to find them if asked. When NT finishes copying the driver files, it will display the protocol name in the Network Control Panel Protocols tab pane as shown in Figure 4-6.

Adding a second, third, and fourth protocol is just as simple as the first. Once they're added, you'll need to configure Windows NT to identify your machine on the network.

Figure 4-5.
You can select from a wide variety of protocol support in NT 4.0.

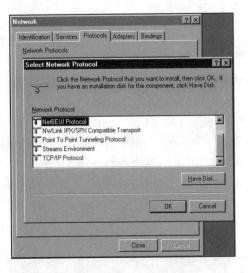

Figure 4-6.
Windows NT makes it simple to install and manage network protocols.

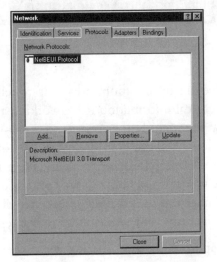

Identifying Your Workstation

Any time you connect a workstation to a network system, you need to be extremely specific about what connections you're going to use, as well as meticulous about the details of those connections:

- Network types used (protocols such as TCP/IP, NetBEUI, IPX/SPX)

- Machine, workgroup, and domain names for Windows NT network installations

- Machine IP address, machine hostname, local network domain name, gateway IP address, and DNS IP address for TCP/IP network installations
- WINS and DHCP capabilities of NT server—based TCP/IP network installations
- RAS host system phone number, user name, and password (for each RAS connection), plus network types (protocols) supported by the RAS connection
- Server name, user name and password for each Novell server (for Novell network installations)

NOTE: See Chapter 6, "Windows NT Communications and the Internet," for general information on TCP/IP and Remote Access Services configuration issues.

Once you have this information, it's a snap to tell NT how to use it. The most critical information in networking any computer system is how you identify that system to the rest of the network. Imagine if suddenly all the house numbers and other addresses were to disappear from every building in your city, or if all the telephones in the world simply rang at random, instead of when a particular number was dialed. That's how important it is to clearly and uniquely identify your workstation to the rest of your network.

This is accomplished by coordinating with other network members for unique names, and configuring your workstation accordingly. To identify your workstation:

1. Open the Network Control Panel and select the Identification tab (shown in Figure 4-7). If no information is in the Computer Name or Workgroup fields, type it in and select Close to accept your entries.
2. If you're changing the computer name, click the Change button and NT will display the Identification Changes dialog (shown in Figure 4-8). Enter your new information and select OK to accept the change.

Figure 4-7.
It's simple to identify your computer on a network—just coordinate your naming conventions with other network members.

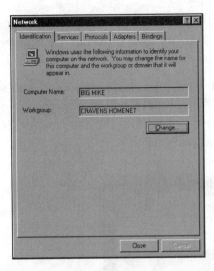

Figure 4-8.
It's just as simple to change network identities.

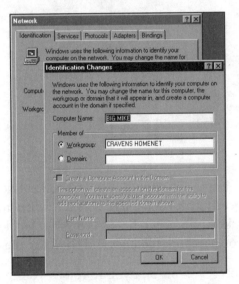

Windows NT will prompt you to restart your machine after any changes to network settings. Whether you restart immediately or later, the new settings won't take effect until you do.

Installing Network Services

There's one more major piece needed for your network connection to work—the network client software. We've already installed your adapter, adapter drivers, and protocol, and we've told your system what name to use on the network, plus what group of computers it belongs to. Now it's time to install the final piece of the puzzle. To install the network services client software:

1. Open the Network Control Panel and select the Services tab. Windows NT will display the tab pane shown in Figure 4-9. Click on the Workstation entry and then click on the Add button.

Figure 4-9.
You need to add network services client software to complete configuring your workstation for network support.

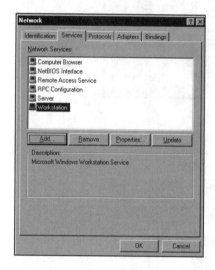

2. Select the client type you desire and click on OK. Setup will need to copy some files, so tell it where to find them if asked. When NT finishes copying the files, it will update your network bindings and complete the installation process.

Windows NT will prompt you to restart your machine after any changes to network settings.

NOTE: Windows NT Workstation will automatically configure client services for Microsoft Networks (NetBEUI) support. You will need to install other client types as you add network types.

Testing Your Connections

Once your system has restarted, you can test to see if your network is working by opening the Network Neighborhood icon on your Windows NT Workstation 4.0 Desktop. You may have to restart other computers on the network as well to get the other workstations to appear on your system.

Windows NT Networking Tools

Once your network installation is configured, you need to know how to use it. In this section, we'll take a look at various tools built in to Windows NT Workstation 4.0 that take excellent advantage of network connectivity.

The Network Session

Windows NT networking begins and ends much the same way as the NT session: you log on to start and then log off or shut down to exit. NT automates most network access from the same logon dialog you use to start your session in NT itself. Depending upon the speed of your machine, the only difference you'll see is a "Logging On" message flash shortly after you enter your password. Windows NT uses password caching (storing frequently used passwords) and user account synchronization (using your user name to automate logging on to multiple resources, such as networks) automatically to make your computing experience even more exciting and luxurious.

Exploring Your Network Neighborhood

As we mentioned briefly above, one of the simplest ways to check your network connections is simply to open the Network Neighborhood icon on your desktop. The Network Neighborhood window (shown in Figure 4-10) is just another Explorer view of another set of resources on your system, or connected to your system, in this case.

Figure 4-10.
The Network
Neighborhood
awaits your excited
exploration.

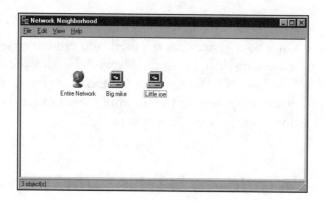

OK, so maybe my home network isn't that exciting, but if I showed you the one at work, as the saying goes, "they'd have to kill me" (and then you). You can access the resources on any system that appears in the Network Neighborhood window simply by double-clicking on the icon to open it.

TIP: You can use the Network Monitor Agent to collect and display information on any type of activity involving your network adapter card. Your administrator can also use it to collect data about computers across the network to help diagnose network problems.

Networking and Security

One of the great strengths of Windows NT lies in its inherent security structures. How can you allow connections to your workstation, or connect to other systems, and really know they're secure?

Security relies upon trust. You need to know any user that you allow to access your system. Windows NT contains a great set of utilities for managing user accounts, logon information, and permissions. There's simply no excuse for any security problems with Windows NT if you use these tools wisely and manage physical access to your systems as wisely.

Conversely, expect to cooperate with other network users in requesting access to their system. Network security is a two-way, and often a two hundred–way, street.

Of course, you'll need the correct rights and permissions to access other systems.

> NOTE: See Appendix B, "Tips on Configuring Windows
> NT," for information on configuring your system security.

File and Folder Sharing

The primary operation in using Microsoft Network services on a Windows NT Workstation is simply enabling sharing for those resources you want to make available to others. To share a resource in Windows NT Workstation:

1. Select the resource (for example, your local C: drive) with the right mouse button and select the Sharing entry from the context menu (as shown in Figure 4-11). Windows NT will display the Properties dialog for that item (for example, as shown if Figure 4-12).

Figure 4-11.
Sharing support is built into the context menu for most objects.

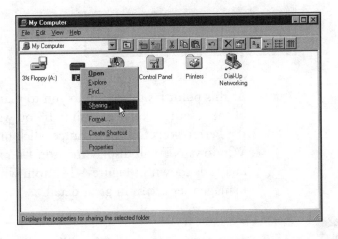

2. You'll need to activate permissions for any users that you want to use your resource. Click on the Permissions button and Windows NT will display the Access Through Share Permissions dialog as shown in Figure 4-13.

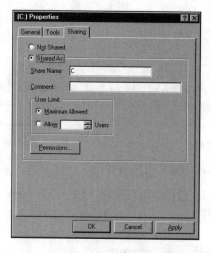

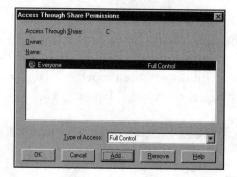

3. At this point it's totally up to you to manage the security of the resource you're exposing. If you want to add or alter the Permissions for this resource, click on the Add button. Windows NT will display the Add Users and Groups dialog as shown in Figure 4-14, from which you can manage user access in great detail.

TIP: See Appendix B for more information on configuring user access via User Manager.

Figure 4-14.
Once a user is
entered in your system
Permissions database,
you can control that
user's rights for any
shared resource.

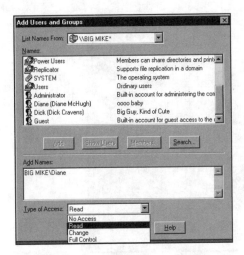

Sharing Devices

Sharing other types of resources such as printers is just as simple. To share a device, open its context menu and select Sharing just as we did in the example above. Windows NT will display the Sharing Properties pane for the device (for example, my crusty HP IIP printer's sharing properties are shown in Figure 4-15).

You can control permissions for your printer by clicking on the Security tab (shown in Figure 4-16).

Figure 4-15.
Windows NT allows
you to specify
additional printer
drivers for enhanced
sharing support
for printers.

Figure 4-16.
In addition to the
Permissions control,
you can perform high-
resolution auditing of
your printer or allow
another user to take
control of it entirely.

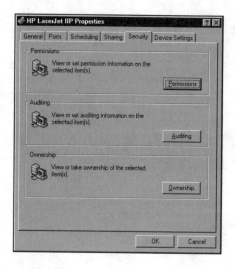

Remote Networking

Another less-publicized but increasingly popular aspect of NT
networking is Remote Access Services support. RAS allows you to
turn your NT Workstation into a communications and
networking server so that you can use Netware, TCP/IP, and
NetBEUI services by calling into your workstation, and accessing
your networks, via a simple modem connection. The same set of
services can be used in client mode to access another NT
Workstation, an NT Server, or any other type of server using
compatible protocols. RAS TCP/IP is now a fairly common
method of Internet access for those not fortunate enough to afford
a persistent Internet connection.

See Chapter 6, "Windows NT Communications and the Internet,"
for detailed information on RAS and TCP/IP networking.

Onwards

Now that we've introduced you to the basics of Windows NT
networking, let's move on and show you how to get your productivity applications running. Chapter 5, "Installing and Running
Applications," will guide you through the basics of operating
common productivity programs under Windows NT
Workstation 4.0.

CHAPTER 5

INSTALLING AND RUNNING APPLICATIONS

Although NT Workstation 4.0 is essentially the same as earlier NT versions "under the hood" in respect to application programs, there are some distinct differences in how programs are installed, managed, and used compared to NT 3.*x.* With the new operating system interface come new application issues, techniques, and tools.

In this chapter we'll take a look at:

- **What type of applications can be used with Windows NT 4.0 Workstation**

- **The differences between Win16, Win32, Windows NT, and Windows 95 applications**

- **Installing common 32-bit Windows productivity applications (such as Microsoft Office for Windows 95)**

- **Running applications**

- **Uninstalling applications**

Understanding Windows Application Types

When the Windows world was young, life was simple: there were MS-DOS applications, Windows applications, and stuff that ran on other computers (Macs and the like). In the good old Windows 3.*x* days, about the most difficult choice you had to make was whether to upgrade from your venerable character-based apps to the newer Windows versions.

The introduction of Windows NT 3.1 brought with it a whole set of application-compatibility issues that are still very much with us. The development of Windows 95 did much to resolve all this, but it's still a bit messy. Here are the different types of applications on the market today that will run under one or more versions of Windows:

- MS-DOS programs (mostly character-based)
- Windows 3.*x* (16-bit Windows applications)
- Windows NT 3.*x* (32-bit Windows applications)
- Windows 95 (32-bit Windows applications using Win95 interface components)
- O/S 2 version 1.*x* programs (mostly character-based)
- POSIX programs

So you can see where all the confusion comes in: how's a user to know what runs with which operating system? Here's a couple of simple rules to help you navigate all this:

- Windows NT 4.0 Workstation will run all the types listed above.
- Windows 95 will run all the Windows and MS-DOS types listed above, but not the O/S 2 and POSIX programs.

NOTE: See Appendix C: Tips on Running Legacy Applications, for more information on running Windows 3.*x* and MS-DOS programs.

What's the Difference between Win32 and Win16 Applications?

If you're around Windows computing very long, it's quite likely that you'll hear the terms "Win16" and "Win32" used fairly frequently. What exactly do these buzzwords mean?

When programmers write Windows applications, they have to follow the rules laid down by Microsoft regarding the structure and operation of Windows itself. The set of rules for Windows 3.*x* (designed to run on 16-bit microprocessors) is referred to as the Win16 API (Application Programming Interface). To write applications for Windows NT and Windows 95, programmers use an API designed to take full advantage of the 32-bit microprocessors required to run those operating systems: Win32. Win32 can actually be described as a superset of Win16, so Win32 operating systems (Win95 and NT) can run most Win16 applications (for example, NT has a Win16 subsystem that supports older Win16 programs).

Can Win32 applications be run on Win16 operating systems? Certainly, with the proper additions to the Win16 system. There's a subset of Win32 (called Win32s, logically enough) that can be installed in Windows 3.*x* and that allows 32-bit Windows applications to run, but they are still subject to all the memory, multitasking, and other limitations of the earlier 16-bit Windows environment (the 32-bit application must also be fully Win32s compatible; some aren't, so check with the application vendor before you assume this is possible).

Windows NT provides the complete solution to all these issues by supplying the best performance and compatibility platform for all Win32 and Win16 applications under one operating system "roof."

There are always exceptions (such as poorly written software) but in general you're safe following these general guidelines. Now, that's not to say that one operating system (NT or Win95) won't run a type of application better than another, but we're assuming that if you're this far in the book you already know the benefits of NT (if not, check out Chapter 1 for a review of the major performance differences between NT and Win95).

Windows 95 versus Windows NT Applications

The part of the previous section that will probably confuse most people is the distinction between 32-bit NT applications (designed for NT 3.x) and Windows 95 applications (which, as everyone should know from the Microsoft Windows 95 marketing blitz, are 32-bit, too). If you've already scratched your head over this one, don't worry, it's truly a fairly subtle distinction (unless you're a true computer geek and spend most of your day studying this type of thing). Here's how it breaks down:

- Windows 95 applications are 32-bit, use the Windows 95 interface tools, and support critical Win95 features (such as TAPI and long filenames); they may offer performance enhancements such as multithreading.

- Windows NT applications are 32-bit, but they don't necessarily use the Win95 interface tools or support other Win95-specific features.

NOTE: See Chapter 6, "What is TAPI," for more information.

So it's quite possible to have a true 32-bit NT application that looks as if it was designed for Window 3.1 instead of NT or Windows 95 (Microsoft released NT versions of Word 6.0 and Excel 5.0 well before Win95 hit dealers' shelves, for example). Some application developers designed their products for NT 3.x, not Win95 or NT 4.0. This doesn't mean that those applications won't work well under NT 4.0; it just means they won't have the same Win95 File Open dialogs and other niceties as applications written specifically for Win95 or NT 4.0.

Is it OK to run Win95 applications under NT 4.0? Please do! Most are designed to work equally well under both operating systems. But don't be surprised if certain specific features don't work the same (for example, NT 4.0 doesn't support 100 percent of the same device drivers for printers or fax modems as Win95). It may take a few months for application developers and hardware manufacturers to catch up with updating some of these items for NT 4.0. Check with your hardware or software vendor if in doubt.

What Is Multithreading?

One major distinction between 16-bit Windows and Windows 95 and NT is that the new 32-bit operating systems support a processing technique know as *multithreading.* This is a fancy term for "doing more than one thing at a time." Multithreading is essentially the same idea as multitasking, except it's defined as being within an application, between various internal application processes, as opposed to occurring at the operating system level (between various applications themselves).

The classic example of multitasking is having a spreadsheet calculating in the background, or a database performing a search, while you edit a document in your word processor in the foreground. Multithreading is similar, but the common example is this: while you edit your document, your word processor spell-checks it and prints another document at the same time, plus it automatically saves the other four you've been working on, all without degrading the overall application performance (if you've used a word processor under 16-bit Windows for more than ten minutes, you know that you usually stop what you're doing while it prints).

If this sounds farfetched, then check out a copy of Microsoft Word 7.0 (for Windows 95 or Windows NT). Multithreaded applications are here today, and Windows NT is the premium environment in which to realize their potential immediately.

Is it OK to run NT applications under Win95? Please do! Odds are you'll see many fewer issues going this way versus the other. Windows 95's designers went to great lengths to ensure compatibility with most existing Win16 and Win32 applications on the market at Win95's release, and any applications released since then should follow Microsoft's guidelines that ensure a fairly high level of compatibility between Win95 and NT 4.0 applications (remember, Microsoft's overarching goal is to have one happy Win32 world, so they've "encouraged" application developers with programming guidelines that ensure good performance in both Win95 and NT 4.0). If a product has Microsoft's official Windows 95 sticker, it should run well under either Win95 or NT, but

Microsoft does allow some "graceful degradation" of performance under NT if it can't be avoided (as there are differences between Win95's and NT's underlying architectures).

Running Applications under NT on Non-Intel Hardware

Although this book is aimed primarily at users with Intel PC systems and this chapter focuses primarily on NT and Win95 apps, we're aware there are other situations and scenarios that you'll encounter in the NT workplace.

Versions of NT (ports) are available for the Alpha, MIPS, or PowerPC processors. However, most common applications are available only in Intel versions. Some application vendors will offer a special version compiled for a RISC NT platform if there is a significant performance advantage to be realized. In other words, for most basic productivity applications, running the Intel version on a RISC NT installation will work fine with no great difference in performance. (How fast can you type data into a word processor, anyway?)

What's a "Port"? What Is "Compiling"?

Most people understand by now that you can't just take a Macintosh program and run it on a Windows computer, and vice versa. Everyone knows that the operating systems, in addition to the hardware, are essentially different.

What's less obvious is that the same level of difference exists between other hardware platforms as well. There's been a lot of buzz about newer RISC (Reduced Instruction Set Computing) processors and all the advantages of their design. Yet few computer users are aware of the differences between "flavors" of RISC computers. Each vendor's RISC machine is as essentially different from the others as a PC is from a Mac. Each RISC platform has its own operating system, so in addition to the Mac versus PC controversy, we now have a multitude of RISC operating systems to contend with. This is a real problem for Information Systems professionals in environments that require all these systems to meet the needs of the enterprise.

What's a "Port"? What Is "Compiling"? (cont...)

Microsoft is addressing this problem of "portability" with Windows NT by offering different "ports" of NT for each of the major RISC hardware platforms: DEC Alpha AXP, MIPS R4000, and PowerPC. With NT, you're no longer tied to the limitations of the Intel platform for Windows computing.

The largest distinction among the platform-specific versions of NT is what compiler is used to customize each version for the specific hardware in use. A compiler is the tool programmers use to convert their program code (written in English-like commands) into language that the computer hardware understands (literally ones and zeros). Every CPU design (whether Intel or any given flavor of RISC) uses slightly different "machine language," so the compiler must be customized for the specific hardware its output is targeted for. By using a compiler tailored to each particular RISC processor needed, Microsoft can move NT to that hardware platform. Although there may be other details required to further customize NT for the other hardware components on a non-Intel machine, this approach is certainly a far cry from starting from scratch for each new CPU design that hits the market!

Application programs are subject to the same general rules requiring design for a specific hardware platform. Windows NT lessens such restrictions considerably by providing a similar set of operating system tools for the application programmer, regardless of the hardware platform in use. But depending upon the specific application, it still may be necessary to perform a port to attain maximum performance. Before purchasing software, consult your application vendor to determine if RISC versions are available for your application, but don't hesitate to use the Intel version if that's all that's available (the performance will probably be very, very acceptable).

For the most part, installing an application on an NT system running with Alpha, MIPS, or PowerPC processors is identical to the process of installing on a Intel system. The biggest consideration in running most Intel-compiled Windows applications on RISC systems is not the installation process, but the general compatibility of the application with the Intel emulation provided in each particular port of NT 4.0. If you're running on one of the supported RISC platforms, please consult the NT documentation for that version regarding specific applications before you install.

Installing Common Business Applications

Enough talk of installing applications; let's see just what's involved in setting up a set of common business programs under Windows NT Workstation 4.0. For this exercise, we'll use what's proven to be a very popular application suite for Windows 95: Microsoft Office Professional. Remember, our goal here is not to make you an Office expert, but to show you how to install any software and ready it for use quickly and easily.

Installing Microsoft Office 95

Odds are pretty good that you're already on the Microsoft Office bandwagon and will want to upgrade to the Windows 95 version with your move to Windows NT Workstation 4.0. Why not use the NT 4.0 version of Office? There isn't one, but Microsoft's guidelines for Windows 95 applications ensures a high level of compatibility under NT 4.0 (see "Understanding Windows Application Types" earlier in this chapter for clarification).

Even if you aren't using Office 95 and you aren't about to, the Office 95 installation example that follows deals with a set of installation issues that will arise with almost any program you'll install. Setup programs may differ slightly, but if your application's developers followed the Microsoft guidelines, odds are you'll feel pretty comfortable with their setup program as well.

For the purposes of this example, we'll assume you're installing Office from your CD-ROM drive. If you're working from floppies (you're a patient soul), the procedure is essentially the same, and we'll give you some tips as well. If you're installing Office from the network, you'll need to see your network administrator for the location of the Office files (see Chapter 3, "Navigating Your Network Neighborhood," if you need help finding a computer on your network).

NOTE: You must have the appropriate rights to install software on a Windows NT system. If you encounter any error messages during application installation regarding security, review Appendix B, "Managing NT 4.0 Security."

The Office 95 Installation Process

To begin installing Microsoft Office under Windows NT Workstation 4.0, follow these steps:

1. Insert the Office CD-ROM into your CD-ROM drive. Within a few seconds, the Microsoft Office for Windows 95 CD-ROM introduction window will appear, as shown in Figure 5-1.

Figure 5-1.
Windows NT 4.0 supports AutoRun for CD-ROMs that have this feature. Once you insert an AutoRun CD-ROM in the drive, the introductory or installation program will automatically appear on your Desktop.

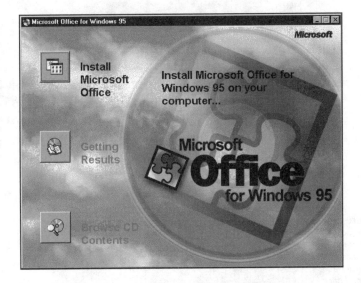

2. Move the mouse cursor to the "Install Microsoft Office" icon and click once. The Microsoft Office for Windows 95 Setup window will appear as shown in Figure 5-2.

3. After you've dutifully read all the legalese, click on the Continue button. Setup will display the Name and Organization Information dialog shown in Figure 5-3. Fill in your information and click once on the OK button to continue.

Figure 5-2.
Clicking on the
Install icon runs
the Office 95
Setup program.

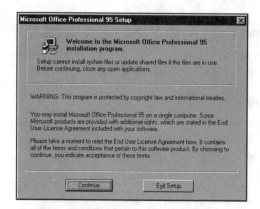

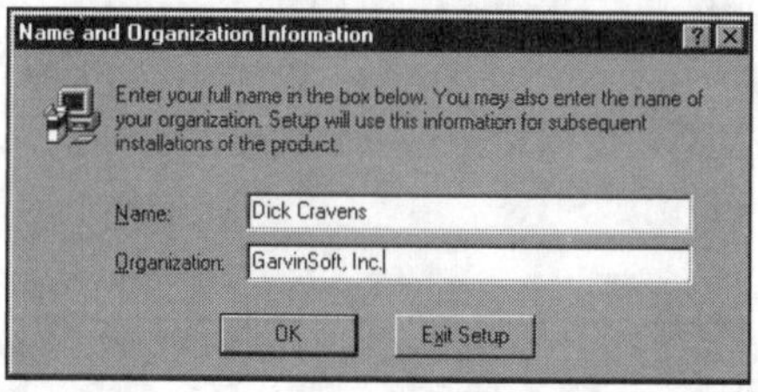

Figure 5-3.
Be sure to provide
your name before
proceeding (the
organization is
optional). Click once
on the OK button
to continue.

4. Setup will display a dialog asking you to confirm the information entered in step 3 above. Click on OK to continue or Change if you made a mistake. Setup will display a dialog asking you to enter your Product ID (as shown in Figure 5-4). Enter your Product ID information and click on OK to continue. Setup will display another dialog verifying the ID number; click on OK again to continue.

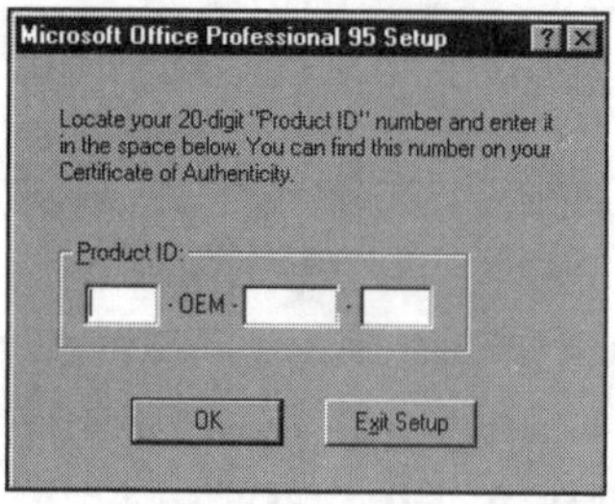

Figure 5-4.
Enter the Product ID
number from the
Certificate of
Authenticity that
came with your Office
95 discs and click on
OK to continue.

5. Setup will now check out your system briefly and then display the dialog shown in Figure 5-5. Click on OK to confirm the installation drive and directory or click on the Change Folder button to tell Setup to use another location.

Figure 5-5.
Confirm the directory
for installing Office by
clicking on OK, or use
the Change Folder
button to select
another.

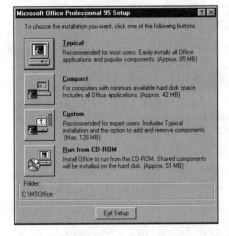

6. Setup will now check out your system more thoroughly to see exactly what program components you have installed. After the search is completed, Setup will display the dialog shown in Figure 5-6. From this dialog you can select which type of installation you desire.

Figure 5-6.
Setup offers you
several choices that
allow you to conserve
drive space, ensure
the fastest program
performance, or let
you skip programs
you don't really need.

7. For this example procedure, let's choose Custom (if you don't need to alter the installation defaults, choose Typical and meet us later at step 9). Setup will display the dialog shown in Figure 5-7.

8. Setup defaults to include the entire Office 95 suite. If you want to lower your disk storage requirements, you can uncheck an entire option here (such as the complete Microsoft Word program) or click on an entry and then use the Change Option button to alter the specific

components of the selection (such as the Templates option under the Word installation). After you've completed selecting which components you wish installed, click on the Continue button.

9. After it has confirmed you have enough drive space, Setup will start copying files to your hard drive as shown in Figure 5-8. When all files are copied, Setup will tell you with one final dialog. Click on OK to return to the Windows NT Desktop.

Figure 5-7.
The Custom Installation dialog lets you pick and choose from Office 95 programs and components.

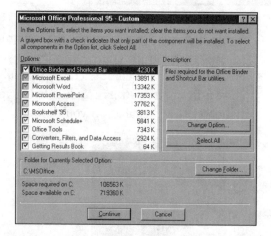

Figure 5-8.
It may take a few minutes to copy all the Office 95 files to your hard drive.

Congratulations! You've just installed Office 95. You'll probably notice that the Office 95 CD-ROM introduction program window is still on your Desktop; click on the Close button in that Window and it will disappear. Or if you prefer, you can run the Getting Results program or select the Browse CD Contents icon to get further acquainted with Office 95.

Installing Office 95 from Floppy Disks

Let's say through some quirk you have a program on floppies instead of CD-ROM (you may have purchased the floppy version by mistake, or your computer doesn't yet have a CD-ROM drive). The procedure for installing Office 95 (or any other program) from floppy is very straightforward. The simplest procedure is as follows:

1. Open the My Computer icon by double-clicking on it. Windows NT will display the My Computer folder window as shown in Figure 5-9.

Figure 5-9.
Use the My Computer icon on the Desktop to open the My Computer folder. This will allow quick access to your floppy drive.

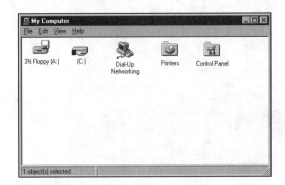

2. Double-click on the icon for your floppy drive (in this case, drive A:). Windows NT will open the folder window displaying the contents of the drive as shown in Figure 5-10.

Figure 5-10.
Double-click on the Setup icon to start the installation process.

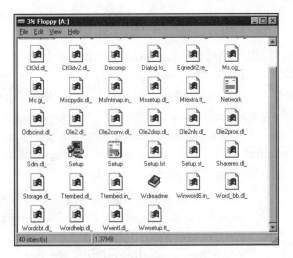

3. Locate the program used to install the software (odds are very, very good that it will be called Setup if it's a Microsoft product; other vendors may use Install or

another name; a big clue is the computer-and-software-box icon type Windows NT uses for these types of programs). Double-click on the program icon to start it. Windows NT will then display the Setup program window as shown in Figure 5-11.

Figure 5-11.
Get ready to swap
those floppies, you're
on your way to
installing Office 95.

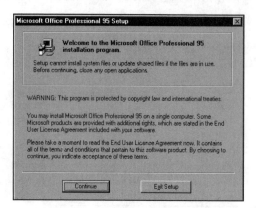

From here on out the installation is the same as outlined starting in step 3 in the section "The Office 95 Installation Process" earlier in this chapter, except you'll be in Floppy Swap Hell for a while (Office 95 is a big program, so it will take quite a few disks). Setup will prompt you when you need to change disks.

Installing from the Add/Remove Programs Control Panel

A less direct but quite useful method of installing new programs is to use the "official" way: the Add/Remove Programs Control Panel. This handy utility walks you through the process of installing your new software with a minimum of fuss. To use the Add/Remove Programs Control Panel:

1. Click once on the Start menu to display the main menu. Select Settings, Control Panel. Windows NT will display the Control Panel folder as shown in Figure 5-12 (your folder may look slightly different depending upon your hardware and software installation).

Figure 5-12.
The Control Panel folder is readily accessible from the Windows NT Start menu.

2. Double-click on the Add/Remove Programs icon. Windows will display the Add/Remove Programs Properties dialog (see Figure 5-13) with the Install/Uninstall pane at the front.

Figure 5-13.
You can install new software or new Windows NT components from the Add/Remove Programs wizard.

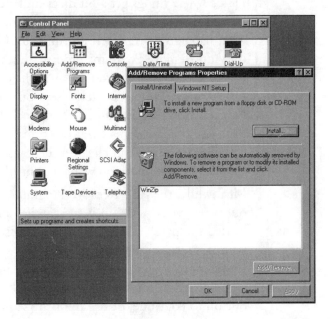

3. Click once on the Install button. Windows will display the dialog shown in Figure 5-14, asking you to insert the program disk or CD-ROM into the appropriate drive. Do so and then click on Next to continue.

Figure 5-14.
Make sure your
program disk or disc
is in the drive before
you continue.

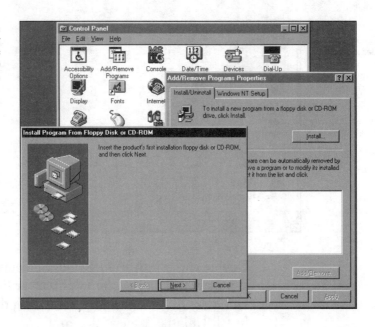

4. Here's where things get a bit dicey and redundant if your
   CD-ROM has the AutoRun feature. Notice in Figure 5-15
   what happens if you insert an AutoRun CD-ROM during
   the Add/Remove Programs process (the AutoRun CD-
   ROM kicked in when you put it in the drive, while the
   Add/Remove Programs wizard kept on doing its thing too).
   Not to worry! If this happens, simply click on the
   Add/Remove Programs wizard to bring it to the foreground,
   and all is well (you can click on the Close icon on the
   Office 95 program if you want to, but it's not required).

5. Meanwhile, the Add/Remove Programs wizard has figured
   out where your program is (it searches any available
   loaded floppy or CD-ROM drives and searches for installation or setup programs). Figure 5-16 shows the Run
   Installation Program dialog with the search results. If this
   is the program you wish to install, click on the Finish
   button to continue, or use the Browse button to correct
   the search results.

6. After the Setup program runs, Windows will display the
   Setup screen seen in Figures 5-2 and 5-11 earlier. The rest
   of the installation process is the same as outlined in "The
   Office 95 Installation Process" earlier in this chapter.

Figure 5-15.
The AutoRun feature can have its drawbacks.

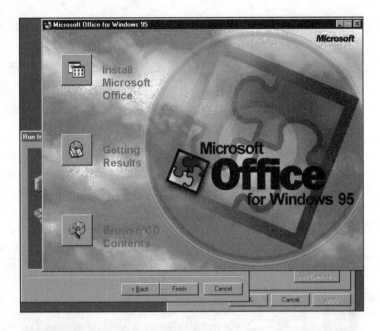

Figure 5-16.
The Add/Remove Programs wizard will search all populated floppy or CD-ROM drives for installation of setup programs. Make sure it's found the right one before you continue.

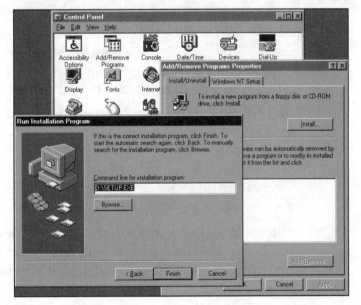

When Setup completes, the Add/Remove Programs wizard will disappear and Windows will return you to the Desktop.

The real benefit of using the Add/Remove Program Control Panel wizard comes when you choose to alter the application installation or uninstall it completely (see "Uninstalling Applications" later in this chapter). However, be aware that not all applications support the full set of features this wizard provides (just using the wizard doesn't mean Windows will be able to automatically uninstall the program, as the application program has to support the wizard as well).

Starting the Office 95 Programs

Now that we've installed a sample application (actually, we installed several, since Office 95 is an application suite), let's look at how to start it. Using an application program under Windows NT 4.0 is a bit different from what it is under previous versions of NT since there have been major changes in the NT Desktop user interface, but you'll be comfortable in just a few seconds after you've run your first application program.

> **NOTE:** For more information on the basics of using the new Windows NT interface, see Chapter 3, "Introducing the NT 4.0 Desktop."

Starting Programs with the Start Menu

As you'll recall if you've read Chapter 3 (or used Windows NT 4.0 or Windows 95 before), you can access almost any feature or installed program via the Start menu button on the Windows Taskbar. If you'll click on the Start menu button once and then select the Programs item, Windows NT will display the Programs menu as shown in Figure 5-17.

This menu may or may not be the complete list of programs installed on your system; if an application doesn't play by Microsoft's setup and installation rules, it may not install an icon for itself here.

TIP: If you need to add a program icon to the Start menu, right-click on the Taskbar and select Properties ➤ Start Menu Programs ➤ Add . . . to run the Create Shortcut wizard.

Figure 5-17.
The Windows NT
Start menu Programs
group will reveal
installed programs.

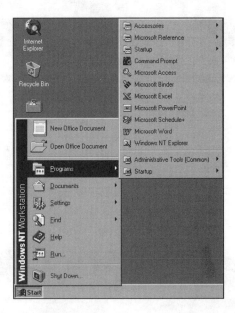

To start an application program, simply move the mouse pointer
to the application shortcut and click once. For example, in Figure
5-18, the mouse cursor is on Microsoft Excel. When the mouse is
clicked, Windows loads Excel as shown in Figure 5-19.

Figure 5-18.
Clicking on the
Application name will
open the program.

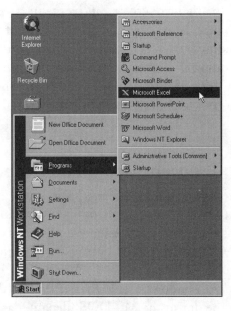

Figure 5-19.
Microsoft Excel loads
quickly from the Start
menu. Notice that the
application is now
registered in the
Taskbar.

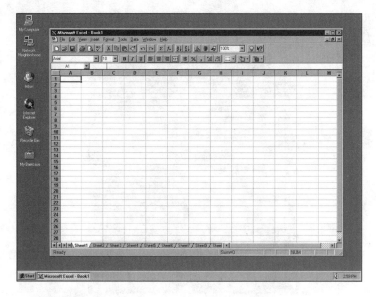

Creating New Documents without Opening Applications

Certain Windows programs also install themselves (or indirectly, their capabilities) in other places besides the Start menu. One of the design principles of the Windows 95/Windows NT 4.0 user interface is the right mouse or *context* menu (so called because the contents change depending upon the context of the cursor when the right mouse button is depressed). Microsoft has taken the liberty of adding a fairly high level of support in this menu for Microsoft Office 95 applications. Figure 5-20 shows the contents of the right mouse menu after the installation of Office 95 and WinZip.

Starting Programs from File Associations

One of the great advantages of the Microsoft Windows interface is the ease with which you can manipulate your documents and applications once they're on your system, thanks to the "smarts" built into Windows regarding data and applications. The primary mechanism here is a basic piece of Windows technology called the *file association*. Windows uses the *file extension* (the last three characters after the dot in the MS-DOS filename) as a basis for the logic required to automate program launching.

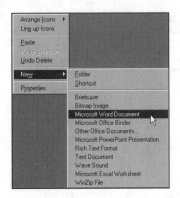

Figure 5-20.
You can create a new Word document on the Desktop or in any folder by using the right mouse context menu.

Let's use the Word document we created just above to demonstrate. Figure 5-21 shows the icon on the Desktop created using the right mouse context menu. By right-clicking on the icon and selecting properties, we can demonstrate that the actual hidden filename extension for this document is .DOC (its full MS-DOS name is NEWMIC~1.DOC, but that's another story).

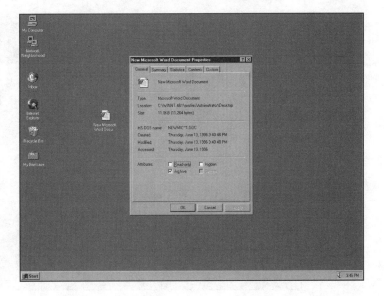

Figure 5-21.
A new Microsoft Word document (created quickly with the right mouse button) and its Properties dialog (displayed quickly with the right mouse button as well).

No, you don't have to preview a document's properties before you open it (we just had you look this one time as an example). You can use the icon to start Word as well, since *Windows knows which application to use based upon the filename extension.* Simply double-click on the icon, and Word will open automatically as seen in Figure 5-22 (this document is empty, of course).

Figure 5-22.
Double-clicking on a document results in Windows using its store of registered file associations to launch the correct application.

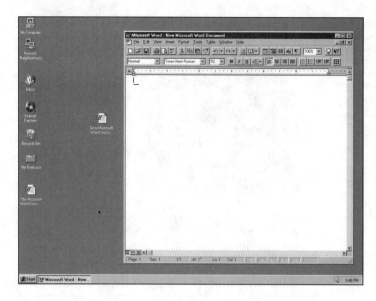

Alternatively, you can also use the right mouse Open command (as shown in Figure 5-23) to open documents as well.

Figure 5-23.
You can use the Open command on the right mouse menu to start an application, too.

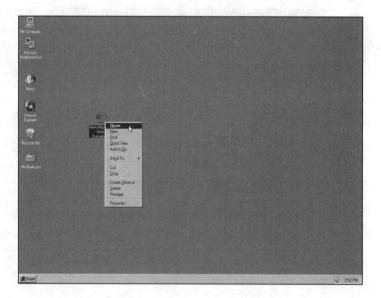

Installing Shareware and Freeware

Commercial applications are not the only ones you'll install on your Windows NT system. You may be the type of power user that simply experiments with every new software gadget that comes down the pike, or you may be solidly tapped in to the Internet, where some of the newest, best software goodies don't come from big commercial software houses, but from student programmers or off-hours hackers with something to prove or just a better idea. Either way, at some point you'll probably want to try some of these shareware or freeware items. By the time you try very many, you're certain to be impressed, and you'll definitely find that some offer the same high quality that you expect from off-the-shelf packages.

A variant on freeware is *public domain* software, freely given with no withholding of any rights whatsoever for the author (and often distributed with the complete source code for the program as well). Much early Internet software was distributed this way. Alteration and redistribution of improved public domain code is usually encouraged by its authors.

Noncommercial software may have installation programs slightly different from what you'll see from Microsoft or Lotus, but don't be dismayed. Shareware installation programs may not be identical to those used by the "big boys," but they're often just as easy to use.

> **TIP:** You can get WinZip in almost any shareware collection, on most BBSs, or at most FTP archive sites. You can also get it direct from Niko Mak computing at their Web site (http://www.winzip.com).

Installing WinZip

Let's take a look at one of the more popular and most excellent examples of Windows shareware, WinZip. To install WinZip:

1. Obtain WinZip95 from the most convenient shareware source (see the Tip in this section for more information). The file you're seeking is called WINZIP95.EXE. Copy it to a empty temporary folder on your hard drive.

2. Run WINZIP95.EXE to begin the installation process (you should know several ways by now to run files in Windows NT; double-clicking on it is the simplest way). The WinZip installation program will display the dialog shown in Figure 5-24. Click once on the Setup button to continue.

What Is Shareware? What's Freeware?

There are many types of software available to computer users today, and almost as many means of distributing that software. Most users are used to the concept of commercial software, available at retail or via mail order. Commercial software is *licensed*; you don't "own" a copy of Microsoft Word when you purchase it, you pay for the right or license to use that copy, and you pay for it in advance. Giving a copy of commercial software to another user is expressly forbidden by the software license, and there are severe legal penalties for duplicating or distributing commercial software without the appropriate license and commensurate fees.

Shareware is different. As the name implies, shareware is software that is available for use before the license fee is paid. You can try shareware for free for a specified period before you pay a license fee, plus you're free to redistribute it (as long as you follow the license guidelines). Most shareware is distributed via online systems. Since shareware authors have a very low cost of distribution, they can pass along great prices on their programs and still make a decent profit. This doesn't mean the quality is necessarily any less than commercial products, it just means the program author has chosen a different distribution method.

Freeware is slightly different from shareware. Although the distribution methods are the same, the author retains all rights to the software; the user isn't charged for the right to use it. Some software authors really are generous in sharing their talents with the world; others may just want feedback on their work before they convert it to a commercial release.

1. After it copies a few temporary files to your system, the installation program will ask you to confirm the directory that WinZip will be installed to (as shown in Figure 5-25). Unless you need to change the entry,

2. The WinZip installation program now displays the dialog shown in Figure 5-26. Unless you have previous experience with archive utilities, click on OK to accept the Express Setup default (Custom lets you set up WinZip to use other compression utilities as well, but you can do this later from within WinZip if you desire).

Figure 5-24.
WINZIP95.EXE is a self-extracting archive that installs the shareware product WinZip.

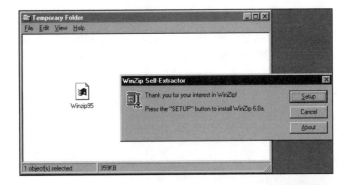

Figure 5-25.
Unless you have an earlier version of WinZip in this directory already, it's probably fine to simply click on OK to accept the default installation directory.

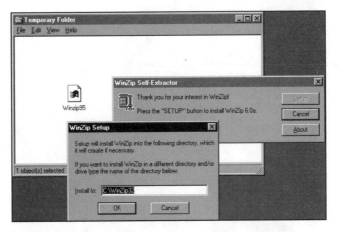

Figure 5-26.
WinZip gives you the option of customizing its configuration during setup. Most users can accept the Express Setup option with no difficulty.

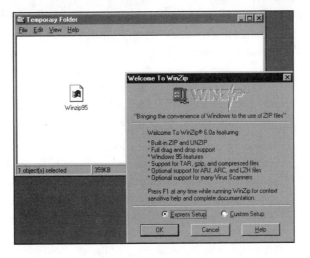

3. WinZip's installation program will next display a dialog full of legalese. Click on the Yes button to scurry past (unless you're really dutiful or enjoy reading such things).

The installation program will then rapidly finish the installation process, run WinZip, and create program icons automatically (as shown in Figure 5-27).

Figure 5-27.
WinZip's installation program automatically creates Start menu icons for you.

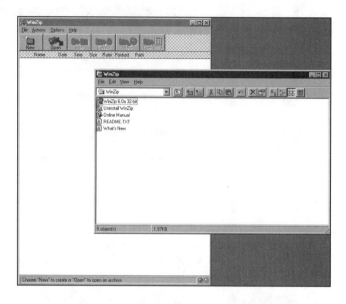

What's a ZIP File?

ZIP files are used for storing groups of other files in a format called an *archive*. File archives are frequently, but not always, compressed to save storage space. It's simply easier to keep large numbers of files in one container or archive when transporting or copying them than to deal with dozens or hundreds. When the files are grouped, it's one transaction, not many.

There are other archive formats (.ARJ, .ARC, .HQX, .LZH, .SIT, .TAR, .Z, .ZOO), each with its own particular format of compressing and storing files. Some of these formats are specific to particular computing platforms or operating systems (.TAR for UNIX, .HQX and .SIT for the Mac), but they all work pretty much the same way: you need a utility to create the archive and an identical or complementary utility to open or decompress the archive. Some archive utilities can create self-extracting archives that appear as executable programs but simply open and decompress their contents when executed.

Installing Self-Extracting Shareware Applications

As you probably noticed if you followed the WinZip installation in the preceding section, the WINZIP95.EXE file is a self-extracting archive (see the *other* sidebar in this section titled "What's a ZIP File"). Even though they contain compressed files like other archives, self-extractors don't need separate programs to decompress them as they have a built-in extraction routine. This slight additional overhead makes them a bit larger than "pure" archives, but the convenience far outweighs the storage bite for most people.

This would all be fine and dandy if all self-extracting programs were as well behaved as WinZip's (which is actually a self-extractor with a little more intelligence built in for the installation process). Most self-extractors simply dump their contents in the current folder or directory, so don't just double-click on any old file you download (you can really mess up a perfectly neat Desktop this way). Do yourself a favor and put the archive in a temporary folder before you execute it.

Most self-extractors won't automatically install their contents. After decompression, you'll need to locate the Setup or comparable installation file and execute it to actually install the archive contents. If in doubt, look for README.TXT or similar files to guide you.

Some self-extracting archives actually contain several disks' worth of data or files. Unfortunately, not all archive utilities are smart enough to handle automatically placing all those files back in the appropriate directory structure upon decompression. If you decompress an archive and then the Setup program can't find files, odds are pretty good it's looking for a subdirectory that didn't get created (all its files are in one big clump instead of neatly tucked away in their appropriate places). For example, most .ZIP-compressed self-extracting archives containing multiple directories need to be run from the Command Prompt with the *-d* argument on the command line, like this:

```
C:\TEMPDIR>ARCHIVE.EXE -D
```

where ARCHIVE.EXE is the name of the self-extracting file.

Not all shareware or freeware programs will be as simple to set up as WinZip, but the quality of such software is improving daily as better and more affordable development tools reach the public. Don't be afraid to try new programs (but do be cautious and test them on a noncritical system before you recommend them to your boss!). You may have corporate guidelines regarding noncommercial programs that you'll need to follow, so if in doubt check with your systems or network administrator before proceeding.

Uninstalling Applications

As simple as it is to install most applications under Windows NT, it's really simpler to remove most programs. Windows NT comes with the ability to remove applications that follow the appropriate installation guidelines. Most recent Windows applications either follow the guidelines closely or come with their own Uninstall program (as shown in Figure 5-28).

Figure 5-28.
WinZip comes with its own Uninstall program.

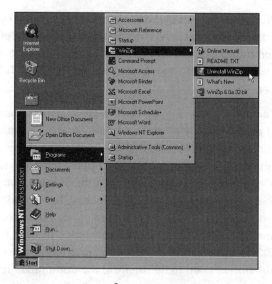

Don't simply delete program files on a Windows NT machine, or any Windows machine, for that matter. Use the program's uninstall utility, or the Windows Add/Remove Programs Control Panel. If you don't, at worst you may destroy or be unable to access data, and at best you may leave remnants of the application strewn across your system (see the sidebar in this section for more information).

> **CAUTION:** Deleting program files or folders without following proper procedures may result in data loss. If in doubt, back up your system before changing it.

Windows Applications Installation Issues

Contrary to the image of a Windows program promoted by the single program icon in the Windows NT Start menu, most applications are not one lone file but often as many as *hundreds* of files, all working together to function as a single application. Some of these files are stored in the applications "home" directory, but most modern applications also place certain support files in the Windows operating system directories and make entries in the Windows Registry as well (see Appendix B, "Working with the Registry," for more information).

Simply deleting a program's home directory and Start menu icon won't automatically remove any program components distributed across the system or correct the Windows Registry. This can lead to "dangling" product components that eat your precious drive space, get loaded into memory when they aren't really needed, and otherwise create a nuisance or system instability. In addition, if the application allowed you to store data in the same directory as the program itself, you may lose valuable information when you delete the program.

Several products are on the market that purport to help you clean up your Windows system to eliminate such situations. Although these products do perform well, it does take some expertise regarding the operating system's and each application's structure to use them without further endangering your system configuration (if you have to ask yourself if you know enough about Windows programs to do this, it's a good clue you don't). Please back up your system before you experiment.

The best method of cleaning your Windows system is not to let it get dirty in the first place. Be sure always to use the appropriate tools to install and remove programs.

Uninstalling with the Add/Remove Programs Wizard

Now let's look at the ideal procedure for removing programs from your Windows NT installation:

1. Click once on the Start menu to display the main menu. Select Settings ➤ Control Panel. Windows NT will display the Control Panel folder.

2. Double-click on the Add/Remove Programs icon. Windows will display the Add/Remove Programs Properties dialog. Be sure to select the Install/Uninstall panel.

3. Select the program you wish to remove from the list at the bottom half of the Install/Uninstall panel (we'll use Microsoft Office Professional for this example). Figure 5-29 shows the Add/Remove Programs Properties dialog with Office selected.

Figure 5-29.
Select the program you wish to remove and click once on the Add/Remove button to continue.

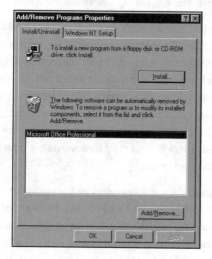

4. Once you've selected the program you wish to remove, click on the Add/Remove button and Windows will start the Office 95 Setup program. Setup will display the screen shown in Figure 5-30.

5. Select the option you want (selecting Add/Remove at this point will let you choose specific Office components, not other programs). For this exercise, we'll remove all by clicking on (logically enough) the Remove All button.

Figure 5-30.
Office 95 Setup takes
over the job of
removing Office.

6. Office Setup, being kind, gentle, and caring, will ask if you really mean Remove All by asking you to confirm with the nice dialog shown in Figure 5-31. If you're serious, click on the Yes button to continue.

Figure 5-31.
Setup is nice enough
to give you a chance
to back out before it
removes Office.

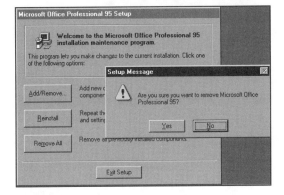

7. When Setup is finished removing Office, it will display the dialog shown in Figure 5-32, which appears to mean that Office was just set up (what it really means is that Office Setup finished the task you gave it, which was to Remove All).

Figure 5-32.
Even though it says
Setup is finished, it just
means Setup is through
with your request to
remove Office (it didn't
set up Office again).

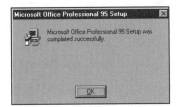

8. Click on the OK button to return to the Add/Remove Programs Properties dialog. You'll notice that Office is no longer listed; you can return to your Desktop by clicking once on the OK button.

Onwards

Our next chapter introduces you to the exciting possibilities that await you with Windows NT 4.0's communications features and shows you how to use them to connect your system to the Internet. We'll also take a look at some of the different resources that await you online.

CHAPTER 6

WINDOWS NT COMMUNICATIONS AND THE INTERNET

In the broadest sense, any form of information exchange constitutes communications. In our study of Windows NT Workstation 4.0, the term "communications" applies specifically to a set of tools used to send and receive data, files, and other information between systems, or from user to user.

Windows NT Workstation offers support for these main communications systems:

- **Multiprotocol networking (NetBEUI, TCP/IP, IPX/SPX, DLC, AppleTalk)**

- **Serial communications (COM ports)**

- **Remote access services (RAS via serial port or ISDN)**

- **Messaging services (MAPI, other mail transports)**

The communications services available to Windows NT are most commonly revealed to the workstation user in the form of the following applications and services:

- HyperTerminal
- Telnet
- Internet Explorer
- Exchange
- Network Neighborhood
- Dial-up Networking

Windows NT Workstation 4.0 also offers limited but robust server capabilities:

- Microsoft Peer Web Services
- FTP server
- NetBEUI file and printer sharing
- Internet Information Server
- RAS Server

So it's important to keep a perspective on the overall capabilities of Windows NT Workstation 4.0 as a communications platform. Although you're better off using Windows NT Server for large group needs, Microsoft has certainly added significant value to the Workstation version of NT in terms of communications and networking tools. We could easily fill several books this size with detailed information on these systems, but in this chapter we're going to look at the parts of the Windows NT Workstation 4.0 communications toolkit most likely to be used by the average desktop user:

- Serial communications using HyperTerminal
- Connecting to the Internet using Dial-Up Networking and Internet Explorer

So let's get you up and running.

Getting Connected to the Outside World: Setting Up Your Modem

The first step in using NT communications is to attach or install your modem. There are two main varieties of modem: internal and external. The internal modem is simply another adapter card that fits inside your computer, just like a sound card or a network card. You plug a phone line into it, and your physical connections are complete. The external modem sits in its own box outside your computer. The phone line connects to it as well, plus there's a cable from the modem to one of the COM ports on the back of your computer (some newer modems use the parallel port, but it's essentially the same set of relationships).

Which type of modem is right for your system? In my book, it's not the form factor of the modem that's critical, it's the speed. Be sure to purchase the fastest modem you can afford, so you can send and receive information in the most efficient manner possible.

Internal modems offer the advantage of slightly improved performance (since it's both modem and COM port in one, the internal modem rarely represents a throughput bottleneck as some older COM ports do) and less desktop clutter. External modems don't take up an expansion slot, often offer diagnostic lights that tell you precisely what's up with your connection, and can be easily moved from machine to machine. I've always preferred an external modem, personally. If my modem needs a reboot (hey, it does happen) then I can reset it instead of the whole computer. Overall, I think external modems are more flexible and a better overall value, even though you'll pay 5–10 percent more for one due to the need for a case, a power supply, a serial cable, and maybe a new high-speed COM port.

> **CAUTION:** Beware the modems that come "bundled" with new computer systems. They *may* be of decent quality, but they rarely are of the latest vintage or offer the highest performance (hey, it's "free," so how much can it be worth?). Spend the extra money and get the latest, fastest modem you can afford. A fast modem can pay for itself in no time (do the math on your online charges).

At the time of this writing, good v.34-standard 28.8 kbps modems can be had for under $200.00, at your corner office supply store. That's a steal, when you consider that ten years ago modems one-tenth that fast went for over three times that amount. Remember, if you're paying by the hour for online service, or if your time is worth practically any amount, a fast modem *saves you money*.

Installing a new modem with Windows NT Workstation 4.0 is simple:

1. Install or connect your modem according to the manufac-turer's instructions. When all the physical connections are made, start your computer and boot Windows NT. Open the Modems Control Panel. Windows NT will run the Install New Modem wizard (shown in Figure 6-1).

Figure 6-1.
Windows NT 4.0
inherits yet another
Windows 95 wizard.

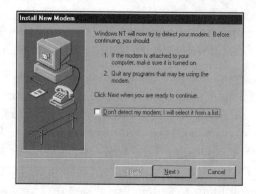

2. Read the instructions, act accordingly, and click on the Next button to proceed. The Install New Modem wizard will test your COM ports and attempt to identify your modem brand and type (see Figure 6-2).

Figure 6-2.
The Install New
Modem wizard will
query your modem
to identify it.

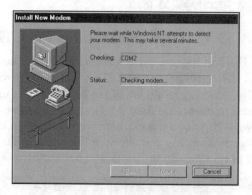

3. The wizard will report which modem, or "Standard Modem" if it can't decide what you have. If the modem ID isn't right, click on Change and select your modem from the list (see Figure 6-3). Click OK when you're finished and then on the Next button to proceed.

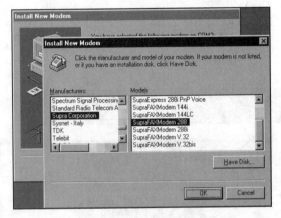

Figure 6-3.
You may have to nudge the wizard and help him ID your modem. If your modem came with Windows NT drivers on a floppy, use the Have Disk button to choose those.

4. The wizard will copy the driver files and install them, then display a dialog saying it's finished. Click on the Finish button to confirm. The wizard will take you to the Modem Properties dialog shown in Figure 6-4.

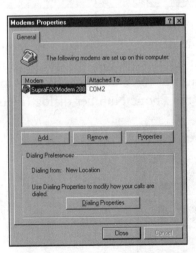

Figure 6-4.
You may further adjust your modem settings from the Modem Properties dialog at any time.

NOTE: For more information on modem configuration, see Appendix B.

Connecting with HyperTerminal

Windows NT Workstation comes with a rudimentary terminal emulation program called HyperTerminal. It's a decent program for connecting to a BBS or other character-based online service. To use HyperTerminal:

1. Go to the Start menu and select Programs ➤ Accessories ➤ HyperTerminal. Windows NT will run the program as shown in Figure 6-5.

Figure 6-5.
The main HyperTerminal screen with the Connection Description dialog. HyperTerminal is session-based, so you have to provide information about the connection you want to make before you gain access to the modem.

2. Enter the name of the system you want to connect to and click on the OK button. Just for old time's sake, I'm going to connect to the Datastorm BBS. HyperTerminal will display the Phone Number dialog (Figure 6-6).

Figure 6-6.
Select the country code, and supply the area code and phone number of the system you're calling.

3. Enter the call information and click on OK to continue. The Connect dialog will appear giving you one last chance to alter your dialing setup. Click on Dial to proceed. HyperTerminal will dial and connect to the BBS.

You'll know you're connected when characters appear in the main terminal screen (as in Figure 6-7).

Figure 6-7.
Characters from the other system show you're connected. Now, what was that password?

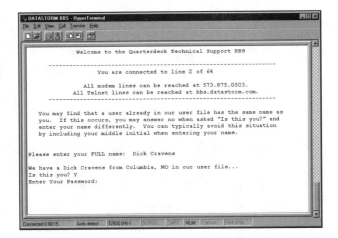

HyperTerminal doesn't keep a central directory of connections, so you'll have to save each set of session settings individually. It's a good idea to do this as soon as you've successfully connected so you know what settings work for that system. To save your session settings:

1. Open the HyperTerminal File menu and select Save. Just like most other Windows programs, HyperTerminal will use the Save As dialog if it's the first time you've saved this data, so you can confirm the name (see Figure 6-8).

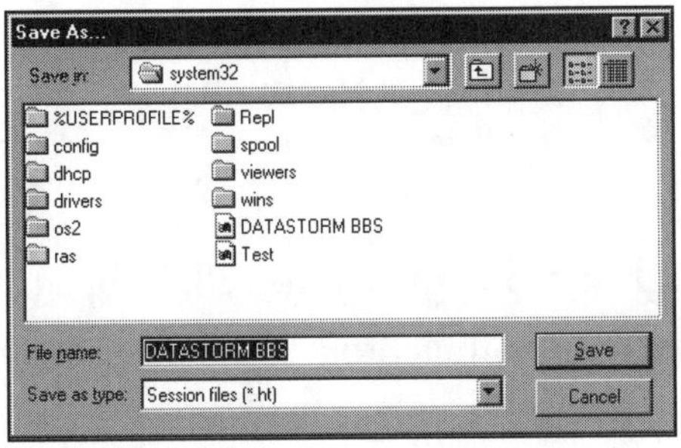

Figure 6-8.
Every session's settings are saved in an individual file.

2. Enter a name and confirm the location you want the file saved to. Click on the Save button to return to HyperTerminal.

> **TIP:** Make a Shortcut to the HyperTerminal settings file for a quick way to place a call to your favorite BBS or online service.

HyperTerminal is a good way to test your modem and other communications hardware. Now that we know all that's working, let's get to the really fun stuff.

Connecting to the Internet Using Dial-Up Networking

Unless you've been under a rock for the last two years, you've heard about this Internet thing. What you probably don't know is that you have everything you need to connect to it right there in Windows NT Workstation 4.0. If you can complete the HyperTerminal example above, you're ready to connect to the Big Kahuna, the Global Internet.

All you need is permission.

Getting an Internet Account

Permission is the part you'll pay for— fortunately not as dearly as in the very recent past. Check your local yellow pages or computer magazine for information on the nearest *Internet Service Provider.* An ISP is the person or company that will let you on to the Internet—for a small fee, of course. Here are the things to look for in an ISP:

- **High-speed connections** (28.8/kbps true v.34 modems)
- **Plenty of connections** (Ask what the user-to-modem ratio is; it should be lower than 10:1.)
- **Decent rates** ($20/month should buy you unlimited connection time.)

- **A local phone number** (Long-distance tolls add up quickly while you're surfing.)
- **A free POP3 e-mail account** (so you can exchange messages)
- **A free news account** (access to global Usenet news)
- **Free storage** (5–10MB of storage on the ISP Web server for your own Web pages)

I'm not trying to be hard on any ISPs out there, but this is a pretty standard package. Why pay more? Not unless you can get other services that are worth something to you (like quality technical support, or gobs more storage space, or your own domain name) or you're really out in the boonies and your market will simply bear more due to lack of competition.

If in doubt, ask other users. Word of mouth is still the most consistent indicator of service quality in any market; service is what you're buying here, consistent connectivity service.

> **NOTE:** Some ISPs will try to convince you they're a better deal because they offer free Internet software. Don't bite. TANSTAAFL (There Ain't No Such Thing As A Free Lunch), as Robert Heinlein's characters say. Usually the software is shareware, and you have to pay a registration fee to remain legal. Besides, Windows NT contains just about everything you need to connect to the Internet, send and receive e-mail, and surf the infamous World Wide Web.

Configuring Your Dial-up Internet Connection

Before we begin configuring your connection, be sure you have all the correct information from your ISP regarding your account. You'll need:

- A user ID
- A password
- Addresses for e-mail and news servers (may be verbose or numeric)

- Gateway and DNS servers (*must* be numeric)
- The phone number for the modems
- The type of connection protocol the ISP supports (PPP or SLIP)
- The type of client addressing the ISP supports (fixed or dynamic IP)

NOTE: You'll need TCP/IP networking installed before you begin to set up a RAS connection. If your system doesn't have this protocol installed yet, add it using the Network Control Panel. See Chapter 4 for more information on installing protocols.

If you've got all that, we can begin:

1. Open the My Computer group and double-click on the Dial-Up Networking icon. Windows NT will run the New Phonebook Entry Wizard as shown in Figure 6-9.

Figure 6-9.
Put in a new name or keep this one, and click on the Next button to continue.

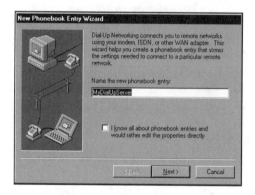

2. The wizard will present a dialog asking you questions about what type of connection you need to make (Figure 6-10). Select the top one regardless, and the other two depending upon what type of connections your ISP supports. Click on Next to continue.

Figure 6-10.
Select the top box
only if your ISP
supports PPP and
dynamic addressing.

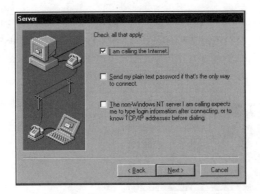

3. The wizard will ask you for a phone number for your Internet connection (Figure 6-11). Enter the number and click on Next to continue and then on Finish in the next dialog. The wizard will take you to the Dial-Up Networking dialog (Figure 6-12), where you may begin your Internet journeys.

Figure 6-11.
Enter your ISP's phone
number when asked.

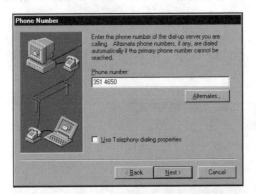

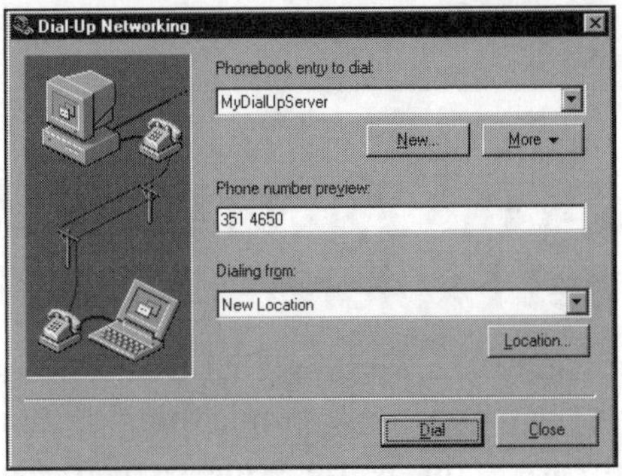

Figure 6-12.
Your connection is
now ready to
be tested.

4. Click on Dial. A dialog will appear (see Figure 6-13) asking you for your user name, your password, and the domain name for the network you're calling. Enter them and click on OK to continue.

5. NT will display a dialog saying "Connecting to MyDialUpServer" (or whatever the connection is named. This dialog will continue to show the status of your connection process progress.

6. When your connection is complete, NT will display the dialog shown in Figure 6-14. Click on OK to begin using your Internet connection.

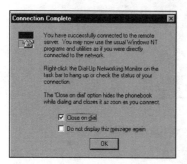

Surfing the World Wide Web with Internet Explorer

Now that you have a working Dial-Up Networking Connection to the Internet, it's a relatively simple thing to start using Internet Explorer to access the World Wide Web. To start Internet Explorer:

1. Start Dial-Up Networking and establish a connection to your Internet Service Provider.

2. When you're connected, double-click on the Internet Explorer icon on the Windows NT Desktop. Internet Explorer will load and display its home page at http://www.msn.com, as shown in Figure 6-15.

Figure 6-15.
Welcome to the World Wide Web!

3. Pick an underlined link on the page and click on it to explore the Web.

For more information on Internet Explorer and the Web, click on the Tutorial link on the Internet Explorer MSN home page, or enter http://www.msn.com/tutorial.default.html in the Address field and press (Enter).

Onwards

Now that you're set up to explore the Web using Microsoft's latest and greatest operating system, be sure to review Appendix E: "Windows NT Information Sources," for more Internet sites of NT interest.

APPENDIX A

INSTALLING WINDOWS NT 4.0

The primary parts of this book (Chapters 1 through 6) have been prepared working from the assumption that Windows NT Workstation 4.0 is already installed on your system. Most users in the corporate environment will have assistance installing major operating system upgrades or will be provided with machines already configured with the new NT 4.0 operating system. Quite a few home or small office users will purchase machines with the operating system preloaded as well.

This appendix, then, is for the rest of you, who don't have help, bought Windows NT Workstation 4.0 after you purchased your computer, choose to do the installation or upgrade yourself, or simply are curious about what's involved in the process of putting NT on a machine. Please don't expect an extreme depth of technical data regarding the multitude of installation options (that can fill a 500-page book all by itself). We're also assuming you've installed Windows before and can follow the Setup instructions without major difficulty.

In this section we'll hit the highlights of

- What information you'll need before you install NT Workstation 4.0
- Minimum hardware requirements
- Major installation options
- Starting installations from different operating systems
- Starting installations from different media sources

By the end of this appendix, you'll have enough information to successfully install NT Workstation 4.0 on most systems.

> **NOTE:** See Appendix E, "Windows NT Information Sources," for assistance in locating detailed technical information on Windows NT Workstation 4.0.

Before You Begin: Installation Requirements

Before you install Windows NT Workstation 4.0 on any system, you will need a fairly thorough understanding of what's required prior to and during the installation. We'll start with detailed information on the hardware and system information requirements, and then we'll move on to other issues that will concern owners of specific hardware.

System Requirements

To install Windows NT Workstation 4.0, you need specific knowledge about your system, both hardware and configuration. Let's start by reviewing the minimum hardware requirements, and then we'll look at the specific configuration information you'll need.

Hardware Requirements

Your system will need the following minimum hardware to
successfully install Windows NT Workstation:

- **Processor:** Intel 80486/33 MHz or higher (or PowerPC,
  MIPS R4x00™, or DEC Alpha AXP RISC processors);
  note that the Intel 80386 is no longer supported. For brisk
  performance, at least a Pentium 90 is recommended, but
  486 machines are acceptable for light use.

> **NOTE:** For more information on hardware
> recommendations, see Appendix D, "Configuring
> Your NT System for Optimum Performance."

- **RAM:** 12MB or more *minimum* for Intel machines (24MB
  or more strongly recommended); RISC—based systems
  require 16MB *minimum*. Don't skimp on RAM—you'll
  really, really regret it.
- **Display:** A VGA (640 × 480, 16 color) display is required.
  You'll want a higher-resolution system with greater color
  depth to fully appreciate the new graphics subsystem in
  NT 4.0.
- **Removable Drives:** for Intel-based computers, a high-
  density 3.5-inch disk drive *and* a CD-ROM drive are
  required (if your system doesn't have a CD-ROM, you'll
  have to install Windows NT Workstation over the
  network, as floppy-only installations are a thing of the
  past). High-density 5.25-inch floppy drives are not
  supported. For RISC computers, a SCSI CD-ROM drive
  is *required*. Support for other removable media (ZIP drives,
  etc.) is provided by third-party vendors, so don't expect
  these peripherals to work without the installation of additional drivers after the basic NT installation.
- **Fixed Drives:** IDE and SCSI drives are supported for
  Intel systems; SCSI drives are supported for all RISC-
  based platforms.

- **File System:** FAT or NTFS file systems are required (HPFS is no longer supported).
- **Mouse:** As with all other versions of Windows, a mouse or other pointing device is pretty useful (since it's intended by the basic logic of the GUI design) but not required.
- **Free Disk Space:** You need one or more hard disks with a minimum of 120MB of free disk space on the partition that will contain the Windows NT Workstation system files (a minimum of 148MB of free disk space for RISC systems). Depending upon the exact options you choose, more drive space may be required (for example, you may choose to specify a larger virtual memory pagefile, which will use more drive space).
- **Network Adapter Cards:** To use Windows NT Workstation with a network, you need one or more network adapter cards. Verify that the network adapter card is on the Hardware Compatibility List before you install NT 4.0.

NOTE: Standard-issue Windows NT Workstation 4.0 for the Intel platform supports either one or two CPUs (special versions from hardware vendors may support more). If you need processor scalability beyond this, investigate Windows NT Server 4.0.

Software Requirements

There really aren't any software requirements for installing Windows NT Workstation 4.0, other than that

- The machine have at least one operating system installed
- The operating system be configured to access the Windows NT Workstation 4.0 installation files
- The Windows NT Workstation 4.0 installation files be present

In other words, the computer must be bootable with at least one operating system that is configured so that you can get to the meat of the matter—the NT Setup files (whether they're on CD-ROM, the local hard drive, or the network).

Setup Information Requirements

Having the right hardware is only part of being prepared to install Windows NT Workstation 4.0. Here's what else you need before you can begin:

- Access to the Windows NT 4.0 installation CD-ROM disc (or network access to the directory containing the installation files for your computer type: Intel, DEC Alpha, etc.)
- A blank 3.5-inch floppy to use as an Emergency Repair Disk
- The three boot disks that came with the installation CD-ROM (unless you're doing the network installation or will select a CD-only installation)
- Three more blank floppies (if you're doing a network installation; not necessary if you're doing a CD-only installation)
- Information on the hardware configuration of your system (more on this later)
- Information on the connectivity configuration of your system (more on this later, too)

Know Your Machine

In addition to the requirements just described, you'll need to know the following about your hardware configuration:

- CPU type (Intel, DEC Alpha, PowerPC, or MIPS)
- Network adapter type
- Display adapter type   SIS   S 30
- Monitor type
- Modem type
- Printer model
- CD-ROM adapter type
- SCSI adapter type

An excellent tool for determining the readiness of your system is the Hardware Compatibility List (shown in Figure A-1).

Figure A-1.
The Hardware
Compatibility List
provides a wealth of
information on specific
products and how well
they will work with
Windows NT.

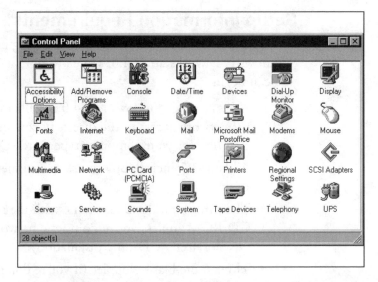

Using the Hardware Compatibility List

It's a really good idea to confirm the compatibility of as many devices in your system as possible, if not your entire system itself, prior to installing NT. The best reference for doing this is the Hardware Compatibility List (referred to as the HCL by NT aficionados). The HCL contains a listing of all tested and confirmed NT-compatible components, as well as complete systems that have been verified by Microsoft to work well with NT.

You can find the current HCL or for NT 4.0 at http://www.microsoft.com/backoffice/ntserver/hcl/hclintro.htm (at the time of this writing). Updates will be issued as new equipment hits the market, so check for the latest version at http://www.microsoft.com/hwtest/ as well.

Although the HCL is a good tool, it's important that you don't interpret it too literally. Just because your device or system doesn't appear on the list doesn't mean it won't work with NT; it just means Microsoft hasn't tested it yet. If your hardware emulates (closely imitates) a device that's on the list, you're probably home free. For example, many network interface cards from relatively unknown manufacturers provide excellent emulations of well-known Intel and Novell models. Another common example includes sound cards that are "clones" of the Creative Labs Sound Blaster series. If the device emulation is of high quality, then you can extend the usefulness of the HCL to those devices as well.

S e n d   U s
Y O U R **C O M M E N T S**

Dear Reader:

Thank you for buying this book. In order to offer you more quality books on the topics *you* would like to see, we need your input. At Prima Publishing, we pride ourselves on timely responsiveness to our readers' needs. If you complete and return this brief questionnaire, *we will listen!*

Name (First) _____ (M.I.) _____ (Last) _____

Company _____ Type of business _____

Address _____ City _____ State _____ ZIP _____

Phone _____ Fax _____ E-mail address: _____

May we contact you for research purposes? ❑ Yes   ❑ No

(If you participate in a research project, we will supply you with the Prima computer book of your choice.)

❶ **How would you rate this book, overall?**

❑ Excellent   ❑ Fair
❑ Very good   ❑ Below average
❑ Good   ❑ Poor

❷ **Why did you buy this book?**

❑ Price of book   ❑ Content
❑ Author's reputation ❑ Prima's reputation
❑ CD-ROM/disk included with book
❑ Information highlighted on cover
❑ Other (please specify):_____

❸ **How did you discover this book?**

❑ Found it on bookstore shelf
❑ Saw it in Prima Publishing catalog
❑ Recommended by store personnel
❑ Recommended by friend or colleague
❑ Saw an advertisement in:_____
❑ Read book review in:_____
❑ Saw it on Web site:_____
❑ Other (please specify):_____

❹ **Where did you buy this book?**

❑ Bookstore (name):_____
❑ Computer store (name):_____
❑ Electronics store (name):_____
❑ Wholesale club (name):_____
❑ Mail order (name):_____
❑ Direct from Prima Publishing
❑ Other (please specify):_____

❺ **Which computer periodicals do you read regularly?**_____

_____
_____
_____

❻ **Would you like to see your name in print?**

May we use your name and quote you in future Prima Publishing books or promotional materials?

❑ Yes   ❑ No

❼ **Comments & suggestions:** _____

_____

_____

TAPE HERE

❽ I am interested in seeing more computer books on these topics

- ❏ Word processing
- ❏ Desktop publishing
- ❏ Databases/spreadsheets
- ❏ Web site development
- ❏ Networking
- ❏ Internetworking
- ❏ Programming
- ❏ Intranetworking

❾ How do you rate your level of computer skills?

- ❏ Beginner
- ❏ Intermediate
- ❏ Advanced

❿ What is your age?

- ❏ Under 18
- ❏ 18–29
- ❏ 30–39
- ❏ 40–49
- ❏ 50–59
- ❏ 60–over

SAVE A STAMP

Visit our Web site at **http://www.primapublishing.com**

and simply fill out one of our online response forms.

PRIMA PUBLISHING
Computer Products Division
701 Congressional Blvd., Suite 350
Carmel, IN 46032

Know Your Connections

If you're going to connect your workstation to any other computer system, you'll need to know what types of connections you're going to use, and specifics about those connections:

- Network types used (protocols such as NETBIOS, TCP/IP, NETBEUI, IPX/SPX)
- Machine, workgroup, and domain names for Windows NT network installations
- Machine IP address, machine hostname, local network domain name, gateway IP address, and DNS IP address for TCP/IP network installations
- WINS and DHCP capabilities of NT server–based TCP/IP network installations
- RAS host system phone number, user name, and password (for each RAS connection), plus network types (protocols) supported by the RAS connection
- Server name, user name, and password for each Novell server (for Novell network installations)

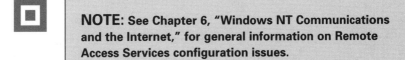

NOTE: See Chapter 6, "Windows NT Communications and the Internet," for general information on Remote Access Services configuration issues.

In other words, you'll be getting to know your network system administrators pretty well if they aren't handling the network configuration part of NT installation for you. Gather the above information before you start your installation, and you'll consume far fewer headache remedies along the way. If you don't know where to get the information, start by asking another NT user in your workplace or user group.

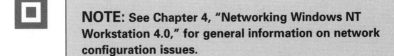

NOTE: See Chapter 4, "Networking Windows NT Workstation 4.0," for general information on network configuration issues.

If you simply can't gather the information before you install, don't panic. Most network options, for example, can be configured after installation as well. It's just simpler to take care of them during installation, if at all possible.

Know Your File System(s)

There are also several basic issues you'll need to be aware of regarding the *methods* and *configurations* used to store information on your drive system, not just the type of drive hardware you have. Be sure to know

- What file systems are already on the computer (MS-DOS, OS/2, NTFS, UNIX)
- How many drive partitions are present, and which file system they each use
- Which if any drives are compressed
- Which file system is in use on the primary boot drive partition

Unfortunately, there's no simple method of describing all the options available in multipartition, multidrive, multi–operating system installations. There's no one-to-one relationship between an operating system and a file system *in all cases.* For example, you can have both NT and MS-DOS on a FAT partition at the same time. The important things to remember when evaluating your installation options are these:

- You can have only one file system (MS-DOS, NTFS, OS/2, or UNIX) per drive partition.
- Some operating systems can work with more than one file system.
- The boot partition must have a file system that each operating system can understand (or you must have a multi-boot utility to help start the operating system).

In other words, if you're really going to tackle a multi-OS installation, be sure that the boot partition of your system uses the "lowest common denominator" file system.

NOTE: See the "Using System Commander in a Multiboot System" sidebar later in this chapter for more information.

What are your options if you need to adjust the partition configuration on your system for the NT installation? You can

- Allow the installation program to perform adjustments to the partition configuration during installation (destroying any data on your system in the process)
- Back up and remove all your data and perform the partition configuration manually using the operating system tools
- Use a partition management product to adjust the system while the data is still in place

Although there are products on the market that claim to allow you to adjust drive partitions without data loss, be wary. Technically there's no reason such products can't work, and I'm not denying that there are good products of this type available (Partition Magic by PowerQuest receives good reviews), but *no product is perfect, or works perfectly on all systems, or under all circumstances.* If you want to use a partition-management application, *please* back up your data before you use it.

CAUTION: Be sure to back up all your data before you adjust drive partitions. Although some products claim to allow partition adjustment without data loss, don't rely upon them to absolutely protect your data (no product, whatever its quality, can unconditionally promise that; just read the liability statements on the software license if you don't believe me). Back up your data before you begin any adjustment to your drive partition, no matter what tools or techniques you use.

NOTE: See "Installing a Multiboot System" later in this chapter.

Windows NT, OS/2, and UNIX Compatibility

Windows NT Workstation 4.0 no longer supports the OS/2 High Performance File System (HPFS). This doesn't mean you can't install NT on a system with OS/2, it just means you can't install it on the same drive partition as OS/2 on that system. If you're installing NT over an OS/2 system (to replace the OS/2 system with NT), you must copy files from any HPFS volumes to an NTFS or FAT volume before upgrading.

The same applies to a UNIX system. Windows NT can't be installed on a UNIX partition without deleting the UNIX file system. You can have both UNIX and NT partitions on a system, but this usually means a reboot to access the alternate file system.

A Windows NT system can certainly communicate and exchange compatible data with both OS/2 and UNIX systems via a variety of connections (network or serial connections, for example), but that's not the same as simultaneously sharing a file system on a drive partition in real time.

Dealing with Compressed Media

If you're installing Windows NT Workstation 4.0 over an earlier version of Windows or MS-DOS, you may have to deal with compressed drive systems. The basic rule of thumb is this: if the drive compression system is compatible with Windows 95, it'll work with NT 4.0.

You may need to reconfigure the ratio of compressed to uncompressed space on your drive system to allow NT the space it needs for its virtual memory pagefile (which cannot reside on a compressed drive).

Keep in mind that although drive compression does represent a certain economy, it can also represent an overall performance hit (it does take time and processor cycles to compress and decompress data). The faster your system, the less consideration you need to give this fact, but it's still worth remembering if you're truly attempting to construct the highest-performance system possible.

Be a Good Neighbor: Coordinate with Your Organization

You've probably already gathered from the above sections that it's important to have a support structure when working with an NT installation in a networked environment. Even if you're handling the NT Workstation installation all by yourself, if you're connecting your machine to a network or any other group systems, be sure to inform everyone responsible for those systems of what you're doing and when. There are two main reasons for this:

- They may help you and save you a ton of hassle.
- Knowing what you're doing may help them and save them a ton of hassle.

Even if you're "Joe NT Stud" and this is your fiftieth installation, you owe it to the network administrators to inform them of any connectivity and other loads that you will impose upon the network. If you're the first person in your organization to use NT 4.0, don't assume everyone else will cheer your sense of adventure and willingness to surf the bleeding edge.

Odds are the information services personnel in your organization already have a transition plan for NT 4.0 and can offer you considerable assistance. Show some respect and play by the rules of your network domain. A single misconfigured network card can bring down an entire network of hundreds of machines if it broadcasts the "right" kind of packet garbage or is using the wrong IP address. Even if you *own* the company, you don't want to have to confess to that one.

Installation Issues and Basics

When you have all the basic information outlined above, you'll need to make some basic decisions about how to get your computer ready for Windows NT 4.0 Workstation. The most basic decision you have to make is whether to install NT 4.0 Workstation over your previous version of Windows, if you have one. If your system doesn't have Windows on it already, you need to decide whether you're going to keep the existing operating system or install NT in addition to it.

Installing Windows NT Workstation over an older Windows installation (using the FAT file system) is a snap. The NT Installation program is designed specifically with this contingency in mind, and it comes equipped with all the tools to take advantage of the information about your system stored in your previous Windows configuration files. If this is the upgrade path you have chosen, your road is fairly flat and smooth ahead. We'll cover the steps to upgrade your older Windows system later in this chapter.

Installing Windows NT Workstation over a non-Windows operating system (or migrating a Windows installation to a Windows NT/NTFS installation) is a bit more complex. To do this, you'll need to decide:

- Which disk partition Windows NT Workstation will reside in
- How to convert all your data to the new file system
- What directory Windows NT will be installed in

We'll cover the basic procedures for these cases as well.

Installation Options

The basic steps to installing NT Workstation are similar regardless of your installation options. They will vary a bit depending upon:

- Which processor type you're using (Intel, PowerPC, DEC Alpha, or MIPS)
- Where your installation files are (local hard drive, CD-ROM, or network)
- What mix of operating systems are on your computer
- What mix of file systems are on your computer
- What type of installation you perform (new, upgrade, or dual-boot)

We're going to start with the simplest type of installation first: a new installation on a machine with only MS-DOS on it. After we cover a basic installation, we'll discuss the most common type, an upgrade from an older version of Windows. We'll also cover installing on a system with Windows 95, and then we'll outline the differences in other cases and give you some tips on how to handle those as well.

The Windows NT Workstation 4.0 Setup program is designed to provide extremely reliable automation for upgrading from MS-DOS (version 6.*xx*), Windows 3.*x*, Windows for Workgroups 3.*x*, and Windows NT Workstation 3.*x*. Unfortunately, because of inherent differences in the design of the registries in NT 4.0 and Windows 95, no automated upgrade path is available for the "cousin" that NT 4.0 most resembles on the surface.

Installing Windows NT on a New Machine

The simplest scenario for installing Windows NT Workstation 4.0 is that of placing it on a machine without any operating system other than MS-DOS loaded. To install NT 4.0 on a workstation with only MS-DOS, you'll need:

- The boot floppy disks from your Windows NT package
- The Windows NT CD-ROM
- Confirmed access to your CD-ROM from MS-DOS

> **CAUTION:** RISC-based systems may have different procedures for program installation, and they commonly will have only a CD-ROM drive for removable media. Please read the manufacturer's instructions before you begin an NT installation on a RISC machine.

Follow this procedure to proceed:

1. Power down your system. Place the Windows NT Setup Boot Disk in drive A: and turn the system on again.

2. The mini–Windows NT operating system on the boot disk will run, copy some temporary files to your hard drive, and then start NT Workstation 4.0 Setup. When Setup prompts you for the second and third floppies, insert them as requested.

3. Setup will ask for the NT 4.0 CD-ROM. Depending upon your hardware configuration, Setup may install directly from the CD-ROM, or it may copy the installation files from the CD-ROM to your hard drive and then restart the system to complete the installation.

Setup will ask you various questions throughout the process regarding your equipment and network configurations. Provide the information as accurately as possible, but if you don't have some information, you can usually configure NT after installation.

Installing or Upgrading from Windows NT 3.x

If you already have a version of NT on your system, you can either

- Replace the older NT with NT 4.0 in the same directory (upgrade)

or

- Install NT 4.0 in a new directory and keep your previous version as well

If you choose to upgrade, your installed applications and configuration settings will be retained, which is generally a good thing. But be aware that along with those, you're also "inheriting" any *problems* your previous installation may have had. If your system is misbehaving, solve the problems before you upgrade, or do a discrete new installation.

> **CAUTION:** If you're using SCSI drive systems on your NT workstation, it's vital that you know the names of the adapters before you run NT 4.0 Setup for a new installation (it's less of an issue if you're upgrading in the same directory as your previous version of NT, but it's still a good idea). Although Setup does an excellent job of identifying most adapters automatically, if you have an unusual one you may need to help Setup by providing accurate identification for it. Before you start NT 4.0 Setup, start your previous version of NT, start the Windows NT Setup application from the Main program group, and choose Add/Remove SCSI Adapters under the Options menu. Record any names there so that you can select the proper device during NT 4.0 Setup.

If you choose the second option and keep your previous installation, you'll have a little higher system overhead in terms of drive storage, but you can return to your older installation simply by selecting it from the NT Boot Loader during system startup. You'll also have to install all your applications again in NT 4.0, but you can save some drive space there by using the same directories for each application that you used in the earlier version of NT.

> **NOTE:** If you're installing NT 4.0 *over* NT 3.51, be sure to remove the Shell Preview from NT 3.51 if you've installed it previously. See the Shell Preview documentation for the uninstall procedure (if you're installing NT 4.0 in a separate directory from NT 3.51 for a dual-boot installation, don't worry about this detail).

To install NT 4.0 from NT 3.*x*:

1. Open the NT Command Prompt and switch to the drive where the NT 4.0 Setup files are located (on your local CD-ROM or a network drive). Move to the directory for your machine CPU type (for example, I386 for Intel machines).

2. At the Command Prompt, type **winnt32** and hit the Enter key (or type **winnt32 /b** if you know NT supports your CD-ROM subsystem, or if you're installing from the network, and you want to skip using floppies during the installation).

3. Setup will run and briefly check your machine configuration. Setup will then ask you to confirm the location of your NT 4.0 installation files (it should be the same directory you started Setup from, unless you're performing a customized installation). Follow the prompts to confirm the location.

4. Setup will display a list of any previous NT installations on your system. If you want to upgrade (replacing a previous installation), select Upgrade and hit Enter to continue. If you want to perform a discrete installation, type the directory location you want for the new installation and press Enter to continue.

5. Setup will ask for the NT 4.0 CD-ROM, or proceed directly from the CD-ROM if it's already loaded, or work from your network files if you're installing from the network. Depending upon your hardware configuration, Setup may install directly from the files, or it may copy the installation files to your hard drive. It will then restart the system to complete the installation.

NOTE: When you upgrade from a previous version of NT, NT 4.0 Setup will try to keep as many of your configuration settings as possible (including any inaccurate ones). If you install NT 4.0 in a new directory, or if you select a dual-boot installation, NT 4.0 will use its internal default settings, and you'll also have to reinstall any applications you want to run under NT 4.0.

Setup may ask you various questions throughout the process regarding your equipment and network configurations. Provide the information as accurately as possible, but if you don't have some information, you can usually configure NT after installation.

CAUTION: If you're installing NT on a system with more than one CD-ROM drive or with a multiplatter CD-ROM drive, be sure to put the NT CD-ROM in as the default disc, or the one that has highest priority on your computer. Also, make a note which drive this is in case you adjust your NT configuration in the future (Setup will want the files to be where it found them last).

Installing or Upgrading from Windows 3.x or Windows for Workgroups 3.11

If you've never had NT on your system but are using an earlier version of Windows 3.x or Windows for Workgroups, the procedure is pretty much the same as that described above for systems with NT already installed, as are the installation options (upgrade or dual-boot). The primary difference is that you'll use a 16-bit version of the NT Setup program to begin the installation.

To install NT 4.0 from a version of 16-bit Windows:

1. Open an MS-DOS Prompt session and switch to the drive where the NT 4.0 Setup files are located (on your local CD-ROM or a network drive). Move to the directory for your machine CPU type (for example, I386 for Intel machines).

2. At the Command Prompt, type **winnt** and hit the Enter key (or type **winnt /b** if you know NT supports your CD-ROM subsystem, or you're installing from the network, and you want to skip using floppies during the installation).

3. Setup will run and briefly check your machine configuration. Setup will then ask you to confirm the location of your NT 4.0 installation files (it should be the same directory you started Setup from, unless you're performing a customized installation). Follow the prompts to confirm the location.

4. Setup will display a list of any previous Windows installations on your system. If you want to upgrade (replacing a previous installation), select Upgrade and hit Enter to continue. If you want to perform a discrete installation, type the directory location you want for the new installation and press Enter to continue.

5. Setup will ask for the NT 4.0 CD-ROM, or proceed directly from the CD-ROM if it's already loaded, or work from your network files if you're installing from the network. Depending upon your hardware configuration, Setup may install directly from the files, or it may copy the installation files to your hard drive. It will then restart the system to complete the installation.

NOTE: Even if you upgrade from a previous version of 16-bit Windows, NT 4.0 Setup will still try to keep as many of your configuration settings as possible. If you install NT 4.0 in a new directory or select a dual-boot installation, NT 4.0 will use its internal default settings, and you'll also have to reinstall any applications you want to run under NT 4.0.

Setup may ask you various questions throughout the process regarding your equipment and network configurations (provide the information as accurately as possible, but if you don't have some information, you can usually configure NT after installation).

Alternatively, you can install NT 4.0 on a system with 16-bit Windows without starting Windows but by running NT 4.0 Setup from the MS-DOS prompt. Be aware NT Setup may not sense your previous 16-bit Windows installation with this method, so if you're upgrading to NT 4.0 from 16-bit Windows, it's best to start 16-bit Windows first.

Installing or Upgrading from Windows 95

As we've mentioned before, Microsoft hasn't had the opportunity to coordinate all the Registry architecture issues between NT 4.0 and Windows 95. This means there's no automated upgrade path for Windows 95 users at present. Windows NT Workstation 4.0 Setup does run well from within Windows 95, but that's not the same as an automatic upgrade (not all your Windows 95 settings will translate into the NT 4.0 configurations).

To install NT 4.0 on a system with Windows 95:

1. Audit your system to make sure NT 4.0 can support all the hardware on your system (Windows 95 is compatible with a wider range of hardware than NT 4.0 at present). See "Using the Hardware Compatibility List" earlier in this chapter for additional information.

2. Insert the Windows NT 4.0 CD-ROM into your drive. The AutoRun feature (if enabled) will start the NT 4.0 Setup program. If AutoRun isn't set up on your Windows 95 system, open an Explorer window and browse the NT 4.0 CD-ROM. Find the Setup program and start it.

3. Install NT 4.0 in a directory separate from Windows 95, creating a dual-boot system (NT Boot Loader will offer Windows 95 as an option when your NT 4.0 installation is completed).

4. When the NT 4.0 installation is over, you'll need to reinstall any applications that you want to use under NT 4.0 (NT Setup can't migrate them automatically in the case of

Windows 95). It's OK to install the applications in the same respective directories under both operating systems (only the application configuration information and some support files are unique to each operating system installation, so the additional drive overhead for dual application installation is minimal).

There's one other trick I want to mention for advanced users: you may optionally manually move application configuration files (.INI files) from your Windows 95 system directory to the Windows NT system directory to maintain your application customizations; unfortunately, more and more applications are moving to a strictly Registry-based installation, so this will only work for a few programs. If you're *really* Windows-savvy, you can try altering the Registry directly, but *please* do your homework before you begin. You'll essentially need to be an expert in both Windows 95 and Windows NT 4.0 Registry structures, which contain significant differences. If it were that easy to do, Microsoft would have automated it, right?

If you don't want a dual-boot system with NT 4.0 and Windows 95, after the above installation is complete, remove any personal data from within the Windows 95 directories and delete them. *Please* be cautious and triple-check that you won't need any of the information in the Windows 95 directories before you do so.

Special Installations

In addition to the fairly standard installations described above, you can install Windows NT Workstation 4.0 in a variety of other ways, using sophisticated tools for customizing and automating the installation or installations. It's even possible to install multiple machines from across the network automatically.

Understanding Boot Options

The most common custom installation is a dual-boot system. The Windows NT Boot Loader allows you to have multiple operating systems installed on one machine, and it lets you select them from a menu at boot time. Dual-boot is a bit of a misnomer (multiboot is more accurate, although a high percentage of users will only have two operating systems on their machine.

NOTE: The Windows NT Boot Loader is designed to allow multiboot installation of Microsoft products only. Don't count on it's supporting all operating systems.

CAUTION: Microsoft doesn't recommend dual-boot installations of Windows 95 and Windows NT. There's no real technical hurdle preventing such an installation, but at the time of this writing Microsoft won't officially support it. You're pretty much on your own. If you do choose to install a dual-boot NT 4.0/Win95 installation, be sure to install applications under both operating systems, as this will not be done automatically by the NT 4.0 Setup program. Also, it's really best if you install NT 4.0 *after* Windows 95, as Win95's Setup is somewhat "predatory" and can reconfigure hardware settings without concern for other operating systems. This can especially be a problem with Plug-and-Play adapters.

Installing a Multiboot System

As we saw in the basic installation procedures earlier in this chapter, the multiboot installation is really as simple as telling NT Setup to use another directory besides your existing Windows one, plus knowing you'll have to duplicate the installations of your applications. There are also a few other issues you should be aware of if you're installing NT on a network:

- You can't totally automate NT installations if they're multiboot; be prepared to do them manually.
- If you are using multiple NT versions, be sure each version uses a discrete, different machine name for network configurations.

Please review the installation procedures earlier in this chapter if you have questions about how to install a dual- or multiboot system.

NOTE: Remember, installing NT in a discrete directory (instead of upgrading) tells NT to use its default settings, not to assume your previous settings from your older version of Windows. You'll need to have all configuration information ready for the NT installation.

Using System Commander in a Multiboot System

If you need to use Windows NT 4.0 with MS-DOS, other versions of NT, and Windows 95, the NT Boot Loader will work pretty well if you can remember all the combinations of keystrokes required to maneuver through the various layers of boot options presented. For example, let's say you need to get to the version of MS-DOS that was loaded before Windows 95, which was loaded before NT 4.0. The NT Boot Loader should let you select Windows 95, and if you select [F8] fast enough, you can get to the Windows 95 boot menu to select your previous version of MS-DOS—if you've had your coffee already.

Or you can use a product like System Commander. It lets you swap partition Master Boot Records and other configuration files on the fly, automatically, from a simple menu displayed when your PC boots. You can install System Commander before or after other operating systems are on your PC, so if you've already put NT on your system, you can add System Commander and then add other operating systems (or other language versions of the same ones) quickly and easily. It works with any Intel-compatible operating system or file system.

You can get System Commander via most major retail software outlets, or directly from V Communications at 1-800-648-8266. Check out the company's Web site at www.v-com.com for further details.

Installing from the Network

If you're going to be installing NT 4.0 from the network, please consult your system administrator for the location of any special NT Setup files or configuration files before you begin (that sounds obvious, but you might be surprised . . .). Your network admin may have special installation disks that will greatly speed up the installation process and even automatically configure all your network protocols and connections for you.

> **TIP:** Check with your Information Systems group or network administrator to see if they've received a copy of the Windows NT Workstation 4.0 Deployment Guide. This set of reference tools provides a valuable reference in leveraging NT's high degree of customization in its automated installation capabilities.

If *you're* the network administrator, it will really pay off if you investigate the Windows NT Workstation 4.0 Deployment Guide before you begin planning system migrations.

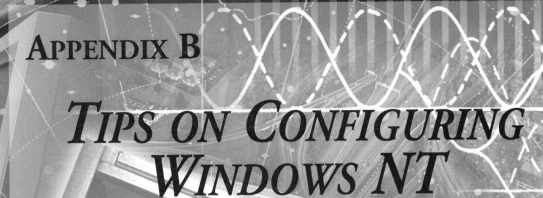

APPENDIX B

TIPS ON CONFIGURING WINDOWS NT

The standard installation defaults that come with your NT Workstation will probably work fine for a very large percentage of users—for now. But computing technology doesn't sit still for long, and odds are you'll add a new something-or-other to your system not long after you purchase it. Even if you're perfectly content with the hardware in your system, you'll eventually want to adjust the display resolution, change your Desktop bitmap, or install a nice toilet flush noise for the Recycle Bin (those of us with a real personality problem will do this several times a day—we know who we are). Regardless of why or when, you'll need to adjust your NT system settings.

Here's how. In this appendix, we'll cover

- NT Control Panels

- Basics of configuring NT Security

Control Panels

Windows NT Workstation 4.0 continues the Windows tradition of presenting the most common configuration controls in a group of utilities called the Control Panel (seen in Figure B-1).

Figure B-1.
You can reach the
Control Panel group
from the Start menu
Settings group.

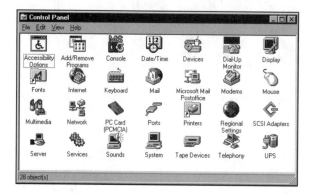

We're not going to go into atomic detail regarding every facet of operation for each Panel, but we'll hit the high points so that you know where to go if you need to dig deeper.

Accessibility Options

Not all users interact with the computer in the same manner, using the same tools. The Accessibility Options Control Panel (Figure B-2) allows you to alter the default behavior of your systems user interface (keyboard, sound, mouse, and so on).

TIP: Remember, you can use the "What's This?" icon next to the Close button at the top right of any Control Panel for context-sensitive help.

Add/Remove Programs

This Panel lets you manage the process of installing or uninstalling applications (Figure B-3), or even Windows NT components (Figure B-4).

Figure B-2.
If you have special needs regarding the physical components of your computer interface, here's where to look.

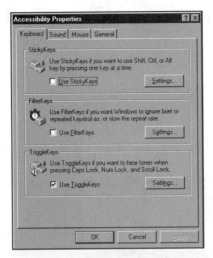

Figure B-3.
The Add/Remove Programs Control Panel helps you withthe process of installing or removing programs . . .

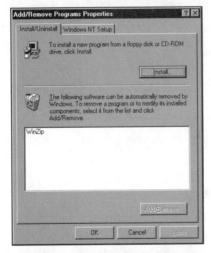

Figure B-4.
. . . or even parts of NT itself.

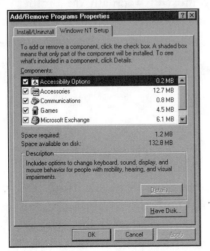

Not all programs can be managed with this utility (a special installation kit must be used by the program as well), but many newer applications support this feature.

Console

The Console Control Panel (Figure B-5) is the same set of Properties panes that are used for the default Command Prompt session.

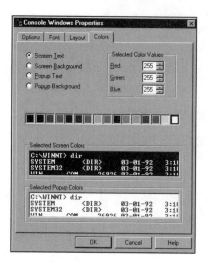

Date/Time

It's important that your computer reflect the correct date and time, especially if you automate tasks based upon the system clock. Unfortunately, most PCs actually do a rather poor job of timekeeping, so you'll probably want to confirm your machine's time settings against an outside reference occasionally. The Date/Time Control Panel (Figure B-6) fits this need, as well as helping you keep track of time zone differentials and Daylight Savings Time.

Devices

The Device Control Panel hasn't had much of a facelift in this version of NT (see Figure B-7), but it really doesn't need one. This panel exists primarily to provide a list of running devices and to allow you to start and stop them on demand, or to let you configure when they are started automatically. You can also link these settings to a particular Hardware Profile.

Figure B-6.
Controls for the date, time, time zone, and Daylight Savings Time, plus a *nifty scrolling map*. What more does a world traveler need?

Figure B-7.
This is actually the control point for device *drivers*.

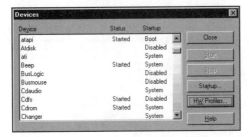

Dial-Up Monitor

This Control Panel (Figure B-8) runs whenever you have a Dial-Up Networking (RAS) connection enabled, whether you're connected or not. It can give you packet-level detail on the status of your Internet or RAS connection.

Figure B-8.
Line Speed at full stop, Captain. All packets at zero CRC. Shall we notify Star Fleet of our status?

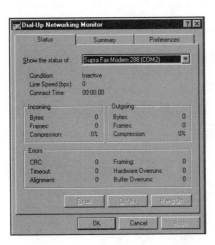

Display

This Control Panel is one you'll probably use quite frequently as you mindlessly adjust your NT Desktop into a hideous array of clashing fonts, colors, and textures. Figure B-9 shows the Background pane, which allows you to change the background bitmap and pattern.

TIP: You can reach this set of panes from the context menu anywhere on the NT Desktop.

Figure B-9.
Nothing quite like inviting a few billion-year-old fossil bacteria onto your NT Desktop.

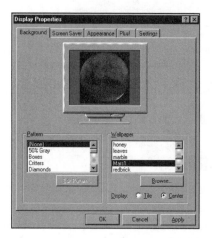

The Screen Saver pane (Figure B-10) lets you choose some eye candy for your coffee break.

Figure B-10.
Put some psychedelia on your desk. Windows NT comes with some great screen savers (unfortunately, this isn't one of them). Hint: there's an NT Developer Favorite Beer List hidden in one of the OpenGL ones.

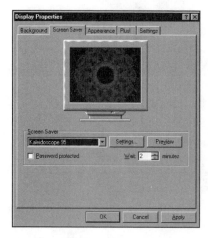

The Appearance Pane (Figure B-11) lets you diddle all the variables in the NT Desktop interface. Fortunately, it's easy to restore the defaults simply by choosing them from the list of Schemes.

Figure B-11.
You can adjust your NT interface fonts and colors 'til the cows come home.

Microsoft's been kind of generous and given NT 4.0 users some of the Windows 95 Plus! features for free. Figure B-12 shows the different interface enhancements that are available to the discerning user.

Figure B-12.
You can change your Recycle Bin icon, stretch your Desktop, smooth your fonts, and color your icons all in one place!

Last, the Settings pane (Figure B-13) lets you manage the screen resolution and color depth of your display system.

Figure B-13.
You can test new
display settings using
the Settings pane.

Figure B-13.
You can test new
display settings using
the Settings pane.

Fonts

TrueType font support in Windows NT 4.0 is simple and straight-forward using the Fonts Control Panel (Figures B-14, B-15).

Figure B-14.
The Fonts Control Panel
windows shows you all
the fonts installed on
your system. Double-
click on any one
of them . . .

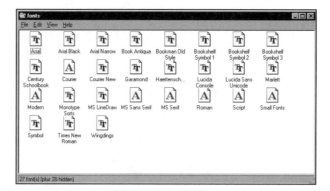

Internet

The Internet Control Panel under NT (Figure B-16) is limited mainly to the configuration of proxy server specifications. Most other Internet connection information can be managed via Dial-Up Networking from the My Computer group.

Figure B-15.
. . . and you can
preview the font at
various resolutions,
and even print
a sample.

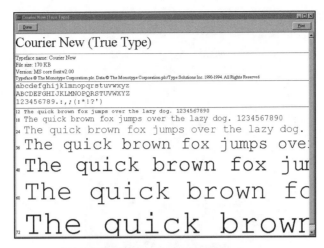

Figure B-16.
Unless you're using
NT 4.0 from inside a
corporate firewall, you
won't need to configure
this Control Panel.

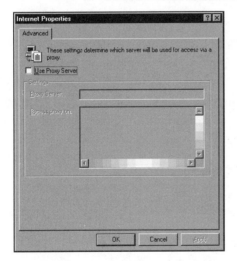

Keyboard

The Keyboard Control Panel (Figure B-17) allows you to adjust the speed, repeat rate, repeat delay, and cursor blink rate for your system, as well as the type of keyboard and what language it was designed for.

Figure B-17.
Satisfy your fingers
and customize that
keyboard *now*.

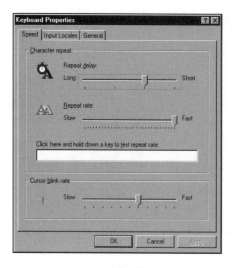

Mail

If you're using Microsoft Exchange for Windows NT 4.0, you'll
want to explore the options here (Figure B-18). The most useful
for many users will be the ability to add Internet Mail support.
You can also manage multiple mail files and address books via
this interface.

Figure B-18.
Use the Mail Control
Panel to configure your
services and resources
for Exchange.

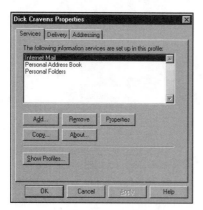

Microsoft Mail Postoffice

If you want to use Microsoft Mail in a small workgroup, you can
create and administer a Postoffice from this Control Panel (Figure
B-19).

Figure B-19.
If you don't have a dedicated Microsoft Mail server, you can use this Control Panel to manage a mail system for a workgroup on a Microsoft Network.

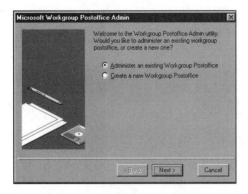

Modems

You can Add, Remove, edit Properties, and adjust Dialing Properties for your modems from this Control Panel (Figure B-20).

Figure B-20.
Manage your modems from one central location.

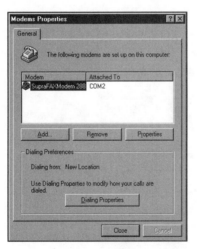

 TIP: See Chapter 6 for more information on installing modems.

The Mouse Control Panel

Not pointing successfully, having trouble clicking? It might surprise you how many options the lowly computer mouse has (Figure B-21). Why, you can even switch the mouse button order and trick your friends . . . no, I shouldn't write that.

Figure B-21.
Adjust your mouse
buttons, change your
cursor graphics, and
tell your mouse to
"snap to."

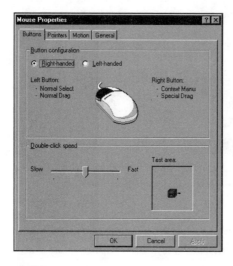

Multimedia

Windows NT has greatly enhanced support for multimedia. This
Control Panel lets you manage and adjust almost every system
parameter for sound, video, and other devices (Figure B-22).

Figure B-22.
Manage your
multimedia hardware
and software from one
central location.

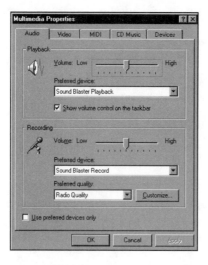

Network

Windows NT's network support is second to none, and you can
control all of it right from this panel (Figure B-23). This is the
same set of panes reached from the context menu Properties item
of the Network Neighborhood group.

TIP: See Chapter 4 for more information on networking with Windows NT 4.0.

Figure B-23.
Network configurations
are consolidated under
Windows NT 4.0.

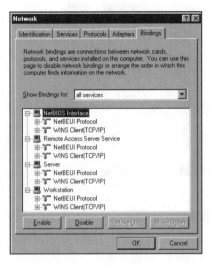

Ports

The Ports Control Panel (Figure B-24) is another one that is so simple and straightforward that it's a little disconcerting. You can add, delete, and configure COM ports from this interface.

Figure B-24.
If you install an
internal modem, you'll
need to configure the
COM port for it here.

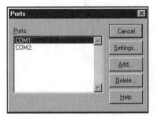

Printers

This is the same set of utilities available from the Settings group in the Start menu. You can add, adjust, and share printers from this group (see Figure B-25).

TIP: See Chapter 3 for more information on installing printers.

Figure B-25.
You can use the Add
New Printer wizard to
automate setting up a
new output device.

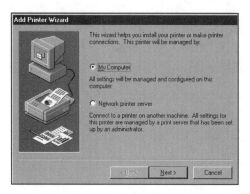

Regional Settings

Microsoft's always made a great effort to make their products as international in scope as possible. Figure B-26 shows the interface for the Regional Settings Properties Control Panel and the wealth of configuration options available there.

Figure B-26.
All the options you can
need for localization
and another *nifty map.*

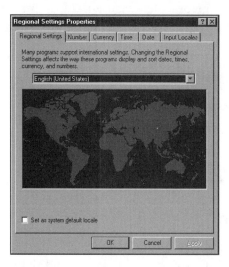

SCSI Adapters

Small Computer Systems Interface adapters are increasingly popular due to their high performance. You can review, but not configure, the installed SCSI systems and the system resources they use in this Control Panel (Figure B-27).

Figure B-27.
Windows NT will classify certain IDE systems as SCSI interfaces.

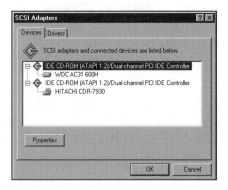

Server

Every NT Workstation is a little bit server at heart. Microsoft provides basic server capabilities to every NT Workstation so that peer-to-peer networking can be fairly robust, without the need for a dedicated NT Server. You can monitor and manage some server resources from this Control Panel (Figure B-28).

Figure B-28.
As you can see, my system's not very busy right now. The cats must be offline.

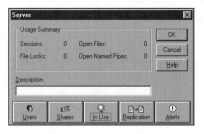

Services

Services are programs that act as resources or perform routine tasks for the system or users. You can manage individual service startup and associate services with Hardware Profiles from this Control Panel (Figure B-29).

Figure B-29.
You can manage
Services/Hardware
Profile relationships
from the Services
Control Panel.

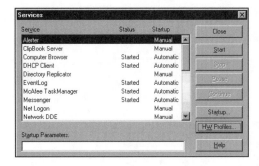

Sounds

A good friend of mine once asked the question "Why can't my
computer be *fun*?" The Sounds Control Panel (Figure B-30) gets
my vote for Best Tool for Making Windows NT Fun. Record
those weird noises and assign them to different events, kids!

Figure B-30.
Sound event
notification can
actually make you
more productive—
no, *really*.

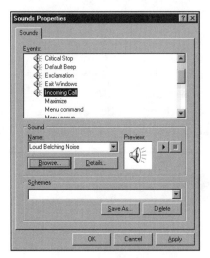

System

This Control Panel gives you access to startup/shutdown controls,
performance information, environment variables, plus hardware
and user profiles (Figure B-31).

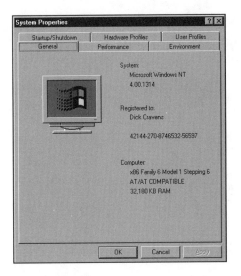

Figure B-31.
This is the same System Properties that can be reached via the My Computer context menu.

Tape Devices

Tape backup devices are cheap, cheap, cheap. So why don't I have one on this machine? If you're smart and do have a tape backup system, here's where you can install, configure, and diagnose it (Figure B-32).

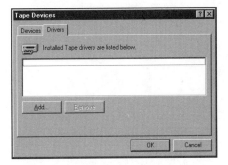

Figure B-32.
Actually, I have a very nice tape drive on my other machine, and I back up across my network, thank you.

Telephony

Microsoft has become communications-happy in the last couple of years, and this Control Panel (Figure B-33) is where you configure NT for the latest Universal Modem Driver (actually called Unimodem). You can also tell NT how to make long distance calls, dial through PBXs, and so on.

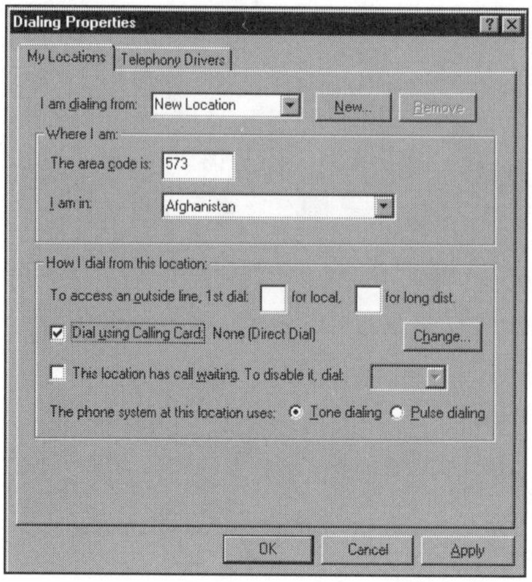

Figure B-33. If you need to update the Microsoft universal modem drivers or configure for dialing while in Afghanistan, you've come to the right place.

UPS

Unfortunately, UPS systems are not yet cheap, cheap, cheap. I still should have one (since my computers are expensive, expensive, expensive). I just faked this setup to show you all the options that NT gives you for automating system shutdown in case of power failure (Figure B-34).

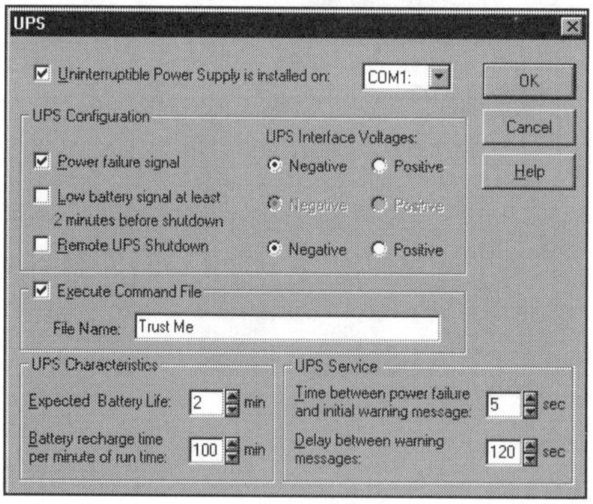

Figure B-34. Your UPS must support notification procedures via a COM port for this Control Panel to offer these functions.

Managing NT Security

One of the elements central to NT's design is integrated security. NT is architected to provide the highest levels of protection for your data. The finest tools in the world, however, are only as useful as the person holding them. It's up to you to *implement* NT security.

NT security begins at the simplest level: logon. By securing the system logon process, NT protects you from your logon sequences being trapped and used against you later. You may also specify a limited number of logon attempts for each account, to prevent automated iterative attempts to derive and test rogue passwords.

At a higher level, NT protects your data by allowing you to define differing levels of access to various parts of your system, per user or group. This method allows security at the internetwork, network, domain, machine, drive, folder, and file level (when using the NTFS file system). You can even secure an NT machine's configuration against its own users (many system administrators have prayed for just such powers).

The primary tool for administering security under NT is the User Manager (shown in Figure B-35). You can access User Manager from the Start menu, Programs, Administrative Tools group.

Figure B-35.
The User Manager interface is clean, simple, and easy to use.

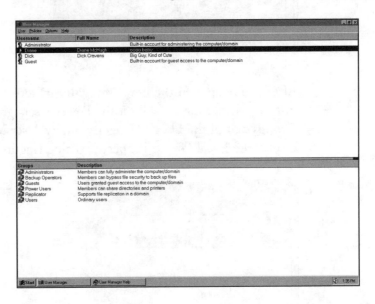

Security specifics can be applied to individuals, or to predefined groups. Group security management allows you to leverage one set of settings by applying them to an individual when you make that person a member of the group. NT User Manager comes with several predefined groups, so you can get started pretty quickly.

TIP: Do yourself a favor and focus on structuring users in groups as opposed to setting up individual accounts with minor access level differences. Try starting with the predefined groups already in User Manager.

To add a user, select User ➤ New from the main menu. User Manager will display the New User dialog (see Figure B-36).

Figure B-36.
Setting up a new user is as easy as filling in the blanks.

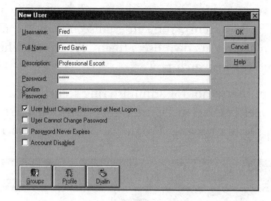

After you've entered the new user, you can add that user to a group just as easily. Double-click on the Power Users group in the Groups half of the User Manager window. User Manager will display the Local Group Properties dialog (Figure B-37).

Figure B-37.
The Local Group Properties dialog shows you the rights that group allows and lets you add new users.

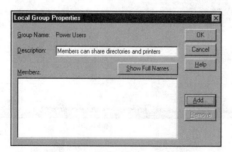

Click on the Add button to see the Add Users and Groups window (Figure B-38). Highlight your new user entry, and click on the Add button to make that person a member of the Power User group. Click on OK when you're finished.

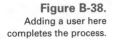

Figure B-38.
Adding a user here
completes the process.

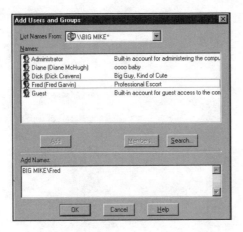

That's the basics to setting up a new user for access to your
Windows NT computer. For additional assistance, be sure to
check out the User Manager Help.

APPENDIX C

TIPS ON RUNNING LEGACY APPLICATIONS

Even if you've made a commitment to push ahead into the world of 32-bit computing, you'll probably run into numerous occasions when you have to use software that just wasn't designed specifically for Windows NT Workstation 4.0. Even software written specifically for Windows 95 can exhibit quirks when running under NT.

In this appendix, we'll look at some of the problems you may encounter with applications designed for:

- MS-DOS
- 16-bit Windows (Windows 3.x, Windows for Workgroups 3.x)
- Windows 95

Plus we'll give you some information on tools in NT to help you configure it for your application's special needs.

Why Legacy Applications Need Special Consideration

We've discussed numerous reasons why Windows NT 4.0 is a superior platform for computing compared to early operating systems, even other 32-bit versions of Windows. The very strengths in NT make running applications designed for other operating systems problematic:

- **Multitasking:** MS-DOS and Win16 applications don't cooperate well in a true preemptive multitasking environment, since they weren't designed for one.
- **Memory management:** Many popular Win16 applications are notorious for poor memory etiquette (this is the source of the infamous GPF).
- **Portability:** Support for multiple processors and different hardware architectures means a higher level of hardware abstraction, which some applications can't handle well. NT also doesn't yet offer as broad support for devices as Windows 3.*x* or Windows 95 due to this fact of design.
- **Security:** Many MS-DOS applications address hardware directly, which is not allowed under NT.

This doesn't mean you shouldn't run legacy applications under NT, it just means you need to be aware of and make use of the special tools Microsoft has provided for their support.

Configuring MS-DOS Application Support

Windows NT uses a basic trick in order to support MS-DOS applications: it fools them into thinking they're running on their own computer. The 80386 and later processors have the ability to segregate and protect memory space in a way that allows creation and management of multiple "virtual machines." Every MS-DOS session under NT is actually an emulation of an MS-DOS operating system and memory configuration, so perfect that the application can't tell the difference. There are several main advantages to this approach:

- NT can create as many virtual MS-DOS sessions as memory allows.
- NT has great control over the emulation parameters.
- NT can control multitasking between multiple MS-DOS emulation sessions and all other Windows applications.

There's one main central control point for all of this for each MS-DOS application: its Properties dialog.

Understanding MS-DOS Application Support

But wait! You say MS-DOS applications don't have Property dialogs! Under Windows 95, and now Windows NT 4.0, they do. Microsoft has migrated the thorough but confusing .PIF (Program Information File) format to one more consistent with the rest of the Windows interface. Since all MS-DOS emulation runs under the aegis of the NT Command Prompt, let's start by taking a look at the Properties for an NT Command Prompt session:

1. From the Start menu, select Programs ➢ Command Prompt. Windows NT will open the Command Prompt session window as shown in Figure C-1 (your window may look slightly different depending upon your display adapter settings and other system variables).

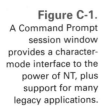
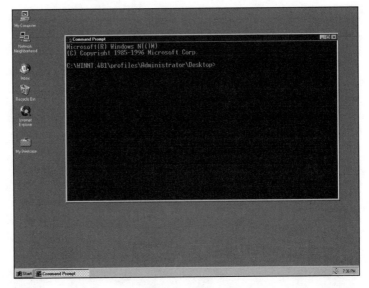

Figure C-1.
A Command Prompt session window provides a character-mode interface to the power of NT, plus support for many legacy applications.

2. Click on the control icon in the upper-left corner of the Command Prompt session and select Properties from the Control menu. NT will display the "Command Prompt" Properties dialog as shown in Figure C-2.

Figure C-2:
The NT Command Prompt Properties dialog allows you to change many of the session parameters for the current Command Prompt session.

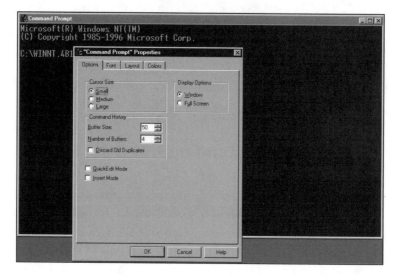

There are four main tabs in the Command Prompt Properties dialog:

- Options
- Font
- Layout
- Colors

Let's take a look at them and the options they contain.

NOTE: All of the Properties settings for the Command Prompt can also be adjusted via the Console Control Panel.

What Is the Command Prompt?

The Windows NT operating system is usually visualized primarily as its GUI. Even though its graphical interface is one of NT's clear strengths, NT "proper" is actually the OS kernel, whereas the GUI "shell" is just one way of presenting NT's capabilities to the user (as was proven in NT 3.51 with the Shell Preview, different user interfaces can be loaded on top of the NT kernel).

Another way of presenting NT's tools is via the character-based Command Prompt. Users migrating to NT from Windows 3.x may assume that the Command Prompt is actually a windowed MS-DOS session (a logical expectation, as Windows 3.x offered just that), but it's not. The NT Command Prompt is a character-based NT operating system terminal session (the terminal is the Command Prompt window). From it you can issue NT commands, start NT applications, and manage NT environments and networks, even on other NT machines. To paraphrase the car ads, "this ain't your daddy's DOS box!"

When you run an MS-DOS session under NT, it starts from an NT Command Prompt session, but NT immediately runs an additional set of drivers to perform MS-DOS specific emulation tasks and provide MS-DOS services in a manner more closely resembling the older operating system. This additional layer of emulation is all but invisible to the NT user, but it's there.

Command Prompt Options Properties

In the Options Properties dialog pane you'll find the following:

- **Cursor Size:** You can adjust the cursor for ease of visibility relative to your other display settings, specifically the Command Prompt fonts.

- **Display Options:** You can preset whether the Command Prompt session runs as a window or full-screen in true character mode.

- **Command History:** Lovers of the MS-DOS DOSKEY command buffer utility will love this option, which allows you to control how many commands can be recalled from the prompt.

- **Insert mode:** You can select whether text typed at the cursor inserts or overwrites.
- **QuickEdit mode:** Allows you to move text with the mouse, bypassing the Edit menu.

Command Prompt Font Properties

Figure C-3 shows the Font pane controls for the Command Prompt Properties:

Figure C-3:
NT doesn't yet offer the full font support found in Windows 95, but it's still fairly flexible.

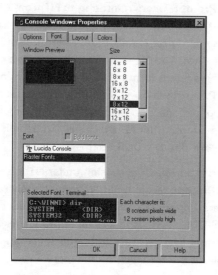

From this pane you can select and preview the font you want to use for your Command Prompt session.

Command Prompt Layout Properties

Figure C-4 displays the Layout controls for the Command Prompt.

Settings in this section apply to both the windowed and full-screen modes of the Command Prompt session. If you run full-screen during a session, NT will match these settings with the closest ones supported by your hardware in character display mode.

Figure C-4:
You can tailor the size and position of your Command Prompt window, as well as its display buffer. The Preview window lets you see the effects of your settings.

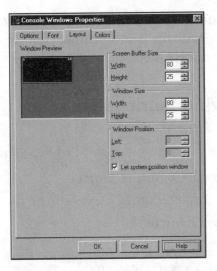

 TIP: Windows NT still supports Alt + Enter for switching between windowed and full-screen Command Prompt sessions. You can also use Alt + Tab for switching between a full-screen Command Prompt session and the Windows NT GUI.

Command Prompt Color Properties

Figure C-5 shows the Color Properties pane:

Figure C-5:
You have full control over the color values of your Command Prompt session.

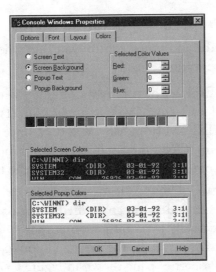

You can adjust almost any color parameter of your session from this interface. Note that you'll be limited in full-screen mode to the character display mode colors your display hardware supports.

Customizing Settings for Your MS-DOS Application

There are several ways to start an MS-DOS application under NT:

- From the Command Prompt
- From Explorer or the Desktop
- From a Shortcut

Any of these will work fine, but if you use them as installed, you'll be running your MS-DOS application using the defaults set up for the NT Command Prompt. These defaults may work fine, but if you need to customize the session parameters due to special needs your MS-DOS application has, you can easily adjust them so that they'll only affect that particular application.

TIP: See Chapter 3 for help in setting up Shortcuts.

MS-DOS Properties Program Settings

Let's look at the additional control you gain when adjusting your MS-DOS application directly:

1. Use Explorer or your My Computer window to navigate and locate any MS-DOS application (I'm going to use EDIT.COM from MS-DOS 6.22 since it's handy on my system). Open the application icon Properties dialog using the context menu. NT will display the Properties dialog as shown in Figure C-6.

2. The General pane can be used to adjust file attributes but is essentially for information purposes. Click on the Program menu for the meat and potatoes. NT will display the Properties pane shown in Figure C-7.

Figure C-6:
Notice that you get additional Properties panes when you open the dialog for a particular application.

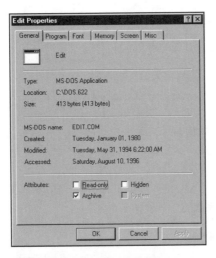

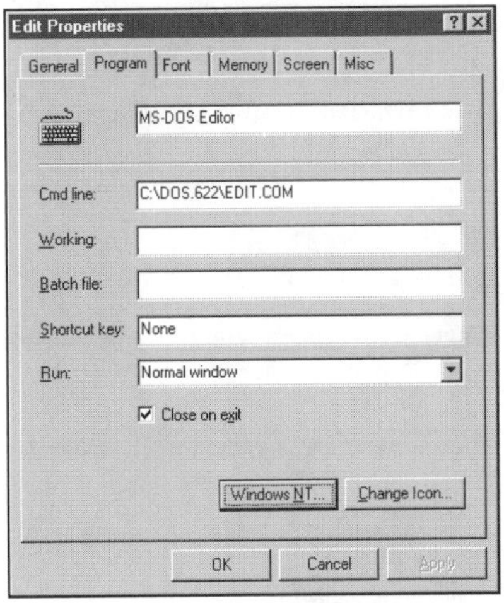

Figure C-7:
This should be familiar territory to Windows 3.*x* users who run MS-DOS applications.

3. From this pane you can adjust what parameters are used when the program starts. To customize the environment the program starts in, click on the Windows NT button. You'll see the Windows NT PIF Settings dialog shown in Figure C-8.

From this set of tools you can leverage great levels of customization for any MS-DOS application requirements. By specifying a different set of configuration files to replace AUTOEXEC.NT and CONFIGURE.NT for a particular application, you can tailor its environment precisely and discretely.

Figure C-8:
These are the files
where NT stores all
the configuration
values used to
initialize the custom
MS-DOS session
emulation settings
for your application.

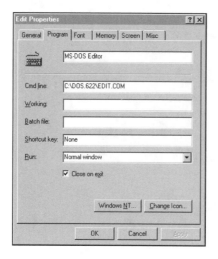

MS-DOS Properties Font Settings

Click on the Font tab, and you'll see the dialog pane shown in Figure C-9:

Figure C-9:
You've actually got a
little more control
over font settings
via this method.

Note that by using the Properties for a specific application icon, NT is giving you more control over the session appearance than it does for the Command Prompt session itself. You can select TrueType fonts as well as the standard system bitmap fonts, in a wide variety of sizes.

MS-DOS Properties Memory Settings

Click on the Memory tab, and you'll see the dialog pane shown in Figure C-10:

Figure C-10:
You can adjust memory parameters to give your application exactly the configuration it needs.

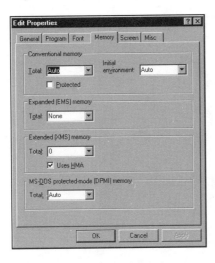

It's really best if you don't adjust these settings unless you know precisely what you're doing. Don't allocate more memory than your application needs, as the rest of NT is hungry enough, already!

MS-DOS Properties Screen Settings

NT gives you a slightly different set of controls for the MS-DOS session display as compared to the Command Prompt, as well. Click on the Font tab, and you'll see the dialog pane shown in Figure C-11:

Figure C-11:
These settings have much the same effect as the Command Prompt settings, but they are presented differently so as to be more familiar to Windows 3.x and Windows 95 MS-DOS users. Note the Performance adjustments.

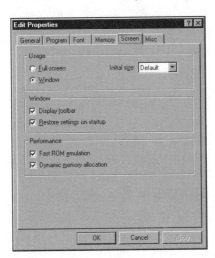

MS-DOS Properties Miscellaneous Settings

Click on the Misc. tab to see the final set of configuration options for customizing your MS-DOS application environment:

Figure C-12:
This pane allows you
to control how your
MS-DOS application
impacts the
performance of the
rest of your NT
environment.

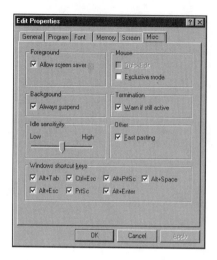

Use these adjustments to control the CPU resources your application uses relative to other running programs.

Running 16-bit Windows Applications

Windows NT offers excellent support for 16-bit Windows applications written for Windows 3.*x* and Windows for Workgroups. There's absolutely no reason you need to hesitate to use this type of program under NT, unless you simply want to upgrade to a later true 32-bit version. True 32-bit programs may offer value above an older iteration of your program, but your 16-bit program's performance won't suffer under NT; it'll be improved due to NT's better overall design for multitasking and memory management.

Running Errant Win16 Programs in Separate Memory Space

NT runs 16-bit Windows applications much as it does MS-DOS programs, in emulation. There are additional layers of emulation for Win16 programs, however. Another difference is that whereas each MS-DOS session runs in a separate virtual MS-DOS environment, Win16 programs by default all run in a shared Win16 subsystem. This default method has all the same benefits and services as using the "real" Windows 3.*x*, plus all the problems. If any one application screws up, the whole Win16 environment can be compromised (32-bit applications are segregated and protected from the Win16 subsystem, so your true NT applications shouldn't be affected). To safeguard against this, NT allow you to run each Win16 application in its own address space, essentially in its own individual Win16 subsystem. You don't want to do this for all Win16 applications, as there is significant additional overhead, but if you have a program that doesn't "play well with others," it's a good option. Another excellent reason to use this feature is if a Win16 program is resource-hungry; many Windows 3.*x* programs run out of System Resources before RAM. Under this method, each application has a complete resource heap to itself.

To run a 16-bit Windows program in a separate address session:

1. Create a Shortcut for that program. Open the Shortcut Properties and select the Shortcut pane (as shown in Figure C-13).

Figure C-13:
NT won't allow you to specify separate memory spaces from the Properties for the program icon itself, so you'll have to use a Shortcut to the program.

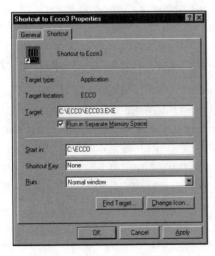

2. Check the Run In Separate Memory Space check box.

That's it. Now your Win16 application can't kick the other programs around.

One caveat: Win16 programs running in separate memory spaces may have difficulty sharing data with other Win16 programs.

Other Win16 Program Issues

The only other problems you're likely to encounter with Win16 programs under NT are simply due to the differences in the interface itself:

- dialogs
- long filenames

Your Win16 applications can't use the new dialogs that 32-bit applications use for Open, Save, and other common functions, nor will they offer support for long filenames. For many users, this is reason enough to demand a 32-bit version of an application.

Running Windows 95 Applications

The single largest issue that will haunt those migrating from Windows 95 to Windows NT Workstation 4.0 (other than the need for more RAM!) will be lack of support for device drivers. Microsoft estimates that Windows 95 supports one-third more devices than NT 4.0 at present. They're working feverishly with equipment vendors to correct the situation, but it probably won't improve much until there's a critical mass of demand for updated drivers.

If you find yourself in this situation, *make noise.* Call or write your hardware vendors and make sure they know that you're a priority. If they are unresponsive, ask them politely if they know of another vendor that publishes NT 4.0–compatible solutions. They'll get the message. A certain amount of patience is appropriate (perhaps even a few months), but don't take no for an absolute, final answer. NT 4.0 is here to stay.

TIP: Ask your hardware vendor if you can help test its new drivers. If you're technically adept and have the time, you perhaps will get support for your hardware months earlier than the general market.

Vexing VxDs

NT will not run Virtual Device Drivers. This particular category of device driver came into popularity, for good cause, in the Win16 and Win95 markets. VxDs conserve scarce MS-DOS conventional memory by running in extended memory through tight integration with the Win16 and Win95 system kernels. The NT security architecture won't allow this method, so VxDs are out. Some vendors offer alternate .DLL-based drivers for their programs (such as Datastorm, for Procomm Plus for Windows 2.0, 2.11, and 3.0).

APPENDIX D

TIPS ON PERFORMING SYSTEM MAINTENANCE

If you've successfully digested the topics in the main section of this book, you've learned the basics of using Windows NT Workstation and you're probably about ready to start dealing with the more mundane (but absolutely necessary) issues of system maintenance. Knowledge of the proper "care and feeding" of any computer system is really just as important as how much you paid for it (or how many hours you've spent learning how to use it) in determining your long-term computing success and satisfaction.

This section of the book covers the following topics designed to help you keep your Windows NT Workstation in fine working order:

- Installing Service Packs
- Tuning NT for better general performance
- Backing up your data
- Protecting your system from computer viruses

We'll also touch on other related miscellaneous maintenance issues as we go.

Maintaining NT Workstation with Service Packs

No software company or design is perfect. Thousands of man-years have gone into the research, design, and production of modern computer hardware and operating systems, and yet they're not perfect (nor will they ever be). So it's in your best interest to get used to the idea that you'll need to occasionally adjust or update your computer system to correct minor problems. It's simply a fact of computing life.

Microsoft has gone to extreme lengths to ensure that NT is as stable and compatible as possible *within the limits of the NT production cycle.* Simply put, every product has to ship sometime; if the software engineering team is allowed to work on a program until it's perfect, it will never reach the public (no disrespect intended, they're just doing their jobs, which is to produce the best product possible). No testing cycle will catch all possible problems with a product (in addition to being tortured by the experts in Microsoft's own Quality Assurance department, NT Workstation has been tested by hundreds of thousands of real users, just like you, before its release). So at some point, a decision is made that the product meets its design criteria with an *acceptable* number of defects, and it is released to the public. Is this irresponsible behavior on the part of the software vendor? No. Or rather, it is only if they then leave the users to fend for themselves in dealing with any of the known problems when the product ships, or problems discovered after release.

The solution? A successful software vendor (like Microsoft) will issue updates (sometimes called *field patches*) to correct problems shortly after a product has already been released, or periodically during the product life cycle (before its successor version is produced). For example, if you'll recall your Windows NT history from Chapter 1, Microsoft started NT with version 3.0 and then released 3.5, followed by 3.51. Version 3.5 was preceded by several *Service Packs* to fix minor problems with version 3.0. (a Service Pack is a collection of improved versions of specific product components, usually several "patched" files) with an installation program to perform the update for you automatically. NT version 3.5 added enough features and increased performance to warrant its own .5 version number increment, and it was followed shortly by 3.51, which fixed several other minor issues. All of these improvements, of course, are now part of NT 4.0.

How frequently can you expect to see NT product fixes issued in Service Packs? Microsoft has produced four Service Packs for NT 3.51 in the year since its release, so you can see how this attests to the company's diligence and commitment to the NT marketplace and users. Although I don't have a crystal ball, I find it likely that they'll continue to be responsive to users' problems by producing fixes to NT 4.0 rapidly, as specific needs arise. Although a quarterly bug-fix cycle may seem interminable if you're the user having to deal with the problem, the realities of software engineering and quality assurance pretty much dictate it as a reasonable minimum time for producing reliable solutions. If every software company fixed bugs as frequently and reliably as Microsoft, the computing world would indeed be a saner place.

Getting NT Service Packs

Now that you know what a Service Pack is and how great a tool it is, you're probably asking "how do I get one?" Well, first off, you're asking the right question, because it's completely up to you to get a Service Pack; Microsoft will not automatically ship you one, tell you when one is issued, or even tell you where to find one. (OK, they do have directions on their Web site and in some of their materials, but it's not like they're taking out magazine ads.) You've got to know to ask, and then you've got to follow through by asking with some regularity over the months you own and use the product. Don't interpret this as indifference on the part of Microsoft, because

- They've got *millions* of users.
- Chances are you'll never need the Service Pack anyway.

It's true. Odds are really pretty darned good that NT will work just peachy exactly the way it was first installed on your system, so you can't really blame Microsoft for not blowing millions of dollars shipping disks to users who don't need them. Conversely, if you think there's a problem with your installation, be sure the Service Pack really solves it before you install it.

Determining If You Need a Service Pack

How do you know if you really need a Service Pack? Here's where the chicken-and-egg part comes in. The best way to know if a specific Service Pack addresses your problem is to read the documentation that comes with it. The "bugs" or product defects that are corrected by a Service Pack are usually listed in the README.TXT file for the Pack (see Figure D-1).

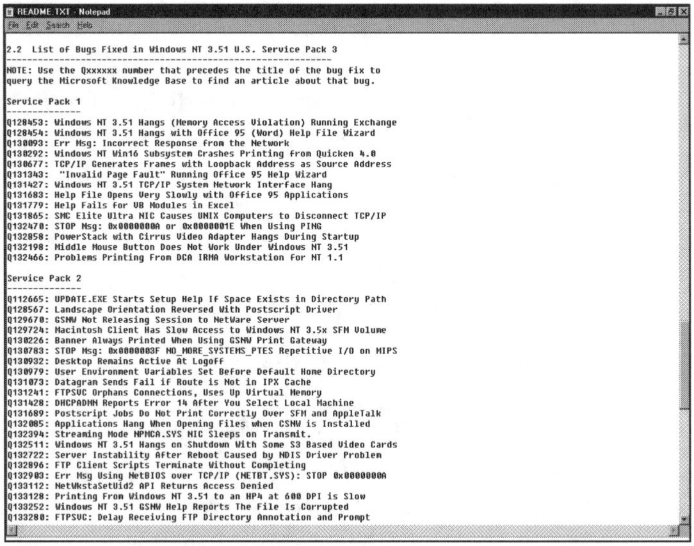

README.TXT - Notepad

File Edit Search Help

```
2.2  List of Bugs Fixed in Windows NT 3.51 U.S. Service Pack 3
-------------------------------------------------------------
NOTE: Use the Qxxxxxx number that precedes the title of the bug fix to
query the Microsoft Knowledge Base to find an article about that bug.

Service Pack 1
--------------
Q128453: Windows NT 3.51 Hangs (Memory Access Violation) Running Exchange
Q128454: Windows NT 3.51 Hangs with Office 95 (Word) Help File Wizard
Q130093: Err Msg: Incorrect Response from the Network
Q130292: Windows NT Win16 Subsystem Crashes Printing from Quicken 4.0
Q130677: TCP/IP Generates Frames with Loopback Address as Source Address
Q131343:  "Invalid Page Fault" Running Office 95 Help Wizard
Q131427: Windows NT 3.51 TCP/IP System Network Interface Hang
Q131683: Help File Opens Very Slowly with Office 95 Applications
Q131779: Help Fails for VB Modules in Excel
Q131865: SMC Elite Ultra NIC Causes UNIX Computers to Disconnect TCP/IP
Q132470: STOP Msg: 0x0000000A or 0x0000001E When Using PING
Q132858: PowerStack with Cirrus Video Adapter Hangs During Startup
Q132198: Middle Mouse Button Does Not Work Under Windows NT 3.51
Q132466: Problems Printing From DCA IRMA Workstation for NT 1.1

Service Pack 2
--------------
Q112665: UPDATE.EXE Starts Setup Help If Space Exists in Directory Path
Q128567: Landscape Orientation Reversed With Postscript Driver
Q129670: GSNW Not Releasing Session to NetWare Server
Q129724: Macintosh Client Has Slow Access to Windows NT 3.5x SFM Volume
Q130226: Banner Always Printed When Using GSNW Print Gateway
Q130783: STOP Msg: 0x0000003F NO_MORE_SYSTEMS_PTES Repetitive I/O on MIPS
Q130932: Desktop Remains Active At Logoff
Q130979: User Environment Variables Set Before Default Home Directory
Q131073: Datagram Sends Fail if Route is Not in IPX Cache
Q131241: FTPSVC Orphans Connections, Uses Up Virtual Memory
Q131428: DHCPADMN Reports Error 14 After You Select Local Machine
Q131689: Postscript Jobs Do Not Print Correctly Over SFM and AppleTalk
Q132085: Applications Hang When Opening Files when CSNW is Installed
Q132394: Streaming Mode NPMCA.SYS NIC Sleeps on Transmit.
Q132511: Windows NT 3.51 Hangs on Shutdown With Some S3 Based Video Cards
Q132722: Server Instability After Reboot Caused by NDIS Driver Problem
Q132896: FTP Client Scripts Terminate Without Completing
Q132903: Err Msg Using NetBIOS over TCP/IP (NETBT.SYS): STOP 0x0000000A
Q133112: NetWkstaSetUid2 API Returns Access Denied
Q133128: Printing From Windows NT 3.51 to an HP4 at 600 DPI is Slow
Q133252: Windows NT 3.51 GSNW Help Reports The File Is Corrupted
Q133280: FTPSVC: Delay Receiving FTP Directory Annotation and Prompt
```

Figure D-1. The README.TXT file in a Service Pack tells you precisely what it will fix, and where to get additional information on specific bugs.

Notice that Service Packs are cumulative. The "List of Bugs Fixed . . . " for Service Pack 3 in Figure D-1 above starts with lists of what fixes were in SP1 (short for Service Pack 1) and SP2 because SP3 *includes them both.* That way you don't need to get all three and install them in order; you just get SP3, and you're current.

Of course, to read this file you'll have to actually have your hands on the Service Pack first.

Finding the Service Pack

There's no big magic involved in getting your SP, but you are the one that will have to get it (as I said earlier, Microsoft won't send it to you, nor will the NT Fairy place it under your pillow). There are two main places to get the current SP for NT:

- Online at Microsoft

  `ftp.microsoft.com/bussys/winnt/winnt-public/fixes`

or

- The Microsoft Developer Network Professional Membership

  `http://www.microsoft.com/ntworkstation/software.htm`

You may also find Service Packs on various commercial information services such as CompuServe, but Microsoft's official distribution is via the methods above (and you'll probably find it cheaper to download from the public sites listed above than from a commercial service). Bear in mind that NT 3.51 SP4 was over 10MB in size, so you'll want to plan for the time the transfer will take. That's one advantage to getting it on CD-ROM as part of the MSDN membership, but if that's the only reason you have for the membership, you may want to look at other ways to get the Service Pack. If you're a member of a user group, check with other members and see if anyone already has the SP you need.

NOTE: See Chapter 6, "Downloading Files with Internet Explorer," for assistance in retrieving files from the Internet.

Please bear in mind that Internet resources are in a constant state of flux. For example, at the Microsoft FTP site listed above, you'll need to do a bit of looking about after you reach the location specified. You'll need to choose additional directory paths to find your target SP file, depending upon which version of NT you're using, what language it's for, and how many Service Packs have been issued. The same goes for the Web address above as well. Microsoft may change its Web server structure at any time, but the address listed should get you close to the information you need.

Remember the part where I said it's best to see the README.TXT *before* you make the installation? It's also wise to check that the SP will solve your problem before you do a 10MB download. Microsoft usually has the README.TXT in the same directory as the SP on their FTP server, so you can just look at the README.TXT before you take a couple of hours transferring the whole Service Pack via modem (if you're lucky, your company has a fast Internet connection and this won't be the case).

NOTE: See Appendix E, "Microsoft Developer Network," for more information.

Installing NT Service Packs

CAUTION: Before you make *any* major change to your operating system, *back up your critical files.* This includes installing a Service Pack. See "Securing Your Data: Backing Up Windows NT," later in this chapter, if you haven't learned how to back your system up already.

Once you've obtained the Service Pack files, installation is really quite simple:

1. Open the Windows NT Command Prompt from the Start menu Programs group.
2. At the Command Prompt, change to the drive that contains the Service Pack medium (floppy, CD-ROM, or fixed or network drive).
3. Change to the appropriate directory for your machine type (i386, MIPS, ALPHA, or PPC for Intel, MIPS, DEC Alpha AXP, or PowerPC CPUs, respectively).
4. Type **UPDATE** at the prompt and hit [Enter]. Windows NT Setup will start copying the Service Pack files as shown in Figure D-2.

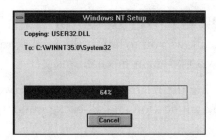

Figure D-2.
Service Pack installation really can't be much easier, since Windows NT Setup does most of the work for you.

5. When Setup is finished copying the Service Pack files, it will prompt you to restart your workstation. It's a good idea to do so immediately.

Configuring Your NT System for Optimum Performance

There are three main areas in which you can increase your NT Workstation's performance with relative ease:

- Mastering multitasking prioritization
- Optimizing memory management
- Improving your overall hardware configuration

In this section we'll take a look at each of these areas. Rest assured that improving your system performance doesn't *necessarily* mean laying out more cash for hard goods—but don't be surprised if you decide it's the best solution to some NT performance problems.

TIP: Microsoft's default settings for Windows NT Workstation are really pretty close to the mark for optimum performance on most systems. If you aren't happy with NT's performance, be sure you have the minimum hardware requirements before you spend much time adjusting your system (see Appendix A, "Installation Requirements," for more info).

Prioritizing NT Multitasking

Windows NT allows you to adjust the level of responsiveness your system offers via two main mechanisms:

- Adjusting the relative prioritization between the foreground application and all background applications and processes
- Adjusting the prioritization of each application relative to others

> **NOTE:** See Chapter 1, "What Is Multitasking?", for more information.

In other words, you can tell NT how to handle CPU access rights for the "active" application versus "inactive" ones (remember, these terms apply to which program has the focus or user console input at any given time, not whether or not the program is actually *doing* anything). You can also use the tools contained in the NT Start command and Windows NT Task Manager to specify how NT should treat one application versus others. You can control relative prioritization of a set of applications while they're all running in the background; or you can tell NT to give a certain application as much CPU time as possible.

Adjusting Foreground Application Performance

Why should you need to adjust the performance of your applications? You may need to if

- A background application hogs the machine so much that your foreground program is sluggish.
- The foreground application is such a hog nothing can happen in the background.
- Your workstation is used mainly by others on the network, with little local use.

In any of the above cases you can perhaps increase performance by making one simple adjustment. You can tell NT how much advantage or "boost" to give the active application (the one that has keyboard and mouse, or *console* focus) by one simple adjustment in the System Properties Performance dialog. Conversely, you can give *all* background applications a boost by *decreasing* the foreground boost in the same way, if that's what's needed.

What type of applications may need this help? It depends upon what the application is, and what you're doing with it. If the foreground application on your workstation is a word processor 90 percent of the time, it's likely you'll never need to make any adjustment. If you then add a database program to your machine and give it large report or index tasks to run in the background while you do word processing, you may suddenly need to boost the foreground app. Or let's say you use your workstation for one thing—running Adobe Photoshop for image processing. You don't care if background tasks get *any* time, so you pump up the foreground app to get the best performance. It's really all a matter of how fast your machine is already, what the applications are you're running, and how you use them.

To adjust the balance between foreground/background prioritization, follow these steps:

1. Right-click on the My Computer icon on your Desktop and select Properties from the context menu. Windows will display the System Properties dialog box.

2. Click on the Performance tab and Windows NT will display the Performance panel as shown in Figure D-3.

Figure D-3.
You can select the appropriate amount of performance boost for the foreground application using the handy slider control.

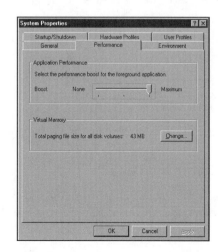

1. Click and drag the slider control to one of the three settings as needed.

2. Click on the OK button to save your changes. Windows NT will display the System Settings Change warning dialog as shown in Figure D-4.

Figure D-4.
If you have no other tasks to accomplish, you can restart NT. You can wait until next time you start NT to test the change if you so desire.

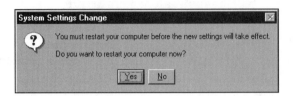

Windows NT will have to change several underlying configuration settings for this adjustment to take effect, so you won't see any difference in performance until you restart.

Adjusting Individual Application Prioritization Using START

If you've attempted to optimize application performance with the Boost control as described above and you're still not satisfied with application performance (especially in the background), you can adjust individual application prioritization using the NT START command (no, not the Start menu Run command, but the START command available from the NT Command Prompt). Windows NT doesn't allow you to alter the priority setting of an application directly (it's hard-coded in the application by its designers when they create the program), but you can override these settings by using the START command. This allows you a great deal of control over how NT prioritizes an individual app versus others. Unlike the boost control, which only controls the balance between *one* foreground application and *all* background programs, START lets you specify this relative priority for an application regardless of where it runs, foreground or background.

The START Command Options

A variety of options are available with the NT Command Prompt START command. START is designed to allow you to control and automate the running of programs from the NT command line, or from .CMD or .BAT files. The basic command structure and syntax are as follows:

```
START ["title"] [/Dpath] [/I] [/MIN] [/MAX] [/SEPARATE |
/SHARED] [/LOW | /NORMAL | /HIGH | /REALTIME] [/WAIT]
[/B] [command/program] parameters]
```

Table D-1 shows information on the arguments or parameters of the START command.

Table D-1   START Command Argument Definitions

Argument	Definition
title	Title to display in window title bar
path	Starting directory
I	The new environment will be the original environment passed to cmd.exe and not the current environment.
MIN	Start window minimized
MAX	Start window maximized
SEPARATE	Start 16-bit Windows program in separate memory space
SHARED	Start 16-bit Windows program in shared memory space
LOW	Start application in the IDLE priority class
NORMAL	Start application in the NORMAL priority class
HIGH	Start application in the HIGH priority class
REALTIME	Start application in the REALTIME priority class
WAIT	Start application and wait for it to terminate
B	Start application without creating a new window. The application has ^C handling ignored. Unless the application enables ^C processing, ^Break is the only way to interrupt the application.
[command/ program]	If it is an internal cmd command or a batch file, then the command processor is run with the /K switch to cmd.exe. This means that the window will remain after the command has been run. If it is not an internal cmd command or batch file, then it is a program and will run as either a windowed application or a console application.
[parameters]	These are the parameters passed to the command/program.

Prioritizing Applications with the START Command

Using START may seem like a bit of a hassle until you see the benefits. Let's look at a couple of ways to use it:

1. Using the Start menu, open the Command Prompt from the Programs group. Windows NT will open a Command Prompt window similar to the one shown in Figure D-5 (your window may be a slightly different size, and the directory name in the prompt may be different depending upon how NT is installed and what your user rights are on the workstation you're using).

Figure D-5.
The Command Prompt window will open to the current directory.

```
Command Prompt
Microsoft(R) Windows NT(TM)
(C) Copyright 1985-1996 Microsoft Corp.

C:\WINNT.4B1\profiles\Administrator\Desktop>_
```

2. At the prompt, type **START WORDPAD /HIGH** and hit the ⌨ key (the caps are optional, it just makes what to type more clear). Windows will run WordPad with a high priority setting.

You can automate this process by creating a .CMD or .BAT file with the START command string in it and then creating a Shortcut to that file. This allows you to create an icon for starting an application with a different prioritization than it normally would receive.

NOTE: See Chapter 3, "Creating Shortcuts," for more information.

Evaluating Application Performance Using Task Manager

Okay, so you may have tried adjusting your application's performance by the methods listed above, and you really can't tell the difference. Chances are it's not your applications that are causing the problem but a lack of other resources such as memory, virtual memory, or drive speed (yes, a slow drive can make even the fastest CPU act sluggish). How can you determine if it's a particular application or some other culprit that's preventing your system from performing at its finest? Fortunately Microsoft has included some really useful tools with NT just for this purpose.

Viewing Application Performance with Task Manager

Windows NT Task Manager provides a number of very useful tools for analyzing your system's performance and managing running applications as well. To use Task Manager

1. Right-click on the Taskbar and select Task Manager from the context menu. Windows NT will display the Windows NT Task Manager window as shown in Figure D-6.

Figure D-6.
The Task Manager window displays all running applications, current processes, and total system performance readouts.

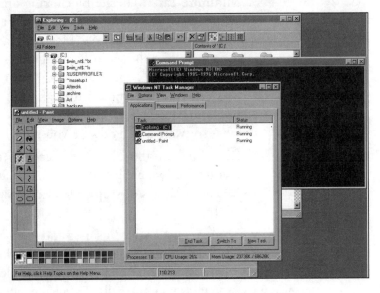

2. Task Manager will probably open to the Applications pane shown in Figure D-6. We want to look at total system performance, so click on the Performance tab if it's not already showing. Task Manager will display the screen shown in Figure D-7.

Figure D-7.
The Performance tab provides details on CPU and total system memory usage (not just RAM).

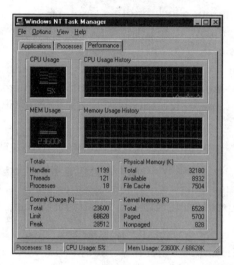

3. Minimize Task Manager by clicking on the Minimize icon at the left of the group of three icons at the upper right of the Task Manager window. Now look at the Taskbar System Tray as shown in Figure D-8 to see the Task Manager CPU Usage display (it'll probably be right between your Volume Control and the Clock as shown, but your System Tray may be different depending upon what software and hardware you have installed).

4. Right-click on the CPU Usage gauge. You'll see a context menu with two choices (Close Task Manager, and Task Manager Always on Top). Deselect Task Manager Always on Top.

Now you can go about your business and keep an eye on your system's CPU usage at the same time. Here's where a bit of common sense and Sherlock Holmes–quality sleuthing comes in: use your system as you normally do, and see when it's loaded down, and when it's not. This may give you some clues whether it's an application that's really hogging your system or it's some other problem.

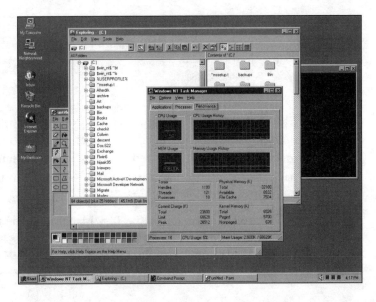

Figure D-8.
The Task Manager CPU Usage gauge shows the percentage of time your system's processor is in use.

For example, the 486 system I'm using right now to write this incredibly useful appendix really has just the minimum stuff for running Windows NT Workstation 4.0, but I'm using it anyway, just to learn more about how NT works on a fairly minimal system.

Thun: "Oh, Father, how I long for the good old days when a 486 DX-4 100 with 16MB RAM wasn't a fairly minimal system; I'm just glad Mother can't see us now."

Sylvester: "Quiet, Thun, I'm trying to see how many CPU cycles are used by this Giant Mouse."

What I've discovered on this system is that even though I have more than the "official" minimum amount of RAM, I still have to be careful to conserve it. My other system, a Pentium Pro with 32MB RAM, is much more responsive, not only because of the faster P6 processor (which is *wicked evil nasty fast*, of course), but because NT has room to load more of itself into memory, and there's less time spent moving chunks of operating system back and forth from the drives to RAM, as on the 486. How did I discover this? By watching CPU usage with one eye while I work. Just typing in Word uses over 75 percent of the CPU time on the 486 (I've got all the multithreaded spell-check doodads turned on, of course); moving a program window is even worse.

NOTE: See "Tips for Optimizing Minimal NT Systems" later in this chapter.

Moral of the story: I've decided that on my 486, there's no sense in mucking about with specific application prioritizations since the machine is basically choked in other ways (I'll tell you some of the tricks I'm using to help my limping 486 later in this appendix).

TIP: You can also get to the Task Manager at any time from the Windows NT Security dialog box by pressing Ctrl + Alt + Del and selecting the Task Manager button.

Adjusting Prioritization Using Task Manager

But you're not me, and you're not using my machine (you can breathe a couple of huge sighs of relief, I'm not offended). So let's look at what other diagnostic tools Task Manager gives you to help you visualize the application processes on your system, and you can decide whether you want to make changes:

1. If Task Manager isn't still open from the example above, open it from the Taskbar right mouse context menu as before.

2. When the Task Manager window appears, click on the Processes tab. Task Manager will display a pane very much like the one shown in Figure D-9.

Figure D-9.
The Processes pane shows you the real low-down on what's running in NT.

3. OK, but you distinctly remember I promised you info on controlling prioritizations from Task Manager. You're right, but you'll have to do some work first, because Microsoft didn't think you'd be that interested in this topic. To see the process priorities, select View ➤ Select Columns from the Task Manager menu. You'll get a dialog much like the one in Figure D-10.

Figure D-10.
You'll need to select the performance variables you want to monitor.

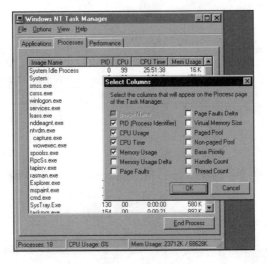

4. For starters, let's just select Base Priority by clicking in the check box to the left of it and then clicking on the OK button. Task Manager will return to the Processes tab pane.

5. But wait! You still can't see anything about priorities, because Task Manager won't resize the window automatically. Grab the right side of the Task Manager window and adjust it until you can see the Base Pri column as shown in Figure D-11 (or click on the Maximize button to take it full screen).

CAUTION: Don't adjust process priorities at random—Microsoft has set them as they are for specific reasons. If you want to experiment with a known specific application, that's great, but don't mess around with parts of the system you don't understand.

Figure D-11.
You can adjust the Task Manager window just like any other to see its complete contents.

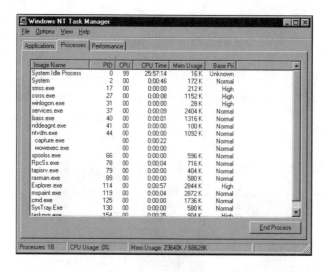

6. Now you can see the prioritizations for each task in your system. Let's take a look at the priority for Paint (listed as mspaint.exe in the process list). Right-click on mspaint.exe in the Image Name column and move the mouse cursor over the Set Priority selection as shown in Figure D-12.

Figure D-12.
Paint's default priority setting is Normal; select another to change it.

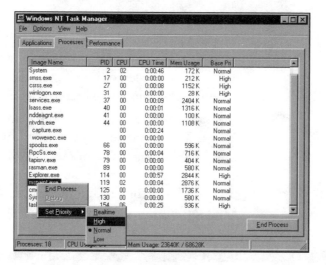

7. Select High from the cascade menu as shown in Figure D-12 above and click once. Task Manager will display a warning message (shown in Figure D-13). Click on Yes to continue. Task Manager will upgrade the priority of Paint and display a new value in the Processes pane.

Figure D-13.
Don't take this warning lightly, and don't go changing things you shouldn't (stick to the application you're testing).

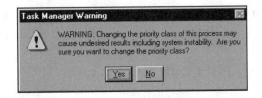

Remember, the point of this example is not to show you how to get under NT's hood and rewire it, the goal is to show you how to use Task Manager to identify an application that might benefit from reprioritizing and test it at a different priority level. You certainly don't want to go into this procedure involving Task Manager every time you run an application. Let's look at some of the other diagnostic display tools available in Task Manager:

1. If Task Manager isn't still open from the previous example, open it from the Taskbar right mouse context menu as before.

2. When the Task Manager window appears, click on the Processes tab. Task Manager will display a pane very much like the one shown in Figure D-14.

Figure D-14.
Click on the column labels in the Processes pane to sort the display by the category you desire (for example, Mem Usage).

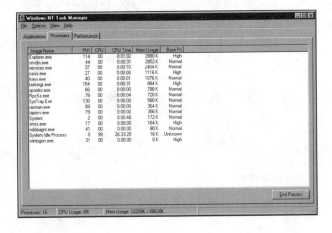

3. Click on the Mem Usage column label. Task Manager will display the current processes sorted by the amount of memory they are currently using. Click on the label again to invert the sort order.

You can use this same trick to view the current system processes by any of the column values in ascending or descending order.

Stopping Tasks with Task Manager

You can also use Task Manager to halt processes, of course. Again, don't go experimenting in the Processes pane unless you have considerable experience with NT and understand what each component process does before you halt it. If your real goal is to stop a running (or formerly running) application, follow this procedure:

CAUTION: Using Task Manager to halt running applications can result in data loss. It's best to close a running application from its own menu. You can switch to running applications quickly from Task Manager by double-clicking on the program name in the Applications pane.

1. If Task Manager isn't still open from the example above, open it from the Taskbar right mouse context menu as before.

2. When the Task Manager window appears, click on the Applications tab. Task Manager will display a pane very much like the one shown in Figure D-15.

Figure D-15.
The Applications pane lists all programs in memory and their status.

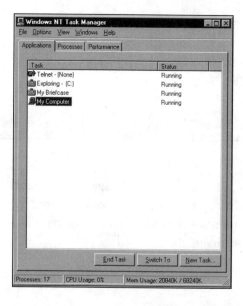

1. Select the Application you want to halt (you should only stop applications listed as "Not Responding") with a single click of the left mouse button.

> **CAUTION:** Task Manager will perform the next step immediately without further warning.

2. Click on the End Task button to halt the task.

I hope you see how this procedure can get you in trouble. Please use it wisely.

There's one more trick I want to show you before we move on. If you're really trying to determine what's using the most memory and CPU cycles on your system, it pays to understand the relationship between Applications and Processes. To see this, start a few applications and open a few windows (say, My Computer and Explorer) and then open the Task Manager window to the Applications pane and right-click on any running program (let's try My Computer). You'll see a display much like the one in Figure D-16.

Figure D-16.
Like most other areas of Windows, Task Manager supports right mouse context menus.

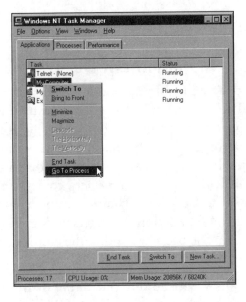

Notice the Go to Process menu entry. Select this, and you should see a pane like Figure D-17.

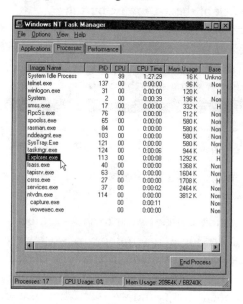

Remember all that stuff in Chapter 3 about how My Computer is actually an Explorer window? Here's proof positive. Try the same exercise on My Briefcase, and you'll see how Microsoft is walking the walk of reusing object code in Windows NT Workstation 4.0.

Memory Management Demystified

There is one immutable fact about memory on any PC: RAM is limited. The good news is that, to some extent, it doesn't matter, as modern operating systems can fool applications into believing a number of things about the machine you're using, including the handy little lie that you have more RAM than you actually do. This neat trick, called *virtual memory,* comes to the PC from mainframe and UNIX minicomputers and allows Windows NT Workstation 4.0 to perform wonders with as little as 12MB physical memory. The bad news is that the cost is decreased performance compared to computers with "the real stuff."

No one I know can afford to put all the RAM on a PC that they can use (anybody out there with extra RAM to give away, please mail it to me in care of the publisher). So it's important to know how to best manage the physical memory you have. Fortunately, NT makes it relatively simple to do this.

What Is Virtual Memory? What's a Pagefile?

Windows NT can use drive space to mimic physical RAM (Random Access Memory) through the technique of virtual memory, which uses special disk files called swap files or *pagefiles*. By mapping the drive space as additional RAM, virtual memory management allows you to run more applications at one time than actual memory allows. Virtual memory operation requires drive space for the swap file and also adds the time to move application memory pages to and from the swap file. This represents a performance decrease as compared to the same workload on a system using the equivalent physical RAM, but as processor and drive speeds increase, the difference in performance is less.

To accomplish these ends, Windows NT's memory management components create a file called PAGEFILE.SYS on your system (you may actually have one on each drive on your system, depending upon how it's configured). NT maps the contents of RAM into the PAGEFILE.SYS structure so that it can swap the contents of working memory to the page file on your drive when other applications or NT itself needs it.

Viewing Memory Configurations in Windows NT

The first step in learning to optimize NT memory is to find out where to view the current memory settings. A swift right-click on the My Computer icon allows you to select the Properties for your NT system, as shown in Figure D-18.

First lesson: the memory value shown in the General tab pane is the installed RAM or *physical memory*. This doesn't tell you squat about what's really going on, other than how much you've got. Click on the Performance tab and then on the Change button in the Virtual Memory section to see the actual *virtual memory* settings for your machine (shown in Figure D-19).

Figure D-18.
Right-click on My
Computer and select
Properties to display
the System
Properties dialog.

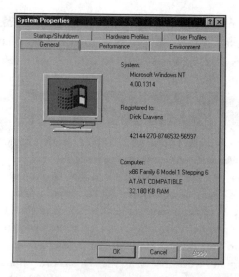

Figure D-19.
Knowing how much
physical RAM you've
got is nice, but you
really need to know
how virtual memory is
configured to know
how much working
memory you have,
and to control your
machine's performance.

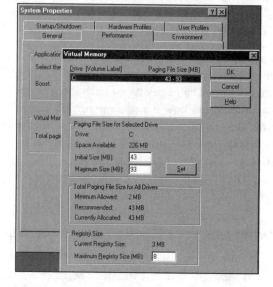

NOTE: *Working memory* is defined as *physical RAM* plus *pagefile size.*

This dialog is where you can actually adjust the amount of virtual memory available to Windows NT by setting the size of the page-file. We'll come back to that in the next section. First let's look at how to tell if you even need to adjust it.

The best tool for seeing the true picture of NT memory usage is the Windows NT Diagnostics program available from the Administrative Tools menu. To start Windows NT Diagnostics, click on the Start menu button and then select Programs ➢ Administrative Tools (Common) ➢ Windows NT Diagnostics. After the Windows NT Diagnostics window appears, click on the Memory tab to see a screen like the one shown in Figure D-20 (yours may be slightly different).

Figure D-20.
The Memory pane gives you a true picture of memory allocation and usage on your system.

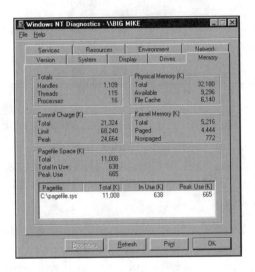

Notice that this screen gives you a wealth of information on the state of memory on your system (probably more than you really wanted to know). We're primarily concerned here with the location, size, and usage of the virtual memory file pagefile.sys. On this system (my P6 Micron) I've got 32MB of physical RAM, plus about 11MB of virtual memory—only 638K has been touched. So this machine has very little virtual memory allocated, or in use. Now consider my other machine, my lowly 486 with 16MB RAM (whose Memory pane is seen in Figure D-21).

You can see I've got pagefiles on each drive on the 486, and each pagefile is about 8MB in size. You can also see these pagefiles get quite a bit more workout than on the P6 with 32MB RAM. C'est la vie, 486/16.

Figure D-21.
Little Joe's got more
virtual memory than
his wealthy cousin
Big Mike.

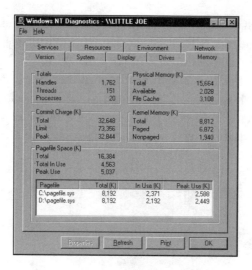

Controlling Memory Configurations in Windows NT

Neither of the machines profiled above has a problem with the current virtual memory settings. If the Peak Use readout on either were to get close to the actual pagefile size, I'd increase the pagefile size as follows:

1. Open the System Properties dialog (either from the context menu for My Computer or from the Control Panel) and click once on the Performance tab to display that pane.

2. Click once on the Change button in the Virtual Memory section. Windows will display the dialog first seen in Figure D-19 above.

3. Enter a new number in the Initial Size (MB) field to suit the requirements of the system (at least as large as the Peak Use setting), and then enter a value twice that size in the Maximum Size (MB) field.

Click on the Set button to commit the changes, and then click on the OK button twice to exit the System Properties dialog. Windows NT will ask whether you want to restart the system now or later to put the changes in effect.

Calculating the Ideal Virtual Memory Settings

Windows NT Workstation 4.0 usually makes a pretty good first estimate of what virtual memory settings to use on your system. If you want to experiment with yours to see if you can increase performance, here are a few rules and recommendations to play by:

- Windows NT requires a minimum of 22MB working memory (remember, *working memory = physical memory + pagefile size*).

- Windows NT will always need 10MB of physical RAM for itself, period.

- Windows NT will always need 2MB of pagefile, period (even if you have gobs of physical RAM)

- The optimum amount of working memory is 40MB. The best way to calculate the optimum pagefile size for this is: 40MB – [(*physical RAM MB*) +10MB] = *pagefileMB*.

- In English: start with 40MB, subtract your installed RAM MB, then add another 10MB for NT itself. Make a minimum pagefile equal in MB to that value. Got it?

- Check the size of your pagefile Peak Usage frequently, and set your minimum pagefile size to at least equal that value. Windows NT will increase the file if it needs to anyway, so save the time by giving it the space up front.

- Be generous in calculating maximum pagefile sizes. You won't use the drive space until you need it, and drive space is cheap compared to RAM, any day of the week.

- *Past a certain point, no amount of virtual memory will make your system faster.* Only more RAM, a faster CPU, or a faster drive subsystem will actually increase system speed. Once you've hit the optimum value for your system, applications, and work habits, more raw MB of drive storage won't actually increase the system speed, ever.

Hardware Purchases: the Last Resort, but Worth Considering

After you've twiddled with prioritization and memory management, you may come to the conclusion that your system simply isn't going to make the grade with NT Workstation for the work you need to do each day. It's OK, you're not alone. Although you can certainly run Windows NT Workstation 4.0 on a minimal system and still benefit from its increased stability and great security features, the fact of the matter is that it does take more hardware to make NT 4.0 run as briskly as earlier versions of Windows. That's simply the price we all pay for progress.

In this section, let's look at some basic hardware areas and how upgrading them can improve the performance of NT Workstation:

- RAM
- CPU
- Drive speed and space
- Display speed

—in that order (from most likely to affect performance to least, top to bottom). The big trick here is understanding the relationships between the major players, and discovering which one is the real bottleneck. The ideal situation is one in which all of these resources are in the optimal balance. Do I have a formula for that? No, Microsoft hasn't shared that information with me yet, but I will give you the benefits of several years' hands-on experience with NT.

RAM, RAM, RAM, Wonderful RAM

Let me say this very, very clearly: there is no other single resource more affecting NT performance than the amount of working memory, or RAM, on your system. More is almost *always* better than less (let's put it this way: I've never been able to afford enough RAM to discover it's bad).

Shouldn't the minimum amount of RAM required for NT be enough, and anything over that simply be just more available for applications? Would that it were that simple. Windows NT uses RAM in several ways:

- For the system kernel (the heart of the NT operating system, plus device drivers and services)
- For the file (drive) cache
- For managing virtual memory
- For applications

—each of which needs to be optimized according to various guidelines not necessarily linearly related to the amount of RAM available. In other words, the percentage of RAM needed by the system kernel will vary according to tasks, not just the amount of RAM on a machine. The percentage of RAM used for file cache will vary as well (on my 16MB machine, I've got a considerably smaller cache than on my 32MB machine). NT will adjust all these values and the balance among them on the fly depending upon *what exactly you're doing with the machine* just as much as *how much RAM you give it*. The more RAM you have, the more of NT gets loaded into memory, increasing overall performance.

NT is much like the giant carnivorous flower in *Little Shop of Horrors*, always yelling "FEED ME!!!" (the good news is it'll probably not try to eat *you* at the end of the day).

Processor Speed

Yes, processor speed is important. No, it's not the be-all and end-all for determining NT performance. To wit, I'd rather have

- A 486 with 32MB RAM

  than

- A Pentium with 16MB RAM

to run most general business productivity software (such as the ubiquitous Microsoft Office). Unless I'm doing image processing or other truly CPU-intensive work, in which case I'd rather have

- A Pentium with 32MB RAM

  than

- A 486 with 128MB RAM

Again, it depends upon what your true task for your NT system is, to determine which type of resource is the most critical. In the case of image processing, no amount of RAM will make the 486 machine outperform the Pentium unless you're using *extremely* large image files, in which case the Pentium as described will be swapping portions of the image file to virtual memory just to view it (yes, some full-color image files are easily that large). Of course, I won't turn down a Pentium with 128MB RAM if it falls in my lap, either.

Drive Performance

Windows NT Workstation 4.0 loves virtual memory almost as much as it loves RAM. NT combines RAM with virtual memory to arrive at a value representing the amount of *working memory* available to NT and applications. It follows, logically, that the slower the drive system, the slower the overall system performance.

What about the Pentium Pro?

If you're considering a completely 32-bit NT system (using few or no 16-bit applications), then please give the Pentium Pro a look. It offers a considerable performance advantage over the Pentium for true 32-bit applications and operating systems. Why does the computer press belittle this processor? Part of the explanation lies in the fact that most of the press coverage during the last two years has been of hardware for Windows 95, which of course contains great big stinkin' chunks of 16-bit code down in its guts. There's no real benefit to using a Pentium Pro on Windows 95, so therefore you don't see many articles praising the true advantages of this processor. The advent of Windows NT Workstation 4.0 will change this, as there is a proven *tremendous* benefit to using the Pentium Pro with this true 32-bit operating system. Pentium Pro systems can outperform a Pentium of the same speed by 50 percent to 100 percent, depending upon the software in use.

Look for this tide to turn quickly in the popular press. At the time I'm writing this (just before NT 4.0's release), you can get Pentium Pro systems for about the same price *or less* compared to Pentium computers (you just have to shop around a bit).

If your system performance is lacking, look first at your RAM and processor profiles, and then at drive subsystems.

It also helps to have plenty of drive space for virtual memory (see the sidebar "What Is Virtual Memory? What's a Pagefile?" earlier in this appendix). You may have a very fast drive, but if NT can't get to enough of it as virtual memory, it will swap more often, which means slower performance as well.

> **TIP:** If you're *really* serious about drive performance, check out Fast-and-Wide SCSI-2 drive subsystems. You'll pay a premium for performance, but you'll get it with near 20MB per second throughput. If you're doing graphics or other disk-intensive work, this may be just the ticket for your system.

Your Display System

During the period when lots of users were migrating to Windows from MS-DOS, it became apparent that some graphics adapters that seemed lightning fast in MS-DOS character mode literally crawled when running in Windows' graphics mode. Early 386 and 486 systems were literally more bound by lack of video performance than any one other factor (excluding RAM, of course) as far as running Windows was concerned. This raises the question: does NT Workstation benefit from a faster display adapter?

The answer is "Yes, of course it does," qualified by "but no more than other versions of Windows." So if you've used your system with Windows before, and you weren't concerned about your display system's speed, then don't spend money on a new display card. Chances are it's better spent in the other areas that we've covered above.

How do you know if your video system is lacking speed? If you drag or resize windows and it takes a while for the screen to "repaint," you need to consider a faster adapter. But first be sure you've eliminated the other areas that can affect performance (a slow hard drive can slow down the entire system, causing video to crawl, for example).

Tips for Optimizing Minimal NT Systems

If you simply can't afford to upgrade your system immediately but want to enhance performance, here are several tips that will cost you almost nothing:

- **Run at a lower color or screen resolution** in the Display Properties Settings dialog. If display resolution or number of colors isn't critical, reduce them to save video and CPU time. Fewer display resources mean faster display performance and more CPU time for other tasks. Try 800×600 resolution at 16 colors instead of 1024×768 at 256.

- **Turn off "Show window contents while dragging"** in the Display Properties Plus! dialog. Believe it or not, this feature eats tons of CPU time just to move a window, which takes CPU time away from background applications.

- **Run fewer applications.** I'm not saying don't multitask when you need to, but don't open any apps you really don't use. Learn to be frugal.

- **Use one Folder window instead of many.** Select View ➢ Options ➢ Folder from the My Computer window, and select "Browse folders by using a single window . . . ". This will reuse the one window as you navigate through folders instead of opening a window for each one as you go.

TIP: You can open another Folder window at any time by Ctrl-double-clicking on the folder you want the new window for. You can open Explorer to that folder by Shift-double-clicking, too.

- **Don't leave a Command Prompt window open.** Every open Command Prompt window sucks about 1MB of memory plus other system resources. If you aren't using the Command Prompt frequently, close it.

- **Don't use wallpaper.** Or if you do, pick a small bitmap and tile it. Large bitmaps use RAM byte-for-byte to display that groovy background for your Desktop. Pick a nice background color and texture instead, and gain back up to almost 1MB of precious real memory.

- **Load the programs you always use and leave them loaded.** Don't open and close programs frequently. If you need the program, open it and leave it open. Windows will swap portions of the program's code to virtual memory if you don't use it for a while, and it will reload just the swapped portions of it automatically when you call the program the next time (which is much faster than loading the whole thing manually from scratch).

- **Minimize background programs.** If you don't need to see the screen of a program in the background, minimize it. If Windows NT has to redraw the Desktop, it can do so more quickly if it isn't working on stuff you really don't need to see anyway. Remember, minimizing a program doesn't stop it from working in the background.

- **Learn to use the Toolbar to switch programs.** Each time you click on a program window, Windows will bring that program to the foreground and redraw the Desktop. Don't go clicking about looking through a maze of windows to find one of your programs, click once on its button on the Toolbar.

- **Set up a pagefile on each drive.** You can speed up virtual memory access by giving Windows more than one pagefile. One pagefile on each drive lets Windows read from one while writing to another, which can speed up performance drastically if you don't have much RAM (see the sidebar "What Is Virtual Memory? What's a Pagefile?" earlier in this appendix).

- **Defragment your drives.** NT doesn't ship with a drive optimization program, but check out third-party products to keep your drives up to snuff. Optimized drives don't *run* any faster, they just *find* critical things faster, which can make all the difference.

None of these tips require major changes in your work habits, so if you're working on an older system with a slower CPU, or one with limited RAM, try them out before you spend money on additional hardware.

Securing Your Data: Backing Up Windows NT

So you set up Windows NT Workstation 4.0 on your bright new computer system, you installed all your new 32-bit applications, you tweaked and prodded your system to get the last bit of performance out of it—and then your hard drive crashed, taking with it every piece of data, every second of your work getting the system just right, each bead of sweat that glistened on your brow as you slaved over the hot CPU day and night creating the perfect NT system configuration. Sucker. You fell for it. You bought the dream. You saw the pretty, shiny lights, you didn't think twice, didn't realize they were the headlamps of a computing nightmare, rolling toward you out of the night—but I digress.

Every computer crashes. Every hard drive fails—eventually. These are simply facts of life. Do you have a cat? Children? Neighbors with chain saws? Do any of your utility companies ever make service calls, and do they own a backhoe? Are there ever thunderstorms in your area? If the answer is affirmative to *any* of the above, then you need to back up your computer, *now.* You'll notice I've not mentioned operator error; I consider that impossible, since anyone intelligent enough to buy this fine book will *never* make a mistake with the power switch, hit reset instead of the CD-ROM access button, drag the wrong folder to the Recycle Bin, spill coffee over the keyboard, or trip over their UPS. You'll be relieved to know that I've consulted my personal psychic nutritionist, and I'm now certain that *none* of my readers will ever suffer from fire, theft, or any natural disasters, either.

Folks, face it. Don't kid yourself. Like death, taxes, and diarrhea, it's going to happen to you—someday. The best you can hope for is to be prepared. Show some respect for your own work, and keep your critical system files and data secure. I'm here to help.

Exploring Your NT Backup Options

All kidding aside: backing up your computer system is a serious business, and it is absolutely necessary. Unfortunately, it gets about the same enthusiasm from most computer users as they show for flossing their teeth. This section will give you the basics on backups and perhaps make it a bit easier to face reality. We'll look at

- Choosing a backup system
- Different types of backups
- Determining what to back up
- Establishing a backup routine
- Using NT Backup

With this head start, you should be able to feel more secure about backing up your computing environment and ensuring the safety of all that hard work you do with it. It's still up to you to follow through.

> **CAUTION:** Store your backups at another site, away from your computer. Don't go to all the trouble to make a backup of your critical system files and irreplaceable data and then watch them be destroyed by the same disaster that claims your main computing system.

Choosing the Right Backup System

There are two main choices for *where* to back up your data. You can back up either to

- Another hard drive

  or to

- Removable media

The main point here is that you should never trust your critical data to a single drive or medium. It's not enough to have another *copy* of your data, you need to have it on another media *system* as well. If a hard drive fails, it can easily take *everything* with it. Never trust a single spindle or device with your work.

Local Hard Drive

It's perfectly OK to back up to another hard drive on the same system (it's on a different spindle). If the entire computer fails and takes your primary drive with it, you can physically move your backup drive to another machine if necessary (this is a hassle and should really be viewed as a last resort). The advantage to using a second local hard drive is speed of access and simplicity. The disadvantage is that it presents limited capacity, and it's really not readily portable.

Network Drive

Backing up to a network server drive offers all the advantages of using a second local drive, plus the server is available even if your primary system fails. In addition, your network administrator should be backing up the entire server at regular intervals, so you're really getting two backups for the price of one. The main disadvantage is the same: limited capacity. Portability is pretty much assumed, if your network is backed up, but don't expect the network admin to hand you the tapes if you need to restore a few files from a month back—expect to politely wait.

> **CAUTION:** Don't back up to a network server without checking with the network administrator first. You can crash an entire network and lose data for all users if you move too much information to a network server without warning.

Floppy Drive

This is the traditional backup system for most computer users. Unlimited capacity meets unlimited tedium with floppy backups. Remember, your time is worth money, too. Although using floppies may seem inexpensive to begin with, about the third floppy swap you'll understand why there's a flourishing market for large-capacity removable media. Floppies are inherently very portable; however, floppy backups are Not Recommended.

Tape Drives

Now you're talking. There are so many decent options available at affordable prices that there's really no excuse for not having at least a minimal tape system on your computer. Low-capacity tape drives (120MB) are available for under $200.00 (prices have probably fallen since this was written, so shop around). Get a tape system with the largest capacity you can afford, but even a 120MB-format system is better than nothing (don't get cheap on me here, waiting around to swap tapes is no more fun than swapping floppies). You can find drives offering up to 4GB of capacity on a single tape, if you really want to back up an entire drive in one swell foop. Portability is a given with tape media, but be aware that you'll usually need an identical drive to restore from a tape. Don't assume compatibility between drive manufacturers or tape backup software.

NOTE: For information on installing a tape drive, see the section "Tape Devices," in Appendix B.

Optical and CD-ROM

These newer technologies offer incredible capacity (600–720MB for CD-ROM, into the GBs for optical media), but they can be a real pain to install and use, in addition to being the most expensive option per MB at this moment in the market, in regard to initial cost for the system and media. Optical drive media mostly only work with the type of drive you create the backup on. CD-ROM backups offer the advantage of being readable on almost any CD-ROM player, but most CD-ROM "burners" come with software designed for mastering CD-ROMs, not automating backups. Most CD-ROM recorders are also single-session, so you can't use a blank more than once (which is potentially very wasteful if you doing daily backups of small incremental changes in your data).

Whatever device you choose, you'll need to check with the vendor to make sure it's compatible with Windows NT Workstation 4.0 before you purchase it. Devices that are on the NT 3.51 Hardware Compatibility List *should* be fine, but check with the vendor for the gospel version regarding NT 4.0 compatibility. This basically means they will have a device driver for their device or will have tested their device with the drivers in NT. Make sure the backup utility software that comes with the device is compatible, too.

Different Backup Types and Methods

Now comes the question of *how* to back up. Whichever media solution you choose, there are two main choices:

- **Full backup**: Basically a copy operation, creating a duplicate of your data on the backup media
- **Incremental backup**: Copying only those files that have changed since the last backup

As you'll see in the examples that follow later in this chapter, there are variations on these two main types, but these are the two main concepts you'll need in order to master your backup techniques.

Choosing a Backup Method

How you actually perform the backup depends upon what system you're using (tape, floppy, or whatever) and what type of backup you need to perform (full or incremental). There are three main procedural techniques for backing up your data:

- **Manual backup:** You can use Explorer to copy your data to floppy media or another hard drive (local or network), or you can use the Command Prompt with the COPY or XCOPY command.
- **Semi-automatic backup:** You can use the NT Command Prompt BACKUP command in a batch file to back up to any local or network drive, or you can use backup software (such as Windows NT Backup) to write your archive to a tape device.
- **Automatic backup:** The better dedicated backup software applications will allow you to schedule full or incremental backups in advance.

I like doing my automatic backup at 5:00 A.M. because it amuses the cats, which keeps them from waking me up when they're bored.

What Data Should You Preserve?

Having backup hardware is good. Knowing *what* to back up will save you hours of time. Don't assume it's best to blindly back up every single byte on your computer. You may be better off backing up selected pieces of data:

- NT system configuration data (the registry, etc.)
- Your work data files
- Your application configuration data

> **TIP:** Most backup utility software written for NT will have an option to automate backing up just the system registry data. You don't need to know all the specific NT data files if this feature is present.

Why not just back up your entire system? Because it changes frequently, and unless you want to do a complete backup frequently, you're better off *securing just the information that makes your system different from a freshly installed one.* You're probably better off, in the case of a total system crash, with reinstalling the NT operating system and your applications and then restoring just the absolutely unique data that represents your customizations to that system.

Plus you'll save a ton on backup media, and a ton of time backing up.

Your Backup Schedule

How often you back up your system will depend upon a wide variety of other variables. If you produce a lot of unique data daily, back up daily. It's good to do a full system registry backup right before you do anything that may change the NT system configuration markedly (such as installing a Service Pack).

> **CAUTION:** Don't back up while you're running other applications. Although it's tempting to use NT's superior multitasking to do "real" work while you're doing a system backup, most backup programs can't copy files that are in use.

The real question you have to ask yourself is: how much time can I afford to lose recreating work I've already done? If you're like me, not much. Learn to strike a balance between doing your work and taking time to ensure its security.

Windows NT Backup

Enough philosophy, let's do a backup. For this example we're going to use the best free backup tool in your NT Workstation system, Windows NT Backup. I'll assume you already have a tape drive on your system, and that the driver software is installed.

> **NOTE:** For information on installing a tape drive or drivers, see Appendix B, "Tape Devices."

Starting a Backup

Let's begin by taking a look at Backup:

1. Click on the Start menu button. When the Start menu appears, select Programs ➤ Administrative Tools (Common) ➤ Backup and click once. Windows NT will run the Backup program and display a window much like that seen in Figure D-22.

Figure D-22.
Backup uses a familiar split-screen display.

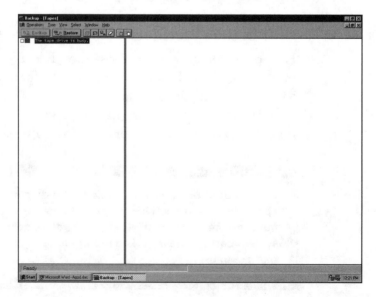

2. Backup will initialize the tape drive as soon as it starts opening. Even though it's not ready to begin a backup operation yet, you can still prepare the backup. Select Window ➤ Drives from the Backup main menu and then click twice on the C: drive icon in the Backup left pane. Backup will scan your C: drive and display a window much like that shown in Figure D-23.

Figure D-23.
My messy C: drive. The left Backup pane shows directories, and the right shows the contents of the current directory (highlighted in the left pane). Since the current directory is the root of C:, all the subdirectories are listed in both panes.

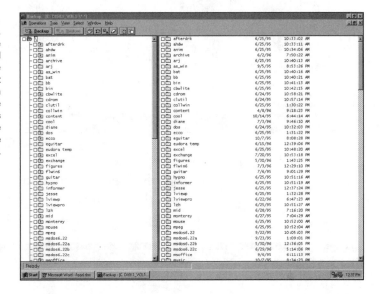

 TIP: You can adjust the view in Backup by adjusting the pane width using the border between the panes. Just grab it with your left mouse button and drag it to the desired location to split the panes to your taste.

3. My goal is to back up all the figures I just shot for another book I'm working on. So I'm going to scroll down to the directory in the left pane and click on it with my left mouse button. Notice what happens in the right pane (shown in Figure D-24).

Figure D-24.
Selecting a directory
in the left pane with a
single click displays its
contents in the right.

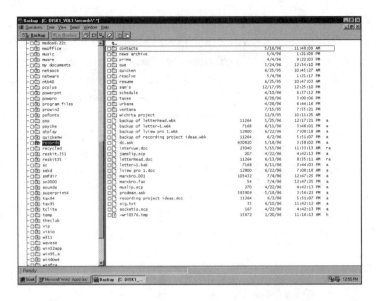

4. I'm in search of a particular directory of files, so I'm going to double-click through the tree control in the left pane until I find just the directory I need. The left pane display will expand as I go (as shown in Figure D-25).

Figure D-25.
Double-clicking on a
directory in the left
pane expands it in
both panes if it has
subdirectories.

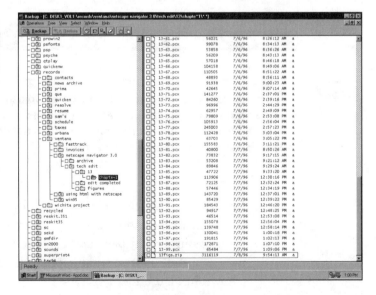

5. Notice that no files have yet been selected; I'm just browsing so far. But wait! there's the file I need to back up, 13FIGS.ZIP. I'm going to click in the box to the left

of the filename in the right pane. Backup marks the file for later and marks all directories above it for visual reference (see Figure D-26).

Figure D-26.
A trail of X's mark the
path to the file marked
for backup.

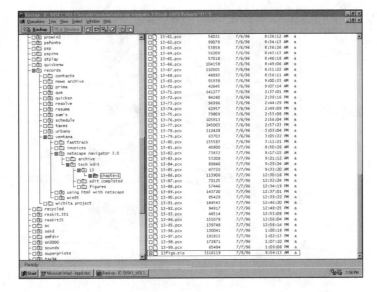

6. Now I need to mark a file on my D: drive. I select the Windows ➤ Drives menu item and click on the D: drive icon in that window. Backup displays the tree for the D: drive as shown in Figure D-27.

Figure D-27.
You can select files
from another drive
before beginning the
backup session.

7. After I've selected the file, I click once on the Backup button at the top left of the screen. Backup displays the Backup Information dialog shown in Figure D-28.

8. NT Backup usually assumes you're using a fresh tape unless you tell it otherwise. Be sure to tell it to Append if you've used the tape before. I also recommend selecting Verify After Backup. I also usually give the backup session a descriptive name to make it easier to recognize should I ever need to restore (see Figure D-29).

9. Now let's set up the options for drive D: by scrolling down in the Backup Set Information section (see that little scroll bar on the right?). Suddenly you'll see another set of options for the D: drive, specifically the Backup Local Registry option (I have NT on the D: drive on this system) as shown in Figure D-30.

Figure D-30.
You can back up your Registry data easily by simply checking the box (this will only appear on the dialog for the drive NT is installed on).

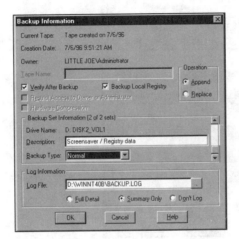

10. Now we're ready to roll. Click on the OK button, and Backup will display the Backup Status dialog as shown in Figure D-31 while it does its job. Best get a cup of coffee, or play with the cats awhile.

Figure D-31.
Backup keeps you notified throughout the backup process. The process starts with a review of all other backup sets on that tape so that Backup knows where to append the new backup set.

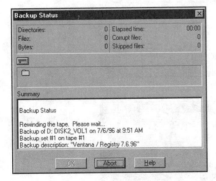

11. Backup will proceed through the backup jobs you've given it. Figures D-32–D-35 show the types of status messages to expect during this process.

Figure D-32.
Backup starts with
drive C: . . .

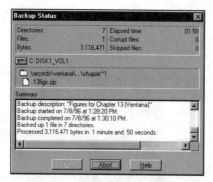

Figure D-33.
. . . moves on
through drive D: . . .

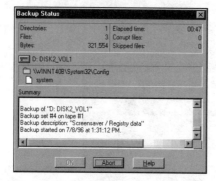

Figure D-34.
. . . rewinds the
tape to begin file
verification . . .

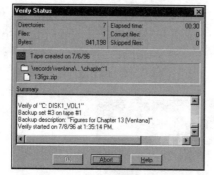

Figure D-35.
. . . then gives you a
full report when
you're finished (you
may have to scroll up
to get some details).

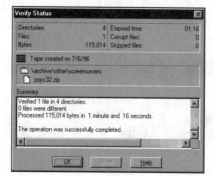

12. Click on the Verify Status dialog OK button to return to the main Backup screen.

It pays to review the report at the end of a backup session to ensure there were no errors in the backup.

Performing a File Restoration with NT Backup

Restoring files from tape is really just the reverse process of creating a backup set. With NT Backup open

1. Select Window ➤ Tapes from the main Backup menu. Backup will rewind the tape and display the Tapes window. The left pane will show the tape title, or the date the tape was first used. The right pane will show any backup sets that have been cataloged since the tape was created.

2. If your last backup set is not listed, double-click on the tape icon in the left pane. Backup will display the Catalog Status dialog and begin to audit the tape. When the Catalog Status window disappears, Backup will redisplay the Tapes window with a complete list of backup sets in the right pane (seen in Figure D-36).

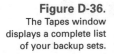

Figure D-36.
The Tapes window displays a complete list of your backup sets.

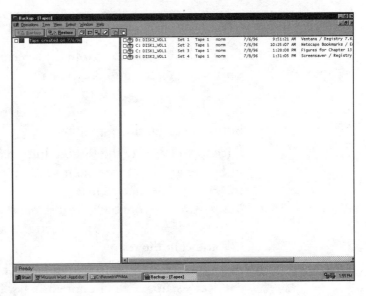

3. Select the backup set you want to view and possibly restore from by double-clicking on it in the right pane (if you know you want to restore the complete contents, skip ahead to step 4). Backup will return to the Catalog Status dialog to prepare the detailed list of that set's file contents, and then it will display the list in the right pane as shown in Figure D-37.

Figure D-37.
You can select the entire backup set, or individual files, for restoration. These are the system registry files for my 486 system.

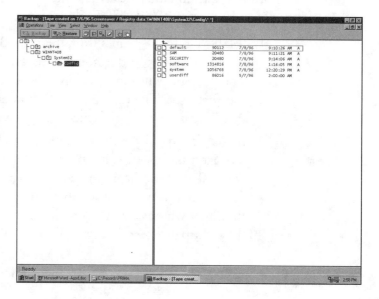

4. I've decided I need to restore the screensaver I backed up earlier, so I'm going to open the tree control and select the file by checking the box to the left of it (you can see it in Figure D-38). Then I'm going to click once on the Restore button to begin the restoration process.

5. Backup will display the Restore Information dialog (seen in Figure D-39). Since I want to be sure the restored file is the same as the tape archive version, I've checked the Verify After Restore box. I've also checked the Restore File Permissions box. When all the settings are correct, click on OK to begin the restore.

6. After your coffee/juice/soda/doughnut break, you can check the status of the Restore process. Backup will display the Verify Status dialog with log text for the session as shown in Figure D-40.

Figure D-38.
Mark the file or folder you want restored, and click on the Restore button to proceed.

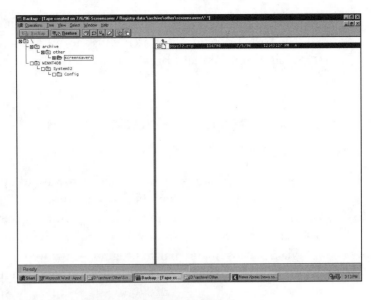

Figure D-39.
You can change the restore drive and path, verify the file, restore file permissions, and restore the system registry all from this dialog. Usually you'll just want to put the file right back where it came from.

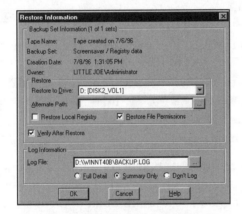

Figure D-40.
When the Restore operation is complete and all files are verified, you can click on OK to return to the main Backup screen.

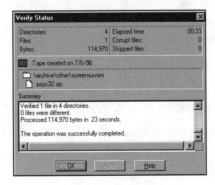

7. Click on OK if the session was successful.

There are other options available in Backup, but you've now seen the basic procedures for archiving and restoring files. Check out Help from the main Backup menu for more information.

Protecting Your System from a Computer Virus

So far in this appendix we've looked at ways to optimize the performance of your Windows NT Workstation by adjusting prioritization, ways to evaluate how to boost performance by adding new hardware, and ways to protect your data and system configuration via a backup maintenance program. Now we need to look at a way to *prevent* problems: performing preventive computer hygiene.

What Is a Computer Virus?

Unless you've been in a cave or on a desert island for the last ten years, you've heard of the evil computer virus. (One even saved the planet Earth from alien destruction in a popular film this summer; wait, that would be a *good* virus?) That doesn't mean you understand how they work, how your system gets them, or what to do if your system has one.

A computer virus is simply a computer program, written to do very special things. The biological term *virus* was applied to this class of program because almost all of them are designed to replicate and spread under the cover of other programs or data (much as biological viruses require a host cell for growth and host organisms for transmission). A computer virus spreads in these ways:

- Downloads via modem from other computer systems, the Internet, BBSs, or commercial online information services
- Files copied or programs run from floppy disks
- Files copied or programs run from CD-ROMs
- Files copied or programs run from your local area network
- Installations of commercial software
- Installations of shareware and freeware
- From compressed file archives

In other words, a virus can come from *anywhere you get data or programs.*

The Scare Factor

Although this section is about a serious topic (the computer virus), some people tend to take it a bit *too* seriously. Yes, the threat is real, and yes, a virus can damage your data and cause you to lose work, but how often will this really happen to you? Although I don't have any statistics at hand on the incidence of viral infections, I can tell you this: with reasonable care and precautions, you have very little to fear. If you purchase software from known vendors and use an antiviral program with some degree of regularity, odds are you'll never see a virus, or at least you'll disable it before it does any damage.

I've been computing over ten years, I've been *extremely* active on bulletin-board systems, online services, and the Internet, plus I've installed *thousands* of commercial and shareware programs, and I can count the times I've seen a real bona fide virus on my computer on one hand. In my five years working for a commercial software company (three years in technical support) my observations of hundreds of other user's experiences were similar: yes, it happens, but not that frequently.

Be assured that commercial software companies, bulletin board sysops, online services, shareware authors, and most other computer professionals do their best to prevent a virus from spreading: their business and income depend upon it.

Don't let the virus scare prevent you from participating in an active computer life.

What does a virus do? Some merely perform harmless pranks (such as writing a message to your screen); others will wipe your hard drive clean as a whistle. How do they do it? There is no "spontaneous eruption" of evil computing code, it has to be written by a human (albeit one of questionable virtue). Virus authors understand the underpinnings of your drive media and operating system and won't hesitate to use their experience to tamper with same. A typical virus may attack the boot sector of your hard drive immediately or replicate itself in hundreds of files on your hard drive, waiting for a certain date or time to cause a problem with your operating system.

How do you know if you have a virus on your system? It's not as simple as it seems. Don't assume that just because your system crashed you've automatically got a virus (there are plenty of other perfectly plausible ways for that to happen, even in Windows NT). Don't let a technical support person palm off an unresolved problem with their product by blaming a theoretical virus infection; request very specific proof. It's also possible you may have a dozen viruses on your system and have absolutely no symptoms, whatsoever.

The good news is that there are very smart people working to provide you with reliable tools to help you identify and deal with any viral attacks on your system. Still, it's up to you to *use* them.

Using Antiviral Software

The best way to *know* that your system is clean of viral infection is use a detection program designed by people who make it their business to know all the different "bugs" out there. Several companies provide programs that can identify all but the latest virus, down to the last few weeks' population sample. Most of these programs offer frequent updates, available via modem or mailed disk, that keep your system as current as is to be reasonable expected.

One Antiviral Program: McAfee VirusScan

One popular program is VirusScan by McAfee. This program is available as shareware, so you can download and test it for free for thirty days (after which nice people will pay McAfee their hard-earned money by registering the product). If you continue to use it, you need to purchase a registered copy from McAfee (which they make very easy to do via their Web site). You can download and purchase VirusScan from http://www.mcafee.com in versions for Windows 3.1, Windows 95, and Windows NT (you can get the Windows 3.1/Windows 95 version at most retail outlets, but I've yet to see the NT version on a shelf, so maybe you should call ahead before you make the trip). It's also available from most mail-order vendors.

> **CAUTION:** If you're not the system administrator for
> your workstation, please always consult that person before
> you install software, especially if you're working in a
> network environment.

At the time of this writing, the NT version is in a file called
WSNT251E.ZIP, which is about 1.44 MB in size . You'll need to
download it and decompress it in an empty directory to begin.
When the file is expanded, you'll have one single file,
SETUP.EXE. To install VirusScan

1. Double-click on the Setup icon in your temporary direc-
    tory (I called mine TEMPORARY). VirusScan Setup will
    run and display a screen much like the one in Figure D-41.

Figure D-41.
The McAfee VirusScan
Setup wizard looks very
much like most other
NT setup programs.

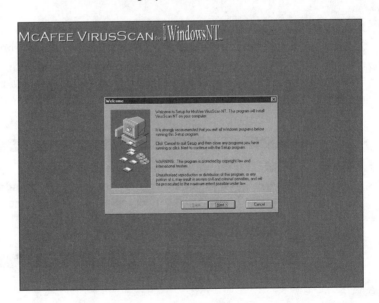

2. Click on the Next button after you've read the warnings
    about other running software and acted accordingly. Setup
    will display the Installer Rights dialog, informing you that
    you must have *administrative* privileges to install
    VirusScan. If you logged in as administrator or have equal
    privileges, proceed by clicking on the Next button again
    (otherwise, please use the Cancel button to exit Setup and
    find your administrator to install the software with you).

Figure D-43.
Accept the default selection here, or Setup will replace your group with the McAfee one.

Figure D-44.
Click on Next to accept these settings and begin the installation.

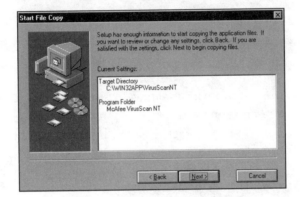

6. Click on Next to accept the installation settings or Back to change them. Setup will copy the VirusScan files to the installation directory and then display the Service Account Information dialog shown in Figure D-45. If you're on a network and want to scan network drives with VirusScan, click on Next to continue. Otherwise click on Skip.

Figure D-45.
If you're not on a network, click on the Skip button to continue.

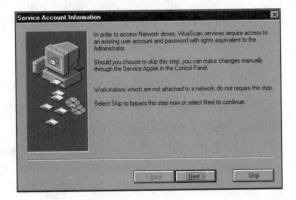

7. If you've selected to enable network scans, you'll see the dialog shown in Figure D-46. Note: you've got to enter a user name and a password to move either Back or Next from this dialog.

Figure D-46.
Enter your NT user name and password and click on Next to continue or Back to change your mind.

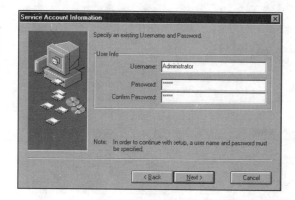

8. Setup will update your system configuration for the options you've selected and display the Start Service dialog shown in Figure D-47. If you're ready to begin using VirusScan, click on Yes to continue.

Figure D-47.
You can use VirusScan immediately if you choose Yes.

9. Setup will display a dialog asking if you wish to read the WHATSNEW.TXT file (sounds like a good idea).

That's pretty much it for installation. It's really a good idea to read the What's New file, as it contains last-minute information on VirusScan and tips on using it most effectively.

Scanning with VirusScan

Now that VirusScan's installed, let's set up a scan session. To start VirusScan

1. Click on the Start menu button. When the Start menu appears, select Programs ➢ McAfee VirusScan NT ➢ VirusScanNT Console with a single click. The VirusScan Console will appear as shown in Figure D-48.

Figure D-48.
Click on the Toolbar icon at the far left to start the VirusScan Wizard.

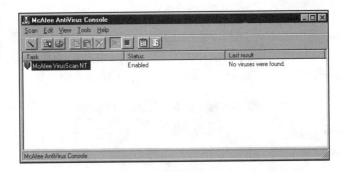

2. Select Scan ➤ Scan Wizard from the main VirusScan menu (or click on the Toolbar icon at the far left). VirusScan will display the McAfee Scan Wizard dialog. Click on Next to continue. The Scan Wizard will display the dialog shown in Figure D-49.

Figure D-49.
You can select additional items to be scanned by clicking on the Add button.

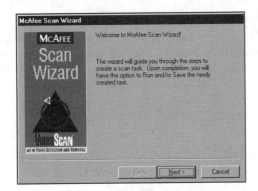

3. Let's scan the entire default C: drive for this run. Without changing any settings, click on Next to continue. The Scan Wizard will display the dialog shown in Figure D-50. Click on Next to accept the defaults for this exercise.

Figure D-50.
You can specify the type of files to be scanned and whether to recurse subdirectories from this dialog.

4. The Scan Wizard now displays a dialog asking you what response you want when it finds an infected file (as shown in Figure D-51). Let's select Continue Scanning for this session. Click on Next to continue.

Figure D-51.
You have several options for how you want VirusScan to handle infected files.

TIP: Be sure to check the McAfee VirusScan Help file for instructions on how to get updates to keep your VirusScan program current.

5. Scan Wizard will now give you three options in the dialog shown in Figure D-52. For this example, let's select the third option, Save and Run Task Now. Be sure to give the Task a descriptive name that you'll understand later.

Figure D-52.
The ability to define and store different scan profiles in a task list makes VirusScan a very powerful tool.

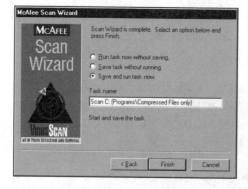

6. While VirusScan runs, a cute animation shows you that it's checking in every folder (see Figure D-53). You can pause or stop the scan using the tape-style controls on the VirusScan Scan window.

Figure D-53.
Hey, time for another dose of caffeine. . . .

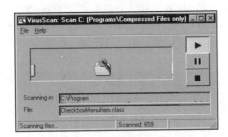

7. While the scan is running, you can view the statistics for the session as it's performed. Select Scan ➤ Statistics from the main menu of the McAfee AntiVirus Console window. VirusScan will display the Scan Statistics window (seen in Figure D-54).

Figure D-54.
Zeros are a good thing, sometimes.

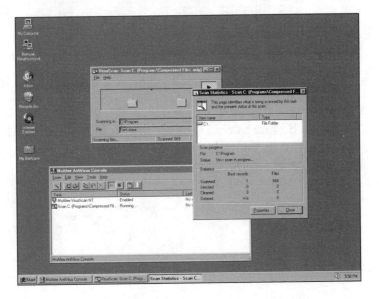

8. When the scan is completed, the result will be present in the main McAfee AntiVirus Console window in the Last Result field. If you want a detailed log of the scan, select the Scan task in the main McAfee AntiVirus Console window, then select Scan ➤ Activity Log from the main menu. The Console will display the detail log (similar to that shown in Figure D-55).

Figure D-55.
You can get detailed information on your scan session from the Console menu.

Be sure to read through the McAfee VirusScan Help file for information on other techniques, such as automating the virus database update process.

APPENDIX E

NT INFORMATION SOURCES

This appendix contains information on a variety of different sources to help you further your knowledge of the Windows NT operating system and its uses. We'll look at these major types of resources for additional information on Windows NT and related technology:

- Information included with Windows NT

- Online information sources

- Additional reference works (hard copy and CD-ROM)

- Vendor information

- Product updates, Service Packs, and device drivers

Microsoft does an excellent job of packaging decent printed documentation with each of its products, and its performance with Windows NT 4.0 is no exception. But no matter how perfect the plan and execution is for product documentation, there is always a need for additional detailed help regarding certain areas or an experienced hand to guide you in specific tasks.

It's a testimony to the power of Windows NT that users continually test its limits, and with each test, they stretch the boundaries of knowledge regarding the operating system and its uses. Learning who these users are, and contacting them, can often make the difference between spending hours or minutes in answering your questions about NT and reaching your goals quickly and easily.

> **NOTE:** Please bear in mind that quite a few of these resources are dynamic in nature and may change after the initial publication of this text.

Information Included with Windows NT

Quite a lot of information comes packaged with Windows NT 4.0 Workstation. The only trick is knowing exactly where to look for it. In this section, we'll look at some excellent resources that are part of your installed Windows NT Workstation, and some that are included in the product but not installed automatically.

The NT Help System

The first place to go for help is, of course, Help. In the new NT interface, the main Windows Help files for the operating system itself are accessed via the Start menu button on the Taskbar (as shown in Figure E-1). You can also start Help by clicking anywhere on the Desktop and then hitting the classic F1 function key (be sure to click on the Desktop first, otherwise you'll get the Help file for whatever application is currently active).

> **NOTE:** See Chapter 3 for detailed information on the Windows NT Help system.

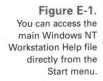

Figure E-1.
You can access the
main Windows NT
Workstation Help file
directly from the
Start menu.

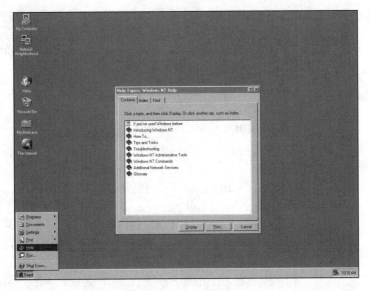

Help is also available from the Command Prompt for Windows
NT commands. Simply type **HELP** and hit the [Enter] key at
the command prompt (or type **HELP** *command name* for the
specific command in question.

Other NT Reference Files

In addition to the standard NT Help system, there are a variety of
other reference files available on the Windows NT 4.0
Workstation CD-ROM. Windows NT 4.0 Setup won't copy the
files to your local drive (saving you several MB of drive space) or
set up icons for the files in your Start menu, but they're readily
available and relatively easy to use.

How do these files differ from the main NT Help in the Start
menu? These files are more oriented toward basic NT 4.0
Workstation procedures and installation problems and really don't
cover in-depth coverage of technical issues. If you prefer a hard-
copy introduction to NT Workstation, you can print these files
and use them as a handy reference.

To access these files, simply browse to them in the Windows NT
4.0 Workstation CD-ROM using Windows NT Explorer. You'll
find the files in the \SUPPORT\BOOKS directory. You can view
or print them in either WordPad or Microsoft Word.

NOTE: See Appendix F, for a very comprehensive glossary of Windows NT and general computing terms used throughout this book.

Hardware Compatibility List

There's another Help file of great interest if you're installing Windows NT 4.0 on several computer systems: the Hardware Compatibility List. The HCL is a rich resource providing the complete list of all peripheral components that have been tested with Windows NT 4.0 Workstation. If you have questions about video cards, drive controllers, printers, or other accessories, you can check them out in advance of attempting an installation. The file even contains a list of complete computer systems so that you can evaluate future purchases.

TIP: Microsoft updates the Hardware Compatibility List file frequently. Check Library 1 of the WINNT (GO WINNT) forum or Library 17 of the MSWIN32 forum (GO MSWIN32) on CompuServe for the latest list. If you have Internet access, you can download the latest file directly from Microsoft's FTP server at ftp://ftp.microsoft.com/bussys/winnt/winnt-docs/hcl (or view an HTML version of the HCL at the Microsoft WWW site at http://www.microsoft.com/NTServer/hcl/hclintro.htm).

You can find the HCL.HLP file on your Windows NT 4.0 Workstation CD_ROM in the \SUPPORT directory. You can create a shortcut icon for the HCL anywhere on your system (use a right-click drag, or see Chapter 3, "Creating Shortcuts"). You can either leave the file on the CD-ROM or create a folder on your local drive and copy it there.

NOTE: There's also a set of Accessibility Tools in the \SUPPORT directory on your Windows NT 4.0 Workstation CD_ROM. Connect to http://www.microsoft.com/ntworkstation for information on installing and using these utilities.

README.WRI and Other Late-Breaking News

It also pays to be familiar with the README.WRI, PRINTER.WRI, and NETWORK.WRI files in your Windows NT system root directory (the main directory where the NT files are stored. These files contain information not available when Windows NT Workstation manuals were sent to production and distribution. If you're having general problems, start with README.WRI; the other two files are most applicable if you're experiencing difficulty with their respective namesake subsystems.

Online Information Sources

The real meat and potatoes of additional Windows NT information lies online in a variety of resources. All you need to access this rich world of additional information is a modem or Internet connection (most commercial online services are now available via TCP/IP as well as conventional dialup connection), plus a membership for each respective commercial service you choose to join.

What's online for the Windows NT Workstation user or administrator? Drivers, Service Packs, utilities, technical articles, trial demos of NT software, and most importantly, other NT professionals with experience in the real world of using NT Workstation, including Microsoft's own technical support group.

CompuServe

Until very recently, Microsoft maintained a very robust set of information and support forums on CompuServe. You'll still find a great number of Microsoft resources there, but don't be surprised if other organizations or entities are running them: Microsoft has announced that its online support efforts are being migrated to Usenet groups. Even after Microsoft pulls up the tent stakes, though, you'll probably want to check out these forums.

The major forum for Windows NT users is the Windows NT Forum (GO WINNT), now run by the Windows User's Group Network (a.k.a. WUGNET). WUGNET is comprised of experienced NT users (many are journalists for major trade publications) that share information regarding the operating system, applications, and other related technologies. WUGNET also maintains the WinNews Forum (GO WINNEWS).

> **TIP:** CompuServe offers free trial memberships, included with most major software packages. If you don't already have a membership, check the literature in your latest software purchase, leaf through a recent computer magazine, or call 1-800-848-8199 for information on other ways to get a startup kit (or check out the CompuServe WWW site at http://www.compuserve.com).

You can also find a variety of other resources if you start your CompuServe visit at the Microsoft Connection (GO MICROSOFT) shown in Figure E-2. The forum menus there will guide you to information on Microsoft applications, other Microsoft operating systems, and a ton of related goodies.

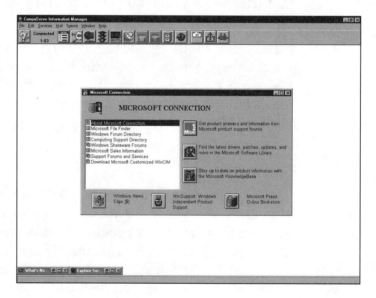

Figure E-2.
The GO MICROSOFT command takes you to the CompuServe Microsoft Connection Forum.

MSN

The word's still out on Microsoft Network client programs for Windows NT, but if you have access to a Windows 95 system with the MSN software, you can find quite a few resources for

Windows NT. Or you can access MSN via the WWW version at
http://www.msn.com with Microsoft Internet Explorer from
within the Windows NT Desktop (shown in Figure E-3). See the
Internet section immediately following for more WWW addresses
specific to Windows NT.

Figure E-3.
Microsoft has already
migrated much of its
own MSN content to
the World Wide Web.

The Internet

As convenient as the commercial online services may be, if you
have a true Internet connection, it's really just as easy to use the
resources available on the network and avoid additional expense
for service memberships, long distance service to the CompuServe
modems, and the like. In this section, we'll look at some of the
various means of gathering information over the Internet.

World Wide Web Resources

The World Wide Web has grown by leaps and bounds in the last
two years. One of the reasons for this is the intrinsic capability of a
Web document to be available 24 hours per day, seven days per
week, at a low relative cost—unlike support personnel. The Web is
a natural for technical support, and Windows NT support
resources abound on the Web.

Microsoft Web Sites

There's little you can do to avoid the obvious: http://www.microsoft.com/support/ is the place to start when looking on the World Wide Web for the latest technical information about any Microsoft product. Microsoft has done a real bang-up job on this part of their site, as shown in Figure E-4.

Figure E-4.
The Microsoft Support page is one great place to start your Web search for NT technical support.

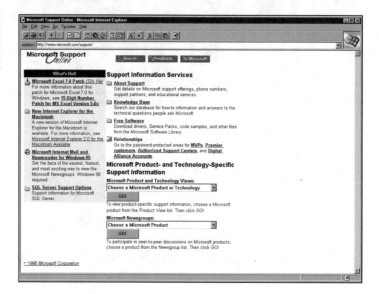

TIP: See "User Groups Resources" later in this chapter for more resource information.

Alternately, you can cut to the chase and go directly to the NT Workstation Home Page at http://www.microsoft.com/ntworkstation/ for the latest information specific to the desktop version of NT. The information here isn't of a highly technical nature, but it's a good place to go to keep up with NT Workstation developments and enhancements. If you're interested in NT Server information and issues, http://www.microsoft.com/ntserver/ is the place to be.

Another gem is the Microsoft Knowledge Base at http://198.105.232.5/isapi/support/kb.idc?Product=Windows+NT&database=KB_winnt. (Yeah, the URL is long, but you get to skip straight to the NT stuff!) Figure E-5 shows the simple interface provided to search literally thousands of documents on NT problems and solutions.

Figure E-5.
Microsoft's Knowledge
Base is a great place
to search for
extremely specific
product information.

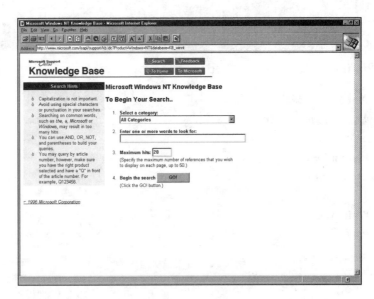

There's quite a bit of depth to the Microsoft Web presence, so use the above addresses as a starting point, and dig in!

Other Web Sites

There's a growing recognition of the inevitable dominance of the Windows NT platform in general computing. This is reflected on the Web by a list of sites that provide detailed information on both NT Workstation and NT Server operation and maintenance. Table E-1 lists some of the best of these sites.

Or, to wrap the whole thing up, check out the mother of all NT Web site lists via *Windows NT Magazine*'s Web site at http://www.winntmag.com/cgi-shl/dbml.exe?template=/WebList/rt vWebList.dbm.

The Microsoft News Server and Other Newsgroups

As mentioned earlier in this chapter, Microsoft is in the process of migrating its product technical support from CompuServe to the Internet, specifically to its Web site and its NNTP News Server. Support is also available from other users via related Usenet groups that are replicated on various servers throughout the world (see "Other Newsgroups" later in this appendix).

Table E-1 NT-Related Internet Sites

Site Name	Address
Chancellor & Chancellor's Windows NT Resource Site	http://www.chancellor.com/ntmain.html
Info Nederland Windows NT Information Site	http://nt.info.nl/english/default.htm
Rick's Windows NT Home Page	http://rick.wzl.rwth-aachen.de/rick/
Windows NT Internet FAQ	http://www.mcs.com/~thomas/www/ntfaq/
Windows NT Administration FAQ	http://www.iftech.com/classes/admin/admin.htm
Windows NT Information Stuttgart	http://www.informatik.uni-stuttgart.de/misc/nt/nt.html
Windows NT InfoCenter at Digital	http://www.windowsnt.digital.com/
Windows NT Magazine	http://www.winntmag.com/
WUGNET Home Page	http://www.wugnet.com/

Microsoft News Technical Support

Microsoft support via NNTP (the Usenet protocol) is available via the Microsoft news server (msnews.microsoft.com), which offers support on these Windows NT-specific topics:

- Applications, OLE, and NetDDE (microsoft.public.windowsnt.apps)
- Domain administration (microsoft.public.windowsnt.domain)

- **File Systems** (microsoft.public.windowsnt.fsft)
- **General** (microsoft.public.windowsnt.misc)
- **NT issues on the Macintosh**
  (microsoft.public.windowsnt.mac)
- **32-bit mail and schedule+**
  (microsoft.public.windowsnt.mail)
- **Netware and Directory Service Manager for Netware add-on products** (microsoft.public.windowsnt.dsmnfpnw)
- **Printing** (microsoft.public.windowsnt.print)
- **General protocol, networking, and connectivity issues**
  (microsoft.public.windowsnt.protocol.misc)
- **Protocol: IPX** (microsoft.public.windowsnt.protocol.ipx)
- **Protocol: Remote Access Service (RAS) and other serial communication issues**
  (microsoft.public.windowsnt.protocol.ras)
- **Protocol: TCP/IP**
  (microsoft.public.windowsnt.protocol.tcpip)
- **Setup** (microsoft.public.windowsnt.setup)

To access these groups, you'll need to set your NNTP client (your newsreader program, or your Web browser if it supports NNTP) to the Microsoft server (msnews.microsoft.com) and subscribe to each of the groups that you are interested in. Don't expect these groups to be replicated throughout the usual Usenet server network, as they will represent a major load for already-bogged news server systems.

Other Newsgroups

There are a more than a few Windows NT–specific newsgroups in the traditional Usenet News universe. Check out the comp.os.ms-windows.nt area of your news server for the latest group offerings, or see the list below.

Don't expect an extremely organized presentation of support information in public newsgroups. What you can expect is to meet the widest possible variety of users, some of whom are the most knowledgeable on the planet. Using newsgroups is a lot like shopping at garage sales (you may have to visit several neighborhoods a few weeks in a row to know which ones have the really juicy sales).

Read the message traffic for a while, get to know the right groups and members, and you'll have hit pay dirt before you know it. You never know when you'll need help with that new SCSI adaptor that Microsoft hasn't heard of yet, but the odds may be good the head of the engineering team for it may be active on the same groups you frequent.

> **NOTE:** Don't be surprised if your news server doesn't carry all of these groups. If it doesn't, talk to your site administrator or service provider about having them added.

- **comp.os.ms-windows.nt.admin.misc**—Windows NT system administration
- **comp.os.ms-windows.nt.admin.networking**—Windows NT networking administration
- **comp.os.ms-windows.nt.advocacy**—Windows NT advocacy
- **comp.os.ms-windows.nt.announce**—Windows NT announcements (moderated)
- **comp.os.ms-windows.nt.misc**—Windows NT miscellany (general discussion)
- **comp.os.ms-windows.nt.pre-release**—Windows NT prerelease (beta Windows NT versions)
- **comp.os.ms-windows.nt.setup**—Windows NT setup (configuring Windows NT systems)
- **comp.os.ms-windows.nt.setup.hardware**—Windows NT hardware setup
- **comp.os.ms-windows.nt.setup.misc**—Windows NT setup miscellany
- **comp.os.ms-windows.nt.software.backoffice**—Windows NT Back Office software
- **comp.os.ms-windows.nt.software.compatibility**—Windows NT software compatibility
- **comp.os.ms-windows.nt.software.services**—Windows NT services software

- **comp.os.ms-windows.programmer.nt.kernel-mode**—Windows NT driver development
- **comp.os.ms-windows.programmer.win32**—General Win32 development

Mailing Lists

One of the simplest methods for gathering information on the Internet involves your mastering technology no more involved than your Internet e-mail system. If you've never used a mailing list, don't be intimidated by the prospect or the process, as there's really nothing simpler. A mailing list is a simple automated service that forwards messages sent to it to everyone that *subscribes* (belongs) to the list. This basic form of group collaboration or conferencing has existed almost as long as e-mail and is one of the most useful services on the Internet when used in moderation. The software that runs the mailing list is usually referred to as the *mail reflector* due to the simple nature of its primary duties (if a message is received, forward it to all subscribers). The various programs used as reflectors have names such as *admin, majordomo, listproc, listserv,* and *SmartList,* but they all work in more or less the same manner.

To join a mailing list, you simply tell the list software that you wish to join by sending it a message to that effect. To do this, you need to know the mail address of the software and the correct command syntax for joining. For example, to join the WinNews mailing list

1. Address an Internet e-mail message to admin@winnews.microsoft.com (use the account you wish the mail to be received by—mail reflectors automatically use your address as the subscription address).
2. Leave the subject line of the message blank.
3. Leave the message body blank except for the line SUBSCRIBE WINNEWS.
4. Send the message.

Within several minutes, you'll probably receive a confirmation of your subscription, along with instructions on how to end it if you so wish (file those instructions carefully, or you may be willing to pay dearly for them later).

> **CAUTION:** One warning: approach mailing list use in moderation. Depending upon the list, it's not unusual to get several *dozen* messages per day from the list server. So try one list, see if you like it, then add another. Some mailing lists (such as WinNews) are really only for distribution, not contribution, so you'll only get one or two messages per month, but others will literally forward every character of any member's contributions straight to your mailbox. So be aware before you sign up, please.

Windows-Specific and Other Mailing Lists

In addition to WinNews (which is simply a PR tool for Microsoft, albeit a useful one), there are many other mailing lists that are useful to Windows professionals. The list of topics in Table E-2 contains the mail address for each list server and the subscription command you need to use to start your service.

Table E-1   NT-Related Internet Mailing Lists

List Topic	Server Address Command (body text)
WinNews	admin@winnews.microsoft.com SUBSCRIBE WINNEWS
Microsoft Windows NT	listserv@peach.ease.lsoft.com subscribe winnt-1
Windows for Workgroups	listserv@umdd.umd.edu subscribe wfw-1
Windows 95	listserv@peach.ease.lsoft.com subscribe win95-1
Remote Work	Majordomo@unify.com subscribe remote-work
TCP/IP for PCs	listserv@list.nih.gov subscribe pcip

Where to Find Other Lists

As you've already noted if you've spent more than a week on the Internet, things change. How do you keep up with new mailing lists? Simple! Subscribe to Lists about Lists! A subscription to New Lists (listserv@vm1.nodak.edu; subscribe new-list) will keep you up to snuff on emerging list-based conferences. To get a list of all known lists run by the listserv software, subscribe to **listserv@list-serv.net** using the command **lists global** as the sole body text.

You can also look for listserv information on other areas of the Internet. On the World Wide Web, try the following addresses:

- http://www.liszt.com
- http://scwww.ucs.indiana.edu/mlarchive
- http://www.nova.edu/Inter-Links/cgi-bin/news-list.pl
- http://www.NeoSoft.com:80/internet/paml/
- ftp://rtmf.mit.edu/pub/usenet-by-group/news.answers/mail/mailing-lists

Or try the following Usenet newsgroups:

- news.lists
- news.answers

FTP Sites

Why list lowly and old-fashioned FTP server sites in this age of the miraculous World Wide Web? FTP sites offer advantages not found on the Web. Depending upon your FTP client application, you should be able to take advantage of batch file transfers (Web browsers limit you to one file per session, or make you run multiple sessions). You can move whole directories in a single transaction using FTP, saving yourself valuable time. Also, some FTP servers are simply less busy than their accompanying Web sites, so you can get the files you need more quickly. That, and some of the best sites haven't "fancied themselves up" to a full Web server yet!

The main FTP site for official Windows NT information is ftp.microsoft.com, of course. Try these other sites as well:

- **The SIMTEL Archive** (oak.oakland.edu/SimTel/nt)
- **University of Texas at Austin** (ftp.cc.utexas.edu/microlib/nt/)

- **University of Cologne** (ftp.uni-koeln.de/pc/win32)
- **Finnish University and Research Network** a.k.a. **FUNET** (ftp://nic.funet.fi/pub/win-nt/)

Additional Reference Works (Hard Copy and CD-ROM)

Perhaps you're more traditional and simply need a good reference book on NT (for yourself, or to recommend to others). Maybe you need a hard-copy reference that's always on the shelf and that will still work even when your computer's down. In any case, there's a good variety of tools, both in conventional softcover and CD-ROM format, to meet your reference needs, from the most general to the extremely specific.

Windows NT Resource Kit

If you're an information systems professional, you probably can make no wiser investment than the Microsoft Windows NT Resource Kit. This series of boxed softcover technical manuals contains several thousand pages of text accompanied by many megabytes of additional documentation and software utilities on the CD-ROM include with the kit. The kit includes

- **Resource Guide** (a complete reference to productivity information for Windows NT)
- **Networking Guide** (information for installing, managing, and integrating Windows NT on all sizes of networks)
- **Messages** (an online Microsoft Access database of all system messages with a glossary of common terms and user responses)
- **Optimizing Windows NT** (basic performance management techniques for tuning system and network performance)
- **Resource Kit Utilities** (for performance monitoring and tuning)

The Resource Kit is available from local resellers or from 1-800-MSPRESS.

Microsoft Developer Network

The Microsoft Developer Network (MSDN) is an annual subscription program with quarterly updates that provides the latest documentation on technology and products from Microsoft. Even if you're not a software developer, if you need to keep absolutely current with the latest Microsoft offerings, this is the best way to do it at minimal cost.

MSDN comes in several different packages suited for your needs:

- **MSDN Library Subscription:** The Library CD gives you product documentation, technical articles, sample code, and the Microsoft Developer Knowledge Base every quarter, plus bimonthly issues of the Developer Network News, two free phone-support incidents, and a 20 percent discount on Microsoft Press books.

- **MSDN Professional Subscription:** It includes the Library Subscription benefits, plus quarterly updates of the Development Platform (software development kits, device driver kits, and Windows and Windows NT Workstations operating systems), plus special shipments of any new operating systems or other major development products that become available between normal subscription issues.

- **MSDN Enterprise Subscription:** It includes the Library Subscription benefits, plus the Development Platform and all of the other Professional Subscription benefits. In addition you will also the BackOffice Test Platform (updated quarterly), with the latest released versions of Microsoft BackOffice, plus special shipments of any new operating systems or other major development products that become available between normal subscription issues.

- **MSDN Library Single Edition:** This is just one release of the Library. If you aren't sure you need a full subscription, this is a good way to check out the MSDN services without a major investment.

For more information, visit the MSDN Web site at http://www.microsoft.com/msdn/ or call the Microsoft Developer Services Team at 1-800-426-9400, 6:30 A.M. to 5:30 P.M. Pacific time, Monday through Friday.

TechNet

Microsoft TechNet is another tool specifically for technical professionals that may prove useful to you regardless of your position or job title. If you're involved in using or recommending new technology, consider this tool carefully. If you evaluate and specify new products and solutions, if you actively administer databases or networks, or if your primary job is to support and train end users, then this is a "no-brainer." Microsoft TechNet will make your life simpler and your job easier. Microsoft TechNet consists of

- Two CD-ROMs every month (over 150,000 pages of current technical information, the latest drivers and patches, data on client/server and workgroup computing, systems platforms, database products, and Microsoft applications)
- The Microsoft Knowledge Base (the library of technical support information developed and used by Microsoft technical support)
- Microsoft Resource Kits (for Microsoft Windows 95, Microsoft Office for Windows 95, Microsoft FoxPro® for Windows, MS-DOS®, Microsoft LAN Manger, Microsoft Windows, Microsoft Windows for Workgroups, Microsoft Windows NT™, and Microsoft Word® for Windows)

For more information, visit the following Microsoft Web sites:

- http://www.microsoft.com/catalog/products /TechNet/default.htm
- http:// www.microsoft.com /technet/
- http:// www.microsoft.com /TechNet/bkoffice.htm

User Group Resources

The computer user group has been and remains a powerful force in the computing industry. Windows NT user groups are no different in this respect. In fact, due to the importance Microsoft places upon its NT product line and strategy, Windows NT users groups actually wield quite a bit of influence over the product and the support Microsoft gives it.

If you're new to NT computing and want to get a feel for the level of interest across the country, here are a few good places to start:

- **Advanced Systems Users Group**
  (http://www.cpcug.org/user/ckelly/new_asug.html)
- **Boston Computer Society Windows NT Users Group**
  (http://www.shore.net/~wihl/nentug.html)
- **Los Angeles Windows NT Users Group—LANTUG**
  (http://www.lantug.org/)
- **Orange County NT Users Group—OCNTUP**
  (http://www.ocntug.org/
- **Windows NT User Group of Indianapolis**
  (http://www.wintugi.org/)

As we can't possibly list all of the major NT user groups here, please don't be offended if yours isn't in this short list. This is intended to get the new NT user started toward making valuable contacts as needed. *Windows NT Magazine* has a pretty darned comprehensive list of Windows NT user groups on its Web site at http://www.winntmag.com/usergroupnt.html, so check it out to find other contacts in your area (or to see if your group is on the list!).

Vendor Information

It's a good idea to have a ready reference to identify sources for new hardware and software. There are many new reference options for this purpose, both online and on CD-ROM.

Computer Select

One outstanding resource for researching products and vendors is the Computer Select product published by Information Access Co. Computer Select gives immediate access to 150 Ziff-Davis periodicals, such as *PC Week, Computer Shopper, Windows Sources,* and *Computer Life.* This rich tool contains product specifications, reviews, technical tips, manufacturers' profiles, and industry news in six main sections:

- **Articles:** Computer Select provides full-text coverage of over 70 computer industry journals as well as abstracts of articles from over 40 additional publications. Each monthly edition covers the previous twelve months' coverage of hardware, software, electronics, engineering, communications, and technology applications.

- **Hardware Products:** Computer Select contains descriptions and specifications of over 28,000 hardware products, from mice to the latest supercomputers.

- **Software Products:** Information is available on 38,000 products, from games to the most vertical business software.

- **Company Profiles:** Detailed contact information is included on over 12,000 companies, including information on key personnel and primary financial information.

- **Glossary of Terms:** Definitions appear for more than 19,000 computer and communications terms and acronyms.

- **Online User Guide:** Instructions are available for using the Computer Select database, plus an appendix of masked words and special characters.

This is a serious tool for computer professionals. If you're in charge of any purchasing or other recommendation process involving computing equipment or software, this is a "must have" item for your information arsenal. Computer Select is available in single-user and network licenses. For more information, call Information Access Co. at 1-800-419-0313, extension 719.

Microsoft InfoSource

Microsoft also provides a tool for vendor and product research: The Microsoft InfoSource Directory. InfoSource is an electronic guide to hardware manufacturers, plus thousands of Microsoft compatible software, hardware, and integrated solutions products, as well as Microsoft Solution Providers. The directory contains information on more than 6,311 hardware, software, and Solution Provider companies and their 8,254 products and services.

The InfoSource directory on CD-ROM can be ordered by calling 1-800-426-9400.

Other Vendor Information

Ziff-Davis Publications provides a search engine on their ZDNet Web site at http://www.zdnet.com/locator/ plus an index of advertisers at http://www.zdnet.com/adverts/adindex.html. This is an excellent set of tools if you're on the Web.

Windows NT Magazine also keeps a list of major Windows NT vendors on its Web site at http://www.winntmag.com/vendors.html plus a search engine for specific product categories at http://www.winntmag.com/cgi-shl/dbml.exe?template=/info/populate.dbm.

Product Updates, Service Packs, and Device Drivers

You'll probably also find that you'll need to obtain the latest updates to your Windows NT Workstation and application software. Or you'll purchase a new peripheral that requires special drivers to work with NT.

The best sources for fulfilling these needs are the same ones we've covered earlier in this appendix. Microsoft and other vendors do an excellent job of providing announcements for new product updates via the commercial online information services such as CompuServe, as well as via the World Wide Web. Microsoft also uses the vast storage power of the CD-ROM to distribute these components in the MSDN and TechNet products described earlier as well. So use the tools and references we've given you above, and you'll be certain to find what you need or at least be able to contact those who know the status of the object of your desire.

APPENDIX F

GLOSSARY

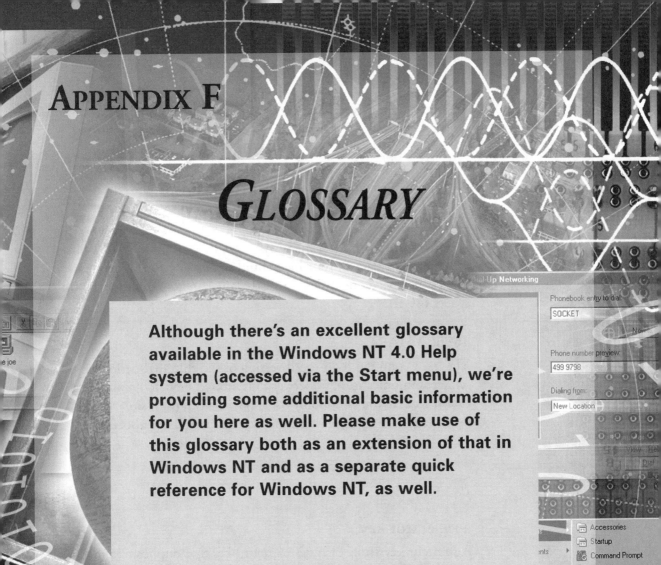

Although there's an excellent glossary available in the Windows NT 4.0 Help system (accessed via the Start menu), we're providing some additional basic information for you here as well. Please make use of this glossary both as an extension of that in Windows NT and as a separate quick reference for Windows NT, as well.

16-bit

Describes the method of accessing memory in two-byte steps. 16-bit CPUs can only process data two bytes (equaling 16 bits) at a time, which also presents an inherent memory address space limitation of 16MB for total system memory. Most Intel-based PC operating systems prior to Windows NT were 16-bit.

32-bit

Describes the method of memory access in Windows NT. 32-bit CPUs process data in four-byte chunks, allowing for higher processing speed and access to vastly larger memory address spaces (4GB).

16550A UART

The most common high-speed version of the chip that performs serial communications. Older versions limited modem communication speeds. If you commonly use modems at transmission speeds exceeding 9600 bps, you need this type of UART. See also *UART*.

A

accelerator key

A shortcut keystroke or series of keystrokes that duplicates a menu function. Using an accelerator key allows you to use the menu commands without taking your hands from the keyboard.

account

See *user account*.

account policy

Windows NT allows the administrator to create rules, or policies, that determine how passwords are used. The policy may apply to all user accounts of a domain or simply to an individual computer.

activate

To bring a program window to the front of the Windows NT Desktop by clicking on it or selecting it in any other manner (such as from the Taskbar). This makes it the active program in terms of keyboard and mouse interaction. See also *active window, focus.*

active window

The window or program in use, at the front of the Windows NT Desktop. The active window has the focus of the operating system for mouse and keyboard interaction. See also *focus, inactive window.*

address book

A database of people, phone numbers, and other contact information used by various Windows NT programs (such as Exchange and HyperTerminal).

administrative alert

Warns if problems occur in security and access areas, user sessions, server power loss, directory replication, or printing, resulting in alert messages being sent to a defined list of users or computers (usually administrators). See also *Alerter service.*

Alerter service

The program that sends messages to administrators or computers if alerts occur. See also *administrative alert.*

Alt + Tab

The keystroke used to switch between running applications. Pressing Alt+Tab simultaneously will display a small window in the center of your screen showing the icons of all open applications. The next application icon in sequence will be highlighted with a square, and its name will appear at the bottom of the window. Releasing Alt+Tab takes you to the currently highlighted application; holding Alt down while releasing and then depressing the Tab key cycles you through the next application, then the next, in carousel fashion. Experienced users prefer this method to using the mouse and the Taskbar as they don't have to take their hands from the keyboard.

anonymous FTP

A generic guest account authentication that most FTP servers use to allow transfer of files without prior user account creation or management. The typical arrangement allows the user to log on to the server with the user name *anonymous* and use their e-mail address as the password (note that it's not *truly* anonymous).

Archie

A program that allows you to search for files on an FTP server.

archive

On an FTP site, a collection of files. Also used to refer to a backup tape or other backup media file sets.

archive bit

Part of the file structure that allows backup programs to determine if a file has changed since the last backup. When a backup occurs, the archive bit is cleared by the backup program; when the file is changed after backup, the operating system sets the bit to indicate that the file has changed. You can manually set a file's archive bit using the ATTRIB command from the command line console or by using the Properties settings for that file from the Explorer or Desktop.

ASCII (American Standard Code for Information Interchange)

The ASCII acronym is the term used to describe a particular character set standard for computing purposes. ASCII data is limited to alphanumeric, punctuation, and transmission control characters. Any ASCII character can be represented using only seven bits of data (each character has a specific numeric value described by a seven-bit number); hence the character set is limited to 128 characters. Originally devised for electro-mechanical teletype equipment, ASCII has been extended in the computing environment with various proprietary character sets that contain graphics and other special-purpose characters, such as the IBM ANSI Graphics character set common on most Intel PCs. Some older computing and network systems will support only seven-bit ASCII data. See also *binary file, UUencode, UUdecode.*

ASCII file

See *ASCII, text file.*

associate

To tell Windows what application to use when opening, printing, or otherwise manipulating a data file. Windows can store information about filename extensions (.DOC, .TXT, and so on) and use the appropriate application to open files using those application associations automatically. However, Windows can store only one association per file type; therefore the last application to register itself with Windows as the associated application for that file type will be the one used. To create or alter the association for a particular type of file, use the View ➤ Options ➤ File Types property sheet from any Explorer window. See also *Explorer, property sheet, registry.*

AT command set

A standard set of commands for configuring and operating Hayes-compatible modems. Not all modems support the AT command set equally. See also *modem, Unimodem.*

attribute

Literally, a property or characteristic. See also *file attribute, property, property sheet.*

Audit policy

A set of configurations that determines the type of security events logged for a domain or for an individual computer and tells NT what to do if the log becomes full.

auditing

Keeping track of user activities by recording events in a security log, or evaluating that security log. You can audit both workstation or server events under Windows NT.

authentication

Checking user logon information. When a user logs on to an account on a Windows NT machine, that machine makes sure the user actually has rights to use the machine. The same holds true when a user logs onto a workgroup domain; in that case any servers present will also perform a check on the user's rights, as will individual machines in the domain as they are accessed. See also *server, trust relationship.*

B

background tasking

Inactive windows may continue to operate in a multitasking operating system such as Windows NT, even though they are hidden by active or foreground windows and tasks. Relative prioritization of background tasks is controlled via the System icon (Tasking button) in the Control Panel. See also *active window, focus, multitasking.*

backup

A set of duplicate files kept as a safety measure against main file failure.

backup domain controller

In a Windows NT Server domain, the server that keeps a copy of all domain policy and security databases, replicated from another machine called the *primary domain controller.* The backup domain controller can also step in to provide authentication services if the primary machine fails or is offline for other reasons. See also *primary domain controller.*

bandwidth

The most data that can be sent at one time over a communications link or network connection.

batch program

A text file using a .BAT or .CMD extension containing Windows NT commands, interpreted and processed sequentially when the file is executed. Batch programs are most commonly used to automate repetitive tasks that are not easily accomplished using the NT graphical interface (for example, copying sets of files ending with different extensions from several internal hard drives to a common archive directory).

binary file

Nontext data, containing eight-bit nonprintable characters. Examples are executable programs, sound files, and graphic files. See also *ASCII, text file.*

binary file transfer protocol

See *file transfer.*

BIOS (basic input/output system)

The firmware (program residing on a chip) on your system motherboard that handles the initial startup of your system and manages communications within the system bus and among system peripherals at the hardware level.

bit

The most basic unit in digital computing; represented by a one or zero. There are eight bits to a byte. See also *16-bit, 32-bit.*

bitmap

A generic term referring to a wide variety of graphics image file types. Also refers to the computer terminal screen in a GUI environment. In a bitmap image, every part of the image matrix is represented by a number, pixel by pixel, to make up the entire field that we see rendered as a graphic. Since the image is a pixel-defined matrix, you must edit individual pixels or groups of pixels to edit the image (parts of the image are not independent objects and cannot be resized or edited separately, unlike scaleable or vector graphics). See also *.GIF, GUI, .JPG, pixel.*

bookmark

A reference point in a document. Commonly used to refer to a shortcut version of the URL format used on the World Wide Web. See also *browser, URL, World Wide Web.*

boot loader

When Windows NT boots, it searches for certain information to tell it how the machine should be configured for startup, such as the location of the startup files for the operating system and what display settings to use. Windows NT will automatically display a menu of any available predefined boot options for a brief period before automatically starting the operating system. You can set the default boot loader settings and time-out values in the Operating System section of the System icon in the Control Panel.

boot partition

The volume that holds the Windows NT operating system. The volume must use the NTFS, FAT, or HPFS file system. A boot partition may be the same as the system partition, but it is not required to be. See also *system partition.*

bps (bits per second)

A basic unit of transmission speed for communications, most commonly applied to asynchronous serial communications using modems. Kbps (kilobits per second) or Mbps (megabits per second) are also commonly used when describing high-speed communications.

branch

A directory and any subdirectories in a file system structure.

browse

To randomly review directories, files, user accounts, groups, domains, computers, or any other type of information, regardless of presentation method. Usually refers to graphical presentations of data. See also *browser.*

browser

A term used generically to refer to HTML viewers for the World Wide Web (such as Netscape Navigator and Microsoft Internet Explorer), but can refer to other information-viewing programs as well. See also *HTML, Internet Explorer, World Wide Web.*

buffer

A place to hold data for temporary use. Contents of buffers are usually lost when a computer application is closed or the computer is reset or shut down. See also *cache.*

built-in groups

Certain default user groups come preconfigured. These groups are given common rights and abilities needed by most users. Assigning a user to a built-in group (such as Administrator) automatically gives them the same rights as all other members of that group. See also *group, User Manager, User Manager for Domains.*

byte

An eight-bit data storage unit. Each character of data takes a byte to store (ASCII text data only requires seven bits, but the eighth bit of each ASCII character is stored as 0 for full compatibility with modern computing systems that work in eight bits or multiples of eight bits). See also *16-bit, 32-bit, ASCII.*

Bulletin Board System (BBS)

An electronic host system usually accessed via terminal emulation over a modem or other connection. Most BBSs are character-based hosts, but some newer BBSs support graphical environments as well. BBSs offer a variety of resources: files, shareware or freeware programs, discussion conferences, news, and mail services. Most BBSs are run on PCs or other microcomputers, with one or more phone lines. Some commercial online systems such as CompuServe, America Online, and others are simply much larger examples of this communications host format. See also *terminal emulation.*

C

cache

An area set aside to store something. See also *buffer, cache RAM*.

cache RAM

Fast RAM used to hold CPU instructions for reuse. The CPU will look first in the fast cache RAM for repetitive instructions before attempting to access slower main dynamic RAM. Cache RAM can dramatically increase the apparent speed of a CPU. See also *CPU, RAM*.

CD-ROM (compact disc read-only memory)

The data version of the popular Compact Disc format. One CD-ROM can hold over 600MB of data.

character-based

Using only ASCII characters or other character sets, not bitmapped graphics, to compose a user interface. MS-DOS is a character-based environment; Windows NT is a graphical environment. See also *ASCII, bitmap, GUI*.

check box

A small box that appears in a dialog box representing an option that you can turn on or off individually by selecting the box; when the selection is active, the box is checked. See also *radio button*.

choose

You must select an item before acting upon it in a graphical computing environment. You will usually have several methods to choose an item (be it using the mouse or keyboard accelerator keys) whether it's from a program menu or a set of icons on the Desktop. See also *click*.

click

Pressing and releasing the left mouse button. In Windows, a single click is generally used to select an icon or list box item, and two clicks are used to activate it (or select the current default action if in a dialog box). Exceptions include the window controls at the top right of program windows and some dialog boxes, which activate with single clicks. Right mouse usage is reserved for special context-sensitive menus and actions and is usually specifically described (if you are instructed to click on something, use the left or "normal" mouse button unless the right mouse button is specified).

client

A computer that uses network resources made available by other computers called servers. See also *server.*

client application

A program that requires a server to operate or provide critical resources. In OLE, the program that use an object provided by another (server) application. See also *object linking and embedding, server.*

client/server

Any computing system in which centralized systems provide data and processing services for use by client applications or workstations. Also referred to as distributed processing.

Clipboard

A system used to move data from one application to another, using a simple "cut-and-paste" metaphor. Most Windows applications support the Clipboard and the same set of Clipboard commands via the Edit menu. Clipboard contents are stored only until the next edit and are lost when the computer is reset or restarted. See also *ClipBook.*

ClipBook

Just as the Clipboard allows you to share data between applications, ClipBook lets you save that data between sessions, even across a network. Each individual computer may have a ClipBook, and ClipBooks may be stored on network servers as well. See also *Clipboard, ClipBook page, ClipBook service.*

ClipBook page

A discrete piece of data permanently stored in a ClipBook. ClipBook pages can be copied using the Clipboard, and they can be shared across the network. See also *Clipboard, ClipBook, ClipBook service.*

ClipBook service

Windows NT must run this service to allow the ClipBook Viewer application to share ClipBooks. See also *Clipboard, ClipBook, ClipBook page.*

Close button

The little button at the top right of a Windows 95 or Windows NT 4.0 application with the X in it. When you click on it, it closes the window and shuts down the application.

cluster

A unit of storage space on a drive medium (literally a group or *cluster* of drive sectors). Any file, regardless of size, takes up at least one cluster (for example, if a drive is formatted with 8K clusters, a 1K file will take up the same drive space as any other file less than 8K). Since the number of clusters per drive is mostly determined by the operating system and the cluster quantity options in its drive formatting utility (not the drive size), larger drives will have relatively larger clusters. To avoid wasting space on large drives due to this unfortunate side effect of the file system, it's best to divide large media into several partitions and logical drives, which will result in smaller individual cluster sizes and a relative savings in drive space.

codec

Rough contraction of *compression-decompression.* A technique or driver for rapidly compressing and decompressing large media files, such as video data. MPEG, Indeo, Cinepak, and QuickTime are all examples of codecs. Codecs can reside in software or hardware (as firmware).

collapse folders

In a directory tree display, to hide unwanted levels of directory information by using the program menu or tree control interface. In Windows NT Explorer, the directory tree control uses small plus and minus symbols to expand and collapse the display. See *Explorer.*

COM

The common name for the asynchronous serial ports on the IBM PC and clones, also known simply as serial ports. Usually used with modems. COM ports are both physical and logical entities; for example, it's very possible to have two COM2 ports on a machine if it's been incorrectly configured, since most physical COM ports can be configured to be any logical port number. See also *modem, serial.*

command line

The line in a character-based terminal interface where instructions are given to the operating system. MS-DOS is one example of a command-line environment. UNIX shell accounts used to access the Internet are another. See also *Command Prompt.*

Command Prompt

Generically, the characters used in a command line environment to denote the command line. Specific to Windows NT, the MS-DOS character-based command line interface environment most often used for the MS-DOS command line emulation for backward compatibility with legacy MS-DOS applications, and to provide command-line capabilities for the Windows NT operating system as well. See also *MS-DOS application.*

compress

To make a file smaller through encoding redundant or recurring information within the file (commonly described as "taking the air out of the loaf of bread"). See also *compressed drive.*

compressed drive

A drive formatted using a compression program that effectively automatically compresses and decompresses all data stored on that drive. Windows NT 4.0 supports the popular DriveSpace disk compression utility.

Computer Browser service

This service provides a list of computers on the network to Windows NT and applications. The Select Computer and Select Domain dialog boxes use this information whenever asked to provide computer or domain names. See also *domain*.

computer name

Every machine in a Windows NT domain must have a totally unique name of up to 15 characters. See also *domain*.

configuration registry

Windows NT stores all configuration settings in a database that allows multiple configurations, remote administration, and other functional benefits. This database can be viewed or edited manually with the RegEdit utility (don't journey there unless you know have experience with registry structure and issues).

connected user

Any user connected to a machine across a network.

connection

Generically, a communications session. In Windows NT HyperTerminal, the configuration file that saves all the information needed to establish a session. See *HyperTerminal*.

Control menu

The menu in the upper left of a program window used to control the program window, accessed via the Control Menu icon. You can Restore, Move, Size, Minimize, Maximize, and Close the current program.

Control Menu icon

The Control menu for a window is accessed via the Control Menu icon, which is usually a smaller version of the icon for that program.

Control Panel

A program folder accessed via the Windows NT Start menu, Settings, Control Panel item. Control Panel contains a variety of different icons each containing configuration items for specific Windows NT functions and services, such as network, display, keyboard, and other settings.

controller

See *domain controller*.

CPU (central processing unit)

The main processor that performs all major system calculations, runs the operating system, and controls communications with peripheral devices.

Ctrl + Alt + Del

This is the classic keystroke used to restart an Intel PC. Under Windows NT, this keystroke is used to begin the logon sequence at boot time, or to access the Windows NT Security dialog box at any time during a session (from which you have many options, including orderly shutdown of NT). Is this a rare glimpse of the Microsoft developers' sense of humor in that they used the "three-fingered salute" to remind users of the stability and security of NT compared to other versions of Windows? See also *Windows NT Security dialog box*.

cursor

The blinking area used to indicate your position of activity or selection in an application or other area of the system interface (such as a dialog box). Depending upon the application and other configuration options, the cursor may appear as an I-bar, a vertical line, or a rectangular dotted "lasso" or marquee. In some applications such as word processors, the cursor will be split, with a vertical blinking line showing the current logical location within the document and a second I-bar that tracks with it until the user moves the mouse to select a new location or indicate a new text selection (when the user clicks on the new location or selection, both cursor parts will rejoin and track until the user intervenes again). In Window NT Explorer and other multipaned applications, the cursor will also change to indicate that the underlying interface element may be moved or resized by clicking and dragging it to the desired Desktop location.

D

DDE

See *dynamic data exchange*.

default button

The button in a dialog with a dark border, which is activated when the (Enter) key is pressed.

default printer

The printer you use most often. You select the default printer by using the Printers icon in the Control Panel, selecting a printer icon in the Printers window, and selecting File ➤ Set as Default.

default profile

See *system default profile, user default profile*.

dependent service

Some services need another service before they can perform their tasks. For example, the Alerter service uses the Messenger service to function.

Desktop

The uppermost level of the Windows NT 4.0 and Windows 95 user interface. Icons, folders, and the Taskbar are common elements of the Desktop.

destination directory

The "target" directory or folder where you copy or move files or directories.

destination document

In Object Linking and Embedding (OLE), the document into which an object is placed. See also *object, object linking and embedding.*

device contention

Peripheral devices (modems, printers, etc.) can be used by only one application at a time, but Windows NT can manage the access from multiple applications to a single device through a variety of techniques, such as print queuing or modem pooling. See also *interrupt request line, queue, TAPI.*

device driver

Specific peripheral devices may require special programs to allow Windows NT to communicate with that device. A device driver is usually installed at the same time the hardware is installed and configured. Windows NT comes with many device drivers for popular peripherals, but a manufacturer may provide alternative or updated drivers as well.

dialup

A type of communications connection established using a modem and POTS (Plain Old Telephone Service) to connect to another computer, network, or the Internet.

dimmed

Unavailable interface controls (buttons, check boxes, etc.) or menu commands are displayed in a tone different from the main one used for active menu or control items, to indicate they are not active.

directory

A structure for organizing a file system (also known as a *folder*). A directory can contain files as well as other directories or folders (called subdirectories). See also *directory tree, folder, root directory.*

directory replication

Windows NT can automate the copying of sets of master directories from server to server, or from server to workstation(s). This eliminates many maintenance issues, since you need only manage a master set of your data. See also *Directory Replicator service.*

Directory Replicator service

A Windows NT program that automates duplication of data between systems. See also *directory replication, service.*

directory tree

Disk directories may be displayed in a variety of ways; the tree method is a branching structure view that displays at minimum two levels of the structure simultaneously. Windows NT Explorer uses a collapsible tree-control display by default. See also *Explorer.*

directory window

The default view in Windows NT Explorer displays the contents of a disk using both a directory tree (left pane) and the contents of the current directory (right pane). See also *Explorer.*

disabled user account

The Windows NT User Manager allows the administrator to manipulate user rights and restore them to enabled status at any time. See also *user account, User Manager.*

disk configuration information

Information included in the Windows NT Registry regarding your drive media (volume sets, drive letters, etc.).

disk duplexing

Windows NT allows you to keep an mirror image of your complete drive on a disk on a completely separate controller.

disk mirroring

Windows NT allows you to maintain a fully redundant copy of one or more partitions on another disk.

disk striping

Windows NT allows managing disk space for maximum utilization by creating disk volumes from free areas on separate drives to create one logically contiguous space, from across 2 to 32 disks.

domain

In Windows NT networks, a uniquely named set of computers sharing a common domain database and security policy. In TCP/IP networks, a set of logical addresses for routing network data to and from a number of host systems. See also *host, subdomain, workgroup*.

domain controller

In a Windows NT Server domain, the server that authenticates logons. The same machine may also maintain the security policy and the master database for a domain. See also *server*.

domain database

See *SAM database*.

domain name

The name used to describe a workgroup on a network. See also *workgroup*.

Domain Name Server (DNS)

A computer that translates TCP/IP network or Internet host computer names (such as fred.garvin.com) to numeric IP addresses (such as 128.127.126.125). The DNS saves you from remembering lots of really boring numbers.

domain synchronization

See *synchronize*.

dot address

See *host address*.

double-click

To click a mouse button twice while on the same object. Used to activate a selection. See also *click.*

download

To move information from a remote system to your own. If you imagine the remote computer as upstairs from yours, it makes sense. See also *file transfer, upload.*

downloaded fonts

Fonts sent to a printer and stored in printer memory until used (or the printer is reset). See also *printer fonts.*

drive icon

An icon in an Explorer window or other menu representing a disk drive.

DriveSpace

A drive compression program included with MS-DOS 6.*x*, Windows 3.*x*, Windows 95, and Windows NT 4.0.

drop-down list

See *list box.*

dual boot

The means by which an operating system can be configured to query the user at system startup to choose an alternative operating system. Although technically the term applies only to a two-operating-system option, it is generally used to apply to multiple-OS boot managers as well. See also *boot loader.*

dynamic data exchange

A method by which two or more applications can exchange data while running, without storing it in an intermediate file or other structure.

E

e-mail

Also known as *electronic mail.* Most commonly used to refer to Internet mail systems using SMTP and POP3 protocols for transmission and delivery of text messages via the Internet. Also applies generically to proprietary mail systems such as Microsoft Mail. See also *Exchange, mail gateway, POP3, SMTP.*

ellipsis (. . .)

The three dots or periods following a menu item indicate a continuance of the menu interface (usually leading to another dialog box or other windowed interface level). The ellipsis is also used on buttons.

embedded object

Data created or manipulated in another application but presented in the current one. For example, a spreadsheet embedded in a word processing document. See also *object, object linking and embedding.*

encapsulated PostScript (EPS) file

A vector-based image file format that will scale in resolution to match your printer's best capabilities.

enhanced meta file (EMF)

The file type produced in the process of changing standard application printer output to the format most closely matching the internal command set of the printer in use (for example, for HP printers, PCL or Page Control Language).

environment variable

A text string (a drive, path, or filename, for example) used by Windows NT to denote a configuration item that will be used dynamically by the operating system and applications. The system path for program execution is the most common example. You may adjust environment variables in the System icon in the Control Panel or from the Windows NT command prompt. See also *path.*

escape code

A text string header used to tell a device to process the data that follows in a certain manner. Escape codes are not intended for display but to instruct the output device regarding the manner of display to use for the data that follows. Terminal emulators, printers, and HTML viewers all use variations of this technology to achieve various effects and results. In terminal emulation, escape codes are used to indicate display and other attributes of the specific session data (for example, bold versus normal text fields). Printer drivers use escape codes to tell the printer hardware which typeface, font size, and attributes to use for text. HTML viewers (Web browsers) use HTML tags (another type of escape code) to indicate how page elements are to be rendered in the finished Web document. See also *device driver, HTML, terminal emulation.*

EtherNet

The prevalent LAN (Local Area Network) hardware standard. See also *LAN.*

event

Any significant occurrence in the system or in an application that requires users to be notified, or an entry to be added to a log.

Event Log service

Records events in the system, security, and application logs.

Exchange

The Microsoft messaging platform for Windows 95 and Windows NT. Exchange Server (a part of the Windows NT BackOffice product line) provides Microsoft Mail compatibility and other database services. Exchange Client offers Microsoft Mail, Internet SMTP mail, CompuServe mail, Microsoft Fax, and other services, and it can be extended with other messaging transports as desired.

Exit

The action taken to begin an orderly shutdown when you are finished with an application, or Windows itself. Choosing Exit from a program or Windows menu will automatically save and close all files and save all pertinent system data before shutting down the application or system (some applications may query you before saving files). Always choose Exit as opposed to simply turning off system power (which will result in data loss). Most applications will also support the ⓐ +$ keystroke for orderly shutdown.

expire

What a password does when it gets too old. Windows NT will then ask you to replace it with a new fresh one.

Explorer

The Windows NT 4.0 program for viewing and managing files. Explorer replaces File Manager.

export path

In directory replication, a path from which subdirectories, and the files in those subdirectories, are automatically exported from an export server. See also *directory replication.*

export server

In directory replication, a server from which a master set of directories is exported to specified servers or workstations (called import computers) in the same or other domains. See also *directory replication.*

extended memory

Memory above the first megabyte of RAM on an Intel PC.

extended partition

Any free space left on a drive after the primary partition is defined may be defined as an extended partition. Additional logical drives may be defined within an extended partition. See also *partition, logical drive.*

extension

See *filename extension.*

external command

A command that is not resident in the operating system kernel but is loaded from disk when used. For example, from the Windows NT Command Prompt, the CD command will execute without additional programs being run, but the XCOPY command requires the file XCOPY.EXE to execute.

F

family set

Tapes forming backup sets.

file allocation table (FAT)

The file allocation table system is the primary method used by MS-DOS to store information about the directory and file structure for MS-DOS media. Windows NT is backwardly compatible with the FAT system. See also *file system, HPFS, NTFS*.

file

Data stored in a defined storage media structure in a computing system. There are many varieties of file types, from simple ASCII text (which can be created from the Command Prompt) to complex binary file types created by applications. See also *ASCII, binary file, file attribute, filename, file system*.

file attribute

A bit setting that indicates the status of the file (such as archive, read-only, hidden, or operating system).

filename

The name used by the file system to identify discrete data files stored on a disk. In MS-DOS systems, a filename consists of two elements: an eight-character name followed by a three-character filename extension (separated by a dot or period). This convention is called the 8.3 filename format, the first part of which is the file name proper (most filenames are not required to have extensions, but it is a fairly useful convention). Windows 95 and Windows NT 4.0 support LFN (Long File Names), which allow up to 256 characters in the complete filename. See also *filename extension*.

filename extension

The period and three characters at the end of a filename. By combining the name and extension components of the MS-DOS FAT 8.3 file system with wildcard character support, you can perform fairly elegant operations upon large numbers of files using simple Windows NT commands. Filename extensions are also used by Windows NT to automate certain application operations. See also *associate, batch program*.

file system

The structure used to name, store, and organize files.

file transfer

Moving a file from one system to another. To perform a file transfer, you must first connect to the other system and then issue instructions regarding the file and how you wish it to be transferred. Depending upon what type of connection you establish and what communications software you are using, this will be accomplished using either a network protocol or a binary file transfer protocol, either of which will ensure against errors in transmission. In a local network environment, most systems are constantly connected, and a file transfer from one machine to another will be performed very much like moving or copying a file from one drive to another on the local machine. In a terminal emulation session, after connection it's likely that there will be a menu on the host system that will provide guidance in performing the transfer, using a binary transfer protocol specifically designed for serial communications (such as XMODEM, YMODEM, or ZMODEM). On the Internet, most file transfers are as simple as clicking on the URL for the file in a Web browser and telling the browser where to store it. See also *FTP, protocol, terminal emulation, URL, XMODEM, YMODEM, ZMODEM*.

firewall

A device placed on a network that lets local traffic out but keeps unwanted outside traffic from getting in. LANs usually employ a firewall when connected to the Internet. See also *Internet, LAN, TCP/IP.*

focus

The program window that is active, or at the front of the Desktop, is said to have the system focus. This is the active window for purposes of keyboard and mouse interaction. See also *activate, active window.*

folder

The name for the icon representing a file directory, or the window displaying the contents of the directory (such as files, programs, and other folders). See *directory.*

folder window

In Explorer, the window that displays the contents of a file folder. See also *directory, Explorer, folder.*

font

In Windows terminology, a type style (such as Times Roman or Courier) and all its variant point sizes and style attributes (bold, italic, etc.). In typography, a specific point size and specific style attribute (bold, italic, etc.) of a particular typeface. See also *monospaced font, proportional font.*

font set

A collection of point sizes and styles for one typeface (such as Times Roman or Courier) for use with a particular display and printer. Windows NT comes with several font sets to allow for different user options in display resolution and relative type size.

free space

The unused portion of a hard disk. Unused space must be partitioned, assigned a logical drive name, and then formatted with a file system before it can be used by an operating system.

FTP (File Transfer Protocol)

A TCP/IP communications protocol designed to allow simple transfer of files between systems. See also *anonymous FTP, file transfer protocol, TCP/IP.*

full name

A user's name, usually in the format last name, first name, and middle initial. The full name is needed by User Manager to define a user account. See also *user account.*

G

gateway

A device that translates transport protocols between two different networks (for example, between IPX/SPX and TCP/IP networks).

.GIF (Graphics Interchange Format)

A popular compressed graphic file format (pronounced "jiff"). CompuServe introduced this format, which offers excellent image quality but is limited to a 256-color image palette. See also *.JPG, palette.*

gigabit

Literally one billion bits; usually used to refer to very high network transmission speeds, as in "gigabits per second."

gigabyte

A unit of storage roughly equal to one billion bytes (some manufacturers calculate a gigabyte as 1000 megabytes, others, as 1024 megabytes).

global account

A normal user account in a user's home domain. If your network has multiple domains, allow users access to other domains via creation of domain trust relationships (this avoids the maintenance of multiple global accounts per user). See also *local account, trust relationship.*

global group

A group that can be used in its own domain, servers and workstations of the domain, and trusting domains; it can be granted rights and permissions and can become a member of local groups but can contain only user accounts from its own domain. This allows the administrator to create groups of users from inside the domain, available for use both in the domain and out of the domain (so that other administrators in other groups can control rights for large numbers of users quickly and easily). Global groups must be created on Windows NT Server, but users can be granted memberships, rights, and permissions at Windows NT Workstations that are members of the global group. See also *group, local group.*

group

In User Manager, an account that is a set of member accounts. Groups are simply a quick way to control sets of capabilities of large groups of user accounts simultaneously. Windows NT Workstation groups are administered with User Manager. Windows NT Server groups are managed with User Manager for Domains. See also *built-in groups, global group, local group, user account, User Manager.*

group memberships

A user account may belong to several groups with different rights and permissions. Windows NT determines these rights and permissions based upon memberships the user account is granted. See also *group.*

group name

A unique name for local or global groups in a Windows NT network. See also *global group, local group.*

GUI (graphical user interface)

A computer interface using symbols, icons, and other visual metaphors, plus pointing devices, in addition to characters. The GUI is based upon the loose premise that it is easier to recognize something and act upon it than to remember something and tell the computer to do it. Each interface has its strengths and weaknesses. GUI interfaces are often promoted as being more "user-friendly" but carry considerable computing overhead in terms of the resources needed to generate and maintain a complex bitmapped graphical environment, with the commensurate loss of performance as compared to the straight character mode interface of the lean, mean command line. Windows NT is primarily a GUI interface, but it contains a command-line interface as well. See also *Command Prompt.*

H

handshake

The part of a protocol negotiation or communications session where two devices or logical entities identify each other and their respective capabilities. The most common example is the squeal of two modems establishing a session link.

HPFS

A file system used with the OS/2 operating system (version 1.2 or later). HPFS offers performance benefits over the FAT system but doesn't offer the security available in NTFS.

HTML (Hypertext Markup Language)

A subset of SGML (Standard General Markup Language) used predominately to format hypertext and hypermedia documents for the World Wide Web or similar intranets. Originally designed for pure hypertext delivery, HTML has been extended several times to include support for other data types such as graphics, sound, and animation. See also *HTTP, hypermedia, intranet, SGML, World Wide Web.*

HTTP (Hypertext Transport Protocol)

The protocol used to deliver HTML documents over the World Wide Web or over similar entities found on intranets. The HTTP protocol also acts as an "umbrella" protocol in terms of supporting addresses for other connection protocols such as telnet, FTP, and Gopher. See also *FTP, Gopher, HTML, intranet, Telnet, URL, World Wide Web.*

header

Information sent to a printer to prepare it for the print job that follows.

heap

The area of Windows memory where dynamic information is stored regarding running applications, their menus, and other system resources in use at the time.

Help file

A document that provides additional information. Specifically refers to Windows Help hypertext files, usually available for each application via the Help menu entry. See also *Help menu, hypertext*.

Help menu

The menu in a Windows application, usually located at the right of the main program menu, that leads to additional information regarding the application.

hexadecimal

Of values using the base-16 numbering system. Most memory address values are stated in hexadecimal, which is convenient in the sense that it beats reading binary values.

hidden file

A file not normally visible from the Command Prompt or Explorer.

high-performance file system

See *HPFS*.

home directory

A directory assigned and accessible to an individual user or group of users. A home directory may be assigned automatically at system logon.

host

An individual computer connected to a TCP/IP network (such as the Internet). Also used to refer to a computer that provides connectivity for terminal or terminal emulation sessions (i.e., a mainframe or minicomputer is host to the terminal or microcomputer terminal emulation). See also *domain, host address, mainframe, microcomputer, minicomputer, subdomain, TCP/IP, terminal, terminal emulation.*

host address

A unique numeric identification for a computer system on a TCP/IP network such as the Internet. The address is usually in the format of four numbers (between 1 and 254) separated by periods or dots (hence the slang term "dotted quad"). Each machine on the TCP/IP network must have its own address (such as 128.127.126.125), but a machine may also have a verbose alias (such as fred.garvinsoft.com). See also *domain, Domain Name Server, host name, subdomain, TCP/IP.*

host name

A unique name for a host computer, which is actually an alias for the numeric host address for that computer. Host names are usually symbolic for easy memorization and arranged hierarchically. For example, the machine fred.garvinsoft.com probably belongs to a guy named Fred on a TCP/IP network at a commercial entity named GarvinSoft. See also *host address, domain, Domain Name Server, subdomain, TCP/IP.*

hypermedia

Documents (usually hypertext) that contain multiple data types, such as text, graphics, sound, video, or animation. See also *HTML, hypertext, multimedia, World Wide Web.*

HyperTerminal

A simple terminal emulation program that comes with Windows NT 4.0.

hypertext

A document or set of documents designed for nonlinear review ("browsing"). Hypertext documents contain links to other documents or resources, allowing the viewer to move from the main topic to related information with great ease (well-designed hypertext allows the viewer to return to the context of the original document easily as well). The hypertext concept dates back to the early work of Ted Nelson and others but has most recently become popularized through the broad acceptance of Windows Help files and of the World Wide Web. See also *HTML, hypermedia, World Wide Web*.

I

I-beam

The shape of the Windows mouse cursor when over an area used for text entry.

import computers

The servers or workstations that replicate directories from an export server. See also *directory replication*.

import path

Where replicated data is stored on an import computer. See also *directory replication, import computers*.

inactive window

Any window or program not at the front or focus of the Desktop. An inactive window may still perform tasks but does not have the focus of the system in terms of keyboard or mouse interaction. See also *active window, background tasking, focus*.

Inbox

The Desktop icon that represents the Exchange messaging client. Also the folder in Microsoft Exchange for incoming messages.

in-place editing

OLE 2.0 allows embedded objects to be edited in the container document, instead of requiring that the linked object's server application be launched. The server application tool menu will appear in the container document's application menu when the linked object is actively edited. See also *object linking and embedding*.

insertion point

The flashing vertical line showing where the cursor is active in the current document. See also *cursor*.

internal command

A command included in the operating system kernel CMD.EXE and thus available from the Command Prompt without loading another file or executable. See also *external command*.

internet

Any network of two or more interconnected TCP/IP networks. See also *Internet, TCP/IP*.

Internet

The worldwide network of TCP/IP internets. Most users are first introduced to the Internet via the World Wide Web, which is actually a subset of the Internet's resources. See also *host, internet, FTP, Gopher, TCP/IP, telnet, World Wide Web*.

Internet Explorer

The Microsoft Web browser included with Windows 95 and Windows NT 4.0. Versions are also available for the Macintosh and Windows 3.x. See also *World Wide Web*.

Internet Assistant

The Microsoft add-in application for Microsoft Word that allows you to author HTML documents in Word. See also *World Wide Web*.

interrupt request line (IRQ)

On the PC, peripheral devices must use an IRQ to notify the CPU when they require service for a particular task (usually sending or receiving information). No two devices may use an IRQ simultaneously, but some can cooperatively share IRQs in a multitasking environment such as Windows NT.

intranet

A TCP/IP network not connected to the global Internet, or the portion of an internal TCP/IP network connected to the global Internet but reserved for internal corporate use and not available to the global Internet. For example, many corporations are implementing Web servers to distribute information internally but don't intend for these resources to be available to general Internet traffic.

IP address

See *host address.*

IP protocol

See *TCP/IP.* See also *protocol.*

IPX/SPX

A set of network protocols developed by Novell for use with Netware.

ISDN (Integrated Services Digital Network)

A type of digital phone connection that allows high-speed remote network and Internet communications. ISDN is common in Europe and most major metropolitan areas of the U.S. east and west coasts but can be difficult to obtain from some regional phone systems (please consult your phone company for details before purchasing any equipment). ISDN service requires special phone lines, modems, or interface cards.

ISP (Internet Service Provider)

A company or entity that delivers Internet connections.

J

.JPG (jay-peg)

A popular compressed graphics file format developed by the Joint Photographic Experts Group. The .JPG file format is very popular on the Internet and on other online communities as it offers excellent compression and full 24-bit color with fairly minimal loss of image quality. Most Web browsers offer support for .JPG files. See also *24-bit, .GIF.*

K

kernel

The part of the operating system responsible for interaction with the hardware and management of processes.

kernel driver

A program (either part of the operating system or used by the operating system) that talks directly to hardware. Windows NT security dictates that no program may access the hardware directly without permission from the operating system. See also *device driver.*

keyboard buffer

An area of memory set aside to allow keystrokes to be stored until the CPU can process them.

keyboard shortcut

See *accelerator key.*

L

LAN (local area network)

A computer network linking systems in a discrete area, such as a building, a set of buildings, an institution, or a company. A LAN can use a variety of hardware and protocol types and can be connected to other networks such as the Internet or a WAN (Wide Area Network). See also *EtherNet, gateway, internet, Internet, WAN.*

leased line

A conditioned, dedicated telephone line used for network connectivity and remote computing.

legacy

A term generically used to describe any software or hardware older than the stuff you just bought.

license

Contrary to popular belief, software is never bought or sold, but *licensed.* Licensing means you have the right to use something in certain very specific ways but you have no further rights to that thing. A software license restricts how you may use the product based upon this fundamental distinction.

link

An area within an HTML or other hypertext document that leads to another resource or document when activated (usually by a mouse click). See also *HTML, hypermedia, hypertext.*

linked object

An image of an object inserted or embedded into a destination document. When changes are made to the original, the linked object is updated automatically. See also *embedded object, object linking and embedding.*

list box

An interface control that lists available choices in a scrolling text list format, usually used in File ➤ Open or ➤ Save dialog boxes.

local

Refers to the machine you are using. See also *host, remote.*

local account

A user account for a domain where a user has no global account or the account is not in a trusted domain. If both the user's original domain and the current domain have trusted relationships, a local account is not necessary. See also *global account, trust relationship, user account.*

local group

A group granted permissions and rights only for its own computer. A local group can also contain user accounts from its own computer, user accounts and global groups (from its local domain and other trusted domains). This allows administrators to create sets of users from both inside and outside the computer, to be used only at the computer. See also *global group, group.*

local printer

A printer connected to a physical port on your computer.

logical drive

A portion of an extended partition on a hard disk, which the operating system sees as another discrete drive letter.

login

See *logon.*

logon

The process of providing a user name and password to a computer system or other resource to gain access to it. See also *authentication.*

logon hours

The days and hours during which a user account can connect to a server. When a user exceeds the allowed hours, the server will disconnect the user or deny any new connections or services.

logon script

A script or batch file that runs automatically at logon, used to customize a working environment for an individual or for groups of users.

logon script path

The local path where Windows NT Workstation stores logon scripts. See also *logon script.*

logon workstations

The computers a user is allowed to log on *from,* defined by the server.

LPT

The common and logical device name used for the parallel port on an Intel PC, commonly used for printing. The term originated as a contraction of "Line Printer."

M

mail

See *e-mail.*

mail gateway

A system that acts as a translator and router of electronic mail messages (for example, a machine that integrates incoming SMTP mail into a Microsoft Mail system and allows Microsoft Mail clients access to SMTP mail). See also *e-mail, POP3, SMTP.*

mainframe

A generic term referring to any large, centralized computer system accessed via terminals.

mandatory user profile

The user profile (defined by the server) assigned to one or more users that must be used at each logon. This profile cannot be changed by the user. See also *personal user profile, user profile.*

maximize button

The middle button in the upper-right corner of an application or other window, with a square in it, visible when the window is less than full screen. When you click on it, it toggles the window to full-screen mode, at which point it becomes the restore button. See also *restore button.*

maximum password age

Windows NT Server can control the period of time a password can be used before requiring the user to change it. See also *account policy.*

media control interface (MCI)

A standard general interface for multimedia devices that lets multimedia programs control multimedia hardware. For example, instead of having to understand how dozens of different sound cards operate, multimedia programmers only have to know the MCI sound interface functions, and it's up to the hardware guys to make their sound cards MCI-compliant.

menu

The available commands for an application or operating system, usually presented as a hierarchical list.

menu bar

The area in Windows applications just below the title bar, where the main program menu is presented. All main menu items are usually available from this area.

Messenger service

A program that sends and receives messages sent by administrators or by the Alerter service. See also *Alerter service.*

microcomputer

A generic term referring to desktop computing systems typified by the IBM PC and clones thereof.

MIDI (Musical Instruments Digital Interface)

A serial communications standard for digital music synthesizers. A MIDI instrument or sound card can reproduce complex musical performances, using a wide variety of instrument voices, from a relatively small set of instructions store in a MIDI file (.MID). These files are not digital recordings but rather digital instructions for performances by the synthesized instruments on the MIDI device (think of them as musical scores). Many PC sound cards now support MIDI synthesis. See also *sound card*.

minicomputer

A generic term for midrange computing systems that approach or surpass the power of mainframes but are smaller both physically and in price. Most minicomputers are intended for use as centralized resources to be accessed via terminals.

MIME (Multipurpose Internet Mail Extensions)

A system for augmenting Internet mail protocols to allow the attachment of binary data types (graphics, audio, video) to text-based mail messages. MIME can use a variety of encoding and decoding methods for compatibility with different mail systems. See also *Exchange, UUdecode, UUencode*.

minimize button

The leftmost button in the upper-right corner of an application window; it displays a minus sign. When clicked, it will reduce the application to an icon on the Taskbar. See also *maximize button*.

minimum password age

Windows NT requires that you use a password a minimum amount of time before you can change it. See also *Account policy*.

minimum password length

The fewest characters a password can contain. See also *Account policy*.

modal

A program dialog box or window that requires interaction, before allowing you to return to the rest of the application or Desktop, is said to be modal. A File ➤ Open dialog box is an example of an *application-modal* dialog (you must select an entry or Cancel before you can use any other part of that application, even though you can see the application window behind the dialog box, but you can use other applications in Windows without closing the dialog box). Certain Windows NT error message dialog boxes are *system-modal* in that you must act upon the message before you can use *any* part of Windows or *any* running application. See also *nonmodal.*

modem

Contraction of "modulator-demodulator." A modem accepts the serial data bit stream from a device (usually a PC COM port) and converts (modulates) it to sound waves that can then be transmitted via the public telephone system or similar means. At the receiving end, another modem reconverts (demodulates) the sound waves into digital data, which is then sent to another device (usually another PC COM port). The modem may also provide other services, such as error correction, data compression, and adaptive call answering. Many modern modems will handle fax (facsimile) transmissions as well. Windows NT allows modems to act as network transport links via RAS (Remote Access Services) and other communications protocols. See also *AT command set, dialup, PPP, RAS, Unimodem.*

monospaced font

A font in which all characters take up the same space, and with the same distance between all characters (as on a typewriter). Monospaced (or fixed-spaced) fonts are needed in certain applications, such as terminal emulation or a Command Prompt session, in which the display is a fixed matrix. See also *font, proportional font.*

mouse pointer

See *cursor.*

.MPG

An audio and video file format popularized by the Motion Picture Experts Group (MPEG).

MS-DOS application

An application designed to run under the Microsoft Disk Operating System (MS-DOS). Although Windows NT provides excellent MS-DOS emulation and support, most MS-DOS applications are simply not designed to behave cooperatively in a multitasking environment. Windows NT allows you to customize the Command Prompt for errant MS-DOS applications (see Appendix C, "Tips On Running Legacy Applications"). See also *program information file*.

multimedia

Information presented using more than one content type simultaneously (sound, graphics, video, text), usually with emphasis on visuals. See also *hypermedia*.

multitasking

The act of performing multiple tasks. Earlier versions of Windows offered limited, cooperative multitasking that relied upon the applications in use to yield the processor. Windows NT offers true preemptive multitasking, which places the operating system in the driver's seat in terms of controlling the amount of time each application receives from the processor. The result is smoother performance.

multithreading

Multitasking within one application. Applications may be designed so that instead of an entire application being one computing process, different functions within the application may be assigned processor time and prioritized according to various task criteria. For example, a multithreaded word processor application can spell-check your document as you type.

My Briefcase

The Desktop icon for using the file-synchronization utilities in Windows NT 4.0.

My Computer

The Desktop icon representing the major resources available from the Desktop. You may view drives, the Control Panel, printers, and the contents of those objects from the My Computer window (it's really just a predefined Explorer view with the left-pane tree control turned off). See also *Explorer*.

N

named pipe

An interprocess communication mechanism allowing one process to communicate with another local or remote process. Named pipe support occurs at a much lower level than dynamic data exchange and is not readily available from the user interface; application designers will implement it at the code level. See also *dynamic data exchange.*

NetBIOS

An IBM network protocol for peer-to-peer (serverless) networking.

NetWare

Novell's trademarked brand name for its server-based network operating system and other network products.

Net Logon service

This operating system program performs authentication of domain logons and also keeps the domain's database synchronized between the primary and other backup domain controllers.

network

A number of computers linked together to enable communications and sharing of resources.

Network DDE DSDM service

The Network DDE DSDM (DDE share database manager) service manages shared DDE conversations and is used by the Network DDE service. See also *dynamic data exchange.*

Network DDE service

The Network DDE (dynamic data exchange) service program provides network transport and security for DDE conversations between applications on different workstations, or from workstation to server.

network device driver

Windows NT provides software controlling communication between the network adapter card (NIC) and the rest of the computer system. Some NICs may require custom device drivers to be provided by the manufacturer. See also *device driver*.

network directory

See *shared directory*.

network interface card (NIC)

The peripheral interface card used to connect a PC to a network (also known as a network adapter). Newer PCs may have the NIC built into the system motherboard.

Network Neighborhood

The Desktop icon that allows you to browse network resources (computers, servers, printers, etc.).

nonmodal

Of a program dialog box or other window that doesn't restrict you from using other parts of the program or Windows. For example, a word processing program may have a Find dialog box that floats above your document but doesn't prevent you from returning to the document between searches. See also *modal*.

non-Windows NT application

Some applications aren't designed to run with Windows NT but were originally designed for other operating systems such as Windows 3.*x*, MS-DOS, OS/2, or POSIX. These applications may work reasonably well under NT but may not be able to take full advantage of all NT features (such as enhanced multitasking and memory management).

NotePad

A Windows applet for viewing and editing ASCII text files.

NT

See *Windows NT.*

NT file system

See *NTFS.*

NTFS

The Windows NT File System is an advanced file system designed specifically for Windows NT. It allows for file system recovery, extremely large storage media, object-oriented file management, and various security features, as well as compliance for the POSIX subsystem.

null modem cable

A special serial cable designed to mimic an asynchronous serial connection. This cable allows two PCs to be linked via a serial port just as if they were connected with modems over a phone line. A true null modem cable supports all major line signals in the RS-232 specification required for high-speed serial connections, especially carrier detect (CD) and hardware flow control (RTS/CTS). You can also convert a standard modem cable to act as a null using a null modem adapter, available at most computer and electronics stores for a fraction of the cost of a full cable.

O

object

In the Windows universe, a piece of information that can be linked or embedded into another document. See also *object linking and embedding.*

object linking and embedding (OLE)

A way to share information between unlike applications (such as a word processor and a spreadsheet) to create compound documents with data persistence and visual integration. OLE differs from DDE in that DDE must occur in real time with both applications running but OLE allows one static document to reflect changes in another after the first is changed (if you embed an Excel spreadsheet in a Word document, close Word, and then tell Excel to change the spreadsheet, you can tell Word to update the embedded Excel spreadsheet automatically the next time the Word document is opened). Later versions of OLE allow in-place editing of embedded objects (clicking on the Excel spreadsheet within the Word document doesn't open Excel but simply allows you to edit the spreadsheet from within the Word file, using Excel toolbars in the Word window). See also *dynamic data exchange, OLE automation.*

OLE automation

The term used to describe an OLE server application sharing its objects with another client application's macro or script language. If a Word macro calls an Excel spreadsheet object to complete a compound document, Word is using OLE automation via the Excel object. See also *object linking and embedding.*

orientation

The direction (vertical or horizontal—portrait or landscape) of printed material in relation to the paper. Modern laser or inkjet printers can orient data on the page to suit the application, whereas older fixed-head printers had to have the paper loaded specifically for each print job orientation.

orphan

A member of a mirror set or a stripe set with parity that has crashed or failed in some catastrophic way. When a member of a volume is orphaned, the operating system relies upon the other members of the set. See also *mirror set, stripe set.*

P

package

Windows represents embedded or linked objects with a package icon. The application used to create the object plays the object (such as a video or sound file) when the package icon is selected.

packet

A unit of data for transmission.

page

A complete ClipBook entry that has been pasted in. As it pertains to memory management, a fixed-size block in a virtual memory page or swap file. See also *ClipBook, virtual memory.*

paging file

See *swap file.*

palette

The number of colors available in a display or reproduction system. In computer color display systems, the color palette is largely determined by the display card memory and software drivers, whereas resolution is a combination of those and the display device (the monitor) itself. Most modern color monitors will display an unlimited range of colors if the display card and software can provide them. Standard VGA settings on Windows systems will deliver a 16-color palette at 640 × 480 pixel resolution. Adding more memory to the display system will allow either greater resolution (for example, 1024 × 768 pixels) or greater color depth (for example, an increased palette of 256 colors) depending upon the display system configuration. See also *pixel, resolution.*

pane

A subdivision of a program window. See *Explorer.*

parallel

Of a method of transmitting data multiple bits at a time. Parallel transmission is technically more efficient but requires more complex wiring, resulting in a shorter effective transmission distance. Most PC printer connections are parallel. See also *LPT, serial.*

partition

A physical disk section defined by low-level formatting that functions as a separate unit from other storage media. See also *system partition*.

password

A string of characters required for user authorization. Every user must have a password associated with that user's name. A password secures your Windows NT Workstation from unauthorized access. Passwords can also be used to restrict access to network resources. A Windows NT password is case-sensitive and can have up to 14 characters. See also *Account policy*.

password uniqueness

Windows NT requires a certain number of new passwords on a user account before you can reuse an old password. See also *Account policy*.

path

Shows the location of a file within a network structure or directory tree. A complete path specification will include the logical drive, the directory name, and the filename if applicable (for example, C:\WINDOWS\SYSTEM.INI). Network paths may also include a machine name (such as \\SERVER1\MAIL\MAILBOX.PST) denoted using UNC path conventions. See also *UNC*.

PC card

Small, credit card–sized peripheral components that plug into slots on laptops and other PCs. PC cards can be used for modems, additional RAM, hard drives, sound cards, etc. Most PC cards support Plug-and-Play and will automatically configure themselves upon installation.

PCMCIA

The previous name (which no one could remember) for PC cards. See *PC card*.

peer-to-peer

Networking without servers. Individual computers each have equal opportunity to share resources on a peer-to-peer LAN. Microsoft Windows Network is a peer-to-peer network. See also *LAN, network.*

permission

A rule used to regulate user access to an object or resource (such as a file folder, printer, or server) as opposed to the entire system. See also *right.*

personal address book (.PAB)

The file format used by the Exchange client and other Windows applications to store address information.

personal information store (.PST)

The file format used by the Exchange client to contain messaging data and structures. You can store your .PST on your own machine or on a network machine.

personal user profile

A server user profile assigned to one user. A personal user profile stores the individual user server settings and restores them upon logon. See also *mandatory user profile, user profile.*

Phone Dialer

A Windows applet that uses the modem for rapid phone dialing.

.PIF

See *program information file (.PIF).*

pixel

Approximate contraction of "picture element." The smallest unit of logical addressability in a display or printing system. A VGA display has a 640×480 pixel field (i.e., a 640×480 resolution), with a color palette or depth of 16 colors. The actual physical size of each pixel is determined by the size of the display device and the resolution of that device (a single pixel on a 13" VGA display is smaller than a single pixel on a 20" VGA display, as both displays have the same *number* of pixels regardless of the actual size of the display tube). See also *palette, resolution.*

Plug and Play (PnP)

A specification for rapid hardware installation and software configuration supported by Microsoft and many hardware vendors. Plug and Play is intended to deliver the user from the IRQ, DMA, BPA, etc. alphabet soup of PC hardware and memory issues. Plug and Play support is required in the operating system, the hardware, and the software drivers for the hardware for it all to work. Windows 95 supports PnP; Windows NT 4.0 doesn't yet.

pointer

The arrow shape used by the mouse cursor in selection mode. See also *cursor.*

POP3 (Post Office Protocol)

The third version of the standard for Internet electronic mail retrieval systems. POP allows one machine to receive and store mail for many host machines (a technique also knows as *store and forward*). See also *e-mail, SMTP.*

port

The physical connection used to attach a peripheral device (modem, printer, scanner, etc.) to your computer. Also refers to the logical memory address the operating system uses to send information to the device or uses to receive information from the device. Common port types on Intel PCs are COM, LPT, and SCSI. See also *COM, LPT, SCSI.*

Postoffice

The machine housing mail messages for a workgroup.

PPP (Point to Point Protocol)

A network driver that allows TCP/IP and other network protocols to be used over a phone line, using standard modems or other devices. PPP is rapidly becoming the most common dialup protocol for Internet access, as it offers some performance improvements, can support multiple protocols, and automates user authentication. See also *authentication, modem, protocol, RAS, SLIP.*

primary domain controller

The Windows NT Server that manages authentication services and maintains the security policy and the master database for a domain. See also *backup domain controller, server.*

primary partition

A portion of a physical disk used by and storing an operating system. Different operating systems each require unique partitions. Each physical disk can be structured into up to four primary partitions (or up to three, if there is an extended partition). Primary partitions cannot be subdivided once created. See also *extended partition.*

printer driver

The software used by the operating system to communicate directly with your printer hardware. Windows NT comes with many different printer drivers, but you may substitute a manufacturer's driver if necessary or desired.

printer fonts

Fonts that reside in your printer firmware, usually in ROM (read-only memory). Also used to describe fonts downloaded to a printer in some systems.

printer window

Windows NT will display a window that shows print job status and other information for all work sent to a specific printer. You can access the printer window by clicking on the printer icon in the tool tray at the far right of the Taskbar, or by opening your printer's icon in the Start menu, Settings, Printers group. See also *queue.*

program file

A file that directly starts an application or program when activated (as opposed to a shortcut or association). Valid Windows NT program files use an .EXE, .PIF, .COM, .BAT or .CMD filename extension.

program group

In Windows NT 3.*x* and Windows 3.*x* Program Manager, a collection of application or file icons in a group window. Windows 95 and Windows NT 4.0 interfaces allow program or file icons (or Shortcuts to those icons) to be stored in the Start menu, in file folders, or on the Desktop.

program information file (PIF)

The file used by Windows NT to control session options for specific MS-DOS based applications. See also *MS-DOS applications*.

program-item icon

The graphic used to represent file and program objects.

property

Values, qualities, or other configuration settings that affect an object.

property sheet

A dialog tab pane that displays the properties or attributes of an object. Usually accessed via the Right Mouse ➤ Properties menu item in Windows 95 or Windows NT 4.0.

proportional font

A font in which character spacing is customized to the actual design of individual characters and spacing between characters is optimized according to the character pairs (also known as kerning). For example, the letter "i" uses less space than "w" in a proportional font, and "ii" placed together uses less space than "ww." Proportional fonts are only possible in a true graphically rendered user interface such as Windows, which allows the display of fonts that are very close to what your printer can produce, resulting in pretty decent WYSIWYG (what you see is what you get, pronounced "whiziwig").

protocol

Simply defined, any set of rules. File transfer protocols such as XMODEM, YMODEM, and ZMODEM are simple sets of rules for sending binary information over serial communications links. Network protocols such as NETBIOS, NETBEUI, TCP/IP, and IPX/SPX are rules for exchanging information over network links. See also *IPX/SPX, NETBIOS, PPP, TCP/IP, XMODEM, YMODEM, ZMODEM.*

Q

queue

Literally, a line of things or people waiting. Print jobs can be sent to a printer queue as a you wait for the printer to finish its current job, freeing up your CPU to get on with life while the printer handles its own work. See also *printer window.*

quick format

Replaces the drive File Allocation Table and root directory, but performs no disk check. See also *file allocation table.*

QuickTime

A popular audio and video format first developed for the Apple Macintosh.

R

radio button

One of a set of round buttons composing an interface control used to offer mutually exclusive options, usually used in program dialog boxes. Just as on a radio, you only get to choose one button.

RAM

Random access memory. This is the main memory used in your computer to store programs and data to be used by the CPU and other subsystems. RAM is volatile (if you lose power during a session, the contents of RAM are lost), which is why you should save your work often.

RAS (Remote Access Services)

A set of programs and drivers that allow a Windows NT Workstation computer to establish network connections to a Windows NT Server via modems and phone line or other devices. RAS supports TCP/IP, NETBEUI, and IPX/SPX protocols. RAS in Windows NT can also be used to connect to any ISP (Internet Service Provider) or other server that supports PPP for Internet access. See also *dialup, IPX/SPX, ISP, PPP, TCP/IP.*

read-only

An attribute of a file meaning that it can be read from but not written to.

Recycle Bin

The icon on the Desktop where you drag stuff you don't want anymore. The object is not actually erased until the computer needs the storage space or you specifically empty the Recycle Bin. While an object is still in the Recycle Bin, you can restore it from the Recycle Bin menu.

refresh

To update the currently displayed information with the latest available data.

RegEdit (Registry Editor)

A program for viewing and editing the configuration registry. *Do not* use this program unless you are versed in Windows NT registry issues.

registry

See *configuration registry.*

remote

The computer connecting to a host. In RAS, the client system connecting to the RAS server. See also *RAS*.

remote access

To share network resources over a remote network link. See also *RAS*.

remote administration

Managing a computer from across a network.

remote procedure call

RPC is a message-passing technique allowing an application access to services across a network.

Remote Procedure Call service

See *RPC service*.

replication

See *directory replication*.

resolution

The degree of sharpness or the ability to render detail in a display, imaging, or other reproduction system. For computer displays, resolution is measured in terms of pixel fields. Standard VGA displays have a resolution of 640 × 480 pixels. Increasing the display card memory can yield higher resolution or greater color palettes, or both, depending upon the amount of memory and the specific configuration options the display system supports. See also *palette, pixel*.

resource

In computing, any device, system, or network component that can be used by another part of the system.

resize button

A triangular-shaped area at the lower-right corner of a program window. When the mouse cursor is over this area, it will become a two-headed arrow, which signifies that you may click and drag the window to resize it. Note that this control will appear only when the window is not full screen (maximized).

restore button

The middle button in the upper-right corner of an application or other window, with two overlapping squares in it, visible when the window is full screen. When you click on it, it toggles the window to sized mode, at which point it becomes the maximize button. See also *maximize button*.

Rich Text Format (.RTF)

A widely used document format supporting font attributes, tabs, and embedded graphics.

right

An access or action that is allowed. Users have various rights, according to their authorizations, to perform certain actions on a computer or network system. Rights apply to the system as a whole, as opposed to specific objects. See also *permission*.

ROM (read-only memory)

Nonvolatile memory used to store information that is used repetitively but not updated. The PC hardware BIOS is an example of ROM.

root directory

See *directory tree*.

routable protocol

A network protocol that supports transmission of packets across internetworks. TCP/IP is the classic example.

router

A network device that receives data packets and sends them to the next machine in the network destination path.

RPC

See *remote procedure call.*

RPC Locator service

The service used by the client side of a distributed application to find server applications. See also *RPC service, service.*

RPC service

The Remote Procedure Call subsystem for Windows NT. See also *remote procedure call, RPC Locator service, service.*

S

SAM

Security Accounts Manager is the Windows NT subsystem that maintains the SAM database and provides access to the database. See also *SAM database.*

SAM database

A database of security information, user account names, passwords, and security policies settings.

Schedule service

A program that supports the Windows NT AT command, which schedules commands and programs to run at specified times and dates.

screen buffer

A memory area used for the command prompt display.

screen fonts

Fonts optimized for screen display as opposed to use by a printer or other output device. Screen fonts are often closely matched to printer fonts to maximize the match between your display and printed output.

screen resolution

See *pixels.*

screen saver

A visually pleasing, animated, usually comic graphic that displays on the computer monitor after a preset period of time. Originally designed to prevent phosphor damage on early color monitors, today's screen savers are mostly used for their cool quality, as most newer monitors are immune to such maladies (sorry to burst any bubbles).

scroll

To move the displayed information on a computer screen to reveal hidden information. Computer displays often cannot display an entire file in a single display screen. Most Windows applications support scrolling via the [Pg Up] and [Pg Dn] keys as well as using scroll bars and the mouse, and they also frequently support automatic scrolling if the cursor is moved beyond the displayed document area. See also *cursor, scroll bar.*

scroll bar

A bar that automatically appears on the edge of an application window or list box control when the display cannot show all available information.

SCSI (Small Computer System Interface)

Pronounced "scuzzy." A peripheral bus for intelligent storage devices (devices that contain their own controller logic for input/output). The SCSI bus and the devices on it (up to seven) manage I/O cooperatively, allowing transfer management to be offloaded from the system CPU, thus raising total system bus throughput. Typical SCSI devices include scanners, disk drives, CD-ROMs, and tape drives. SCSI-2 is a standard that doubles throughput by allowing enhanced device queuing and simultaneous transfers with dissimilar devices (a tape drive and a CD-ROM, for example).

security accounts manager

See *SAM*.

security database

See *SAM database*.

security ID (SID)

A unique name for each user or group of users in a security system.

security identifier

See *security ID*.

security log

Windows NT can record events to allow review of system activities. See also *event*.

security policies

Windows NT Workstation security policies consist of the Account, User Rights, and Audit policies, managed with User Manager. For Windows NT Server, domain security policies consist of the Account, User Rights, Audit, and Trust Relationships policies, managed with User Manager for Domains. See also *permissions, rights, User Manager*.

Selection cursor

See *cursor*.

serial

Of a method of transmitting data one bit at a time. Most PC modem communications are serial. See also *parallel*.

server

A computer that shares resources (files, printers, databases, modems) with one or more network users. See also *client, share*.

Server Manager

An application used to manage domains, workgroups, and computers on a Windows NT network.

Server service

Provides RPC support, file, print, and named pipe sharing. See also *named pipe, RPC, service*.

service

A program (or operating system process) that performs a specific function available to other programs, computers, and services. Windows NT services are RPC-enabled and can be called from remote computers. See also *RPC*.

SGML (Standard General Markup Language)

A typographic markup language that allows for consistent complex document formatting across multiple delivery platforms. See also *HTML*.

share

To make resources available to network users.

shared directory

A directory or file folder users can connect to over a network.

shared folder

See *shared directory*.

shared network directory

See *shared directory*.

shared page

In ClipBook, a page that others may access.

shared resource

A device, a program, or data used by more than one other device or program, either on the local computer or across a network.

sharename

The name used to identify a shared resource.

shortcut

An icon that represents another file or program object at another location. Shortcuts act as system "aliases" without creating duplicate data, and most shortcuts support the same functions as the objects they represent (dragging a document to a printer shortcut will have the same result as dragging the document to the original printer icon itself). Systemwide OLE support in Windows NT makes shortcuts possible. See also *object linking and embedding*.

shortcut key

See *accelerator key*.

SID

See *security ID*.

SLIP (Serial Line Internet Protocol)

A protocol that allows transmission of TCP/IP network communications over a modem and a phone line. The term is sometimes incorrectly used generically to refer to any type of dialup network connection. See also *PPP, RAS*.

SMTP (Simple Mail Transfer Protocol)

The system for exchanging electronic mail between Internet hosts. SMTP was designed for direct, immediate host-to-host transmission of simple text messages via Internet protocols. Since a growing number Internet-capable machines are not on the Internet at all times, a combination of SMTP and POP3 systems is common. See also *host, POP3*.

sound card

A peripheral interface card providing sound reproduction support for the operating system, applications, and games. There are two prevalent standards for sound on the Intel PC, the Creative Labs Sound Blaster and MIDI. The Sound Blaster and compatible cards provide basic sound synthesis (the ability to create fairly realistic musical sounds from mathematical formulas) and the ability to record and play back digital sound files (the most popular digital sound format is the .WAV file). Most Sound Blaster and compatible cards also support the MIDI (Musical Instrument Digital Interface) standard. See also *MIDI*.

source directory

The directory or file folder containing the file or files you intend to copy, move, or transfer.

source document

The document containing the original information used in a linked or embedded object.

split bar

Windows NT Explorer and other programs use a vertical or horizontal bar to divide different program areas (for example, to display a file directory window in two parts, the directory tree on one side, and the contents of the directory on the other). The relative sizing of the two windows is controlled by grabbing the bar with the cursor and moving it. See also *cursor*.

spool

A temporary holding area for print jobs. See *queue*.

Start menu

The hierarchical pop-up menu at the left or top of the Taskbar. The Start menu contains program shortcuts for most major components of Windows and any applications you have installed. The Start menu is also fully configurable. This menu and the Taskbar are actually the replacements for Program Manager in the Windows 95/Windows NT 4.0 interface.

Startup folder

Placing programs or program shortcuts in the Startup folder causes Windows to run them when it starts. You can drag items or their shortcut to the Startup folder in Explorer, and you can view your Startup folder contents from the Start menu Programs group.

status bar

A line of information at the bottom of a program window.

string

A sequence of characters, usually text.

subdirectory

A child directory within a parent directory. Most PC file systems allow nesting file directories, so you may have subdirectories of subdirectories in a hierarchy. In Windows 95 and Windows NT 4.0, directories and subdirectories are also referred to as folders.

subdomain

Any subdivision of an Internet domain. For example *mizzou1.missouri.edu* is a subdomain of *missouri.edu,* and *missouri.edu* is a subdomain of *.edu* as well. The machine *bozo.mizzou1.missouri.edu* is then a host in the subdomain *mizzou1.missouri.edu.* See also *domain, host.*

swap file

A file used to page virtual memory data to and from disk when physical RAM resources are depleted. Also called a paging file.

synchronize

To replicate the domain database from the primary domain controller to other servers. See also *directory replication.*

syntax

The order in which computers expect commands and command arguments to be submitted for processing.

system default profile

The user profile that is loaded when Windows NT Server is running, before any user is logged on. See also *user default profile, user profile*.

system partition

The volume that contains the hardware-specific files needed to load Windows NT. See also *partition*.

T

tab

In a dialog box, the interface extension element used to access a pane of information in a dialog box. In word processing, an ASCII character that represents a value used to represent a tab keystroke for spacing.

TAPI (Telephony Application Programming Interface)

This set of programming tools provides a semi-universal way for program designers to address modems and manage COM port contention. The goal of TAPI is to provide the same type of device independence for modem communications that the Windows printer drivers do for printers (applications don't have to understand individual printers, since Windows handles the individual printer differences). See also *device driver*.

Taskbar

The area at the bottom of the Windows NT 4.0 Desktop that displays the Start menu and buttons representing any running programs. Clicking on a program button brings that program to the front of the Desktop and makes it the active application. The Taskbar can be resized by dragging on its upper edge, and it can be moved to any side of the Desktop by dragging it in the middle. See also *Desktop*.

Task Manager

A utility that shows all running programs and allows you to switch to them, end them, or arrange their position on screen. In Windows NT 4.0, the Task Manager is available when you right-click on an open area of the Taskbar, and as part of the Windows NT Security dialog box that appears after you press `Ctrl`+`Alt`+`Del`. See also `Alt`+`Tab`, `Ctrl`+`Alt`+`Del`, *Taskbar.*

TCP/IP (Transmission Control Protocol/Internet Protocol)

A combination of protocols used for Internet communications. TCP takes care of preparing data for transmission, tracks what data was sent, and resends it if there were any errors; IP takes care of getting the data from host to host. For TCP/IP to function, every computer on a TCP/IP network must have a unique identifier, or *host address.* The term TCP/IP can also refer to a suite of other protocols (telnet, FTP, and others) commonly used on the Internet. See also *domain, host address, host name, protocol, sub-domain.*

telnet

One of the suite of Internet protocols that allows remote connections to host computers. A contraction of Terminal Emulation via Network, telnet allows you to extend your local console to a machine anywhere across a TCP/IP network. The term Telnet also applies to any number of terminal emulation/telnet protocol applications that use the telnet protocol as a transport for a terminal emulation session. Windows NT comes with a rudimentary Telnet application that supports the basic DEC VT terminal emulations. See also *TCP/IP, terminal, terminal emulation.*

Telnet

An application for terminal emulation using the telnet protocol. See *TCP/IP, telnet, terminal, terminal emulation.*

terminal

A computer console (display and keyboard) with minimal local processing and storage capabilities (terminals don't have processing power in the sense that a PC does). Hardware terminals are used to access centralized timesharing computing systems such as mainframes and minicomputers, via direct connection, network connection, or modem. Some hardware terminals have local printing capabilities. Most terminals have only character-based interfaces. See also *mainframe, minicomputer, terminal emulation.*

terminal emulation

The act of emulating a hardware terminal via software. Also describes the software product that emulates a hardware terminal. Terminal emulation software allows a PC to duplicate most if not all of the functions of a dedicated hardware terminal for communications with a variety of host systems such as mainframes and minicomputers, usually via serial communications over a modem and phone line. This type of program saves PC owners the cost of dedicated terminal hardware, frees the desktop real estate that would be required for the dedicated terminal, and gives users capabilities for local data processing and storage that no hardware terminal can provide. Most terminals emulators support only character-based interfaces. Windows NT comes with HyperTerminal, a simple terminal emulation program. See also *telnet, terminal.*

text file

A file containing only ASCII characters, with no formatting information other than that supported by the ASCII character set (e.g., tabs, linefeeds, and carriage returns).

thread

See *multithreading.*

tile

To arrange windows so that all can be viewed at once. The more programs, the smaller the programs are when tiled.

time-out

How long a computer will wait before performing an action. Some programs have time-out values preset for certain functions (if the desired result does not occur within a time-out period, a predefined action will be taken).

time slice

The processor time allocated to a process or an application.

title bar

The area at the top of a program window that shows the program title. It also houses other window controls and is the main area to use for click-dragging or moving the application window without resizing it.

toolbar

A set of shortcut buttons directly below the menu bar in most applications. Some applications allow you to configure or customize the toolbar.

TrueType

Microsoft's version of scalable font technology. One font file can be used at a variety of point sizes without loss of type quality. The main advantage of TrueType fonts is that they can be used with common laser and inkjet printers that don't have the expensive PostScript capability used for high-end typesetting.

trust

See *trust relationship*.

trust relationship

Links between domains allowing user accounts in one domain to access the entire network (also known as pass-through authentication). Accounts and groups in a trusted domain can be granted rights and resource permissions in a trusting domain, without creating separate accounts in the trusting domain's database (the trusting domain honors the account user names and passwords of a trusted domain). See also *global groups, groups, local groups, User Manager for Domains*.

U

UART

Acronym for Universal Asynchronous Receiver Transmitter. The UART is a chip that performs serial communications tasks in the PC COM port or internal modem. See also *16550A UART*.

UNC (Universal Naming Convention)

The syntax for addressing logical paths on other network machines without assigning them a logical drive letter.

Unimodem

A Windows driver that provides configuration support for modems using the Hayes AT command set "standard." Unfortunately, not all modems support the Hayes AT command set equally, so this driver may not work well with all modems. See also *AT command set, modem.*

uninstall

To completely remove a program and its components from your computer system. Most Windows applications install some files in the Windows System directory as well as in their own, and they may make several entries into the system configuration registry. Therefore, simply deleting program files from their directory (for example, C:\EXCEL) won't restore your system to the state it was in prior to application installation. "True" Windows NT applications *should* make use of the facilities in the Add/Remove Programs Control Panel, but not all do.

uninterruptible power supply (UPS)

See *UPS.*

UNIX

The multitasking operating system used on most Internet hosts. Most versions of UNIX used for dialup connection servers are character-based (also known as "shell accounts").

upload

To move data from your local machine to the host system you're connected to. If you think of the host as upstairs from your system, it makes sense. See also *download, file transfer.*

UPS

Uninterruptible power supply; a battery-operated power supply that maintains system power for a limited time during a power failure. Many UPSs also supply power-conditioning and surge-suppression services as well.

UPS service

A Windows NT service that controls certain configuration options and monitors the status of the uninterruptible power supply connected to the Windows NT computer. The UPS icon in the Windows NT 4.0 Control Panel provides a simple interface to the available UPS service options. See also *UPS*.

URL (Universal Resource Locator)

A format for describing the location of resources on a computing system, usually the Internet or other TCP/IP network (such as an intranet). The basic format for a URL is *[protocol]://[hostname.subdomain.domain]/[resourcepath]*. For example, *http://www.microsoft.com/news.htm* refers to a HTML page named *news.htm* on the Microsoft World Wide Web server *www.microsoft.com* that will be transferred using the *http* protocol. URLs can also specify a wide variety of other Internet resource and protocol types, such as *telnet://*, *ftp://*, *gopher://*, and others. Files on local media may be accessed via URL with most HTML browsers using the *file://* prefix, for example.

user account

The information that defines a user (user name and password for logon, group memberships, rights, and permissions). For Windows NT Workstation, user accounts are managed with User Manager. For Windows NT Server, user accounts are managed with User Manager for Domains. See also *group, User Manager, User Manager for Domains.*

user account database

See *SAM database.*

user default profile

The user profile loaded by a server when a user's assigned profile cannot be accessed or when a user doesn't have an assigned profile, logs on for the first time, or logs on to the Guest account. See also *system default profile, user profile.*

User Manager

A program used to manage user accounts, groups, and security policies. In Windows NT 4.0, User Manager is found in the Start menu, Programs, Administrative Tools group. See also *permissions, rights, trust relationship, User Manager for Domains.*

User Manager for Domains

A program used by Windows NT Server to manage security. Just as User Manager does for workstations, it administers user accounts, groups, and security policies for a domain or an individual computer. See also *permissions, rights, trust relationship, User Manager.*

user name

A name for a user account on a Windows NT workstation or network. A user name must be totally unique and cannot duplicate any other group name or user name in its own domain or work-group. See also *user account.*

user profile

Configuration information (the Desktop arrangement, screen colors, screen savers, network connections, printer connections, etc.) is stored on a user-by-user basis in user profiles in the system Registry. This user profile is loaded and the Windows NT environment is configured accordingly at user logon. See also *logon, registry.*

User Profile Editor

A Windows NT Server program that creates, edits, and saves personal user, mandatory user, user default, and system default profiles. See also *user profile.*

user right

See *right.*

User Rights policy

A set of configuration options that assigns rights to groups and user accounts. See also *policy.*

UUdecode

The process of converting seven-bit ASCII text encoded with eight-bit binary data to the original eight-bit binary data after reception. May also refer to a program that provides the service of encoding/decoding. See also *MIME, UUencode.*

UUencode

The process of converting eight-bit binary data to seven-bit ASCII text for transmission via SMTP mail systems. May also refer to a program that provides the service of encoding/decoding. See also *MIME, UUdecode.*

V

virtual memory

Windows NT can use drive space to mimic physical RAM (random access memory) through the technique of virtual memory, which uses special disk files called *swap files* or *page files.* By mapping the drive space as additional RAM, virtual memory management allows you to run more applications at one time than actual memory allows. Virtual memory operation requires drive space for the swap file and the time to move application memory pages to and from the swap file. This represents a performance decrease as compared to the same workload on a system using the equivalent physical RAM, but as processor and drive speeds increase, the difference in performance is less. See also *swap file, page file.*

virtual printer memory

PostScript printers segregate memory into two main types, one for print job data and another for font and other resources used over and over for multiple print jobs. Virtual printer memory is that reserved for resident and downloaded fonts.

volume

A partition or collection of partitions formatted for use by a file system. Windows NT allows construction of volumes via several methods. See also *stripe sets, mirror sets.*

W

wallpaper

A bitmap graphic used as the background for the Desktop. To set the wallpaper, right-click anywhere on the Desktop. Select Properties and then the Background tab. Use the Wallpaper list box to select a pattern or graphic.

WAN (wide area network)

A network linking computers that are quite distant geographically. For example, a dedicated network link between two LANs in separate cities would be defined as a WAN. Some companies are now using the public Internet as a transport for WAN connectivity. See also *internet, Internet, LAN.*

.WAV

The prevalent digital sound format for Windows.

wildcard

A character used to represent one or more characters in an operating system command syntax structure. The question mark (?) can be used to represent any single character, and the asterisk (*) wildcard can be used to represent any character or group of characters. By using these wildcards in combination with the MS-DOS FAT 8.3 filename structure, Windows NT Command Prompt commands, and batch programs, you can automate repetitive tasks with amazing power and dexterity. See also *batch program.*

Windows NT

The 32-bit, scalable, fully preemptive-multitasking version of Microsoft Windows. Unlike earlier versions of Windows, NT is a true operating system and requires no other operating system (such as MS-DOS) to function. Unlike other versions of Windows, NT is portable (is available in versions for a variety of hardware platforms), secure (offers C2-level security, suitable for many governmental, institutional, and corporate tasks), and scalable (provides multiprocessor support); it also offers an advanced file system with long filenames. NT comes in two primary version, Server and Workstation. See also *NTFS, Windows NT Server, Windows NT Workstation.*

Windows NT Security dialog box

The dialog box that appears when the Ctrl+Alt+Del keystroke is used in an NT session. The intent of trapping the classic Intel PC reboot keystroke is to prevent unauthorized users from gaining access to the machine by simply rebooting it. In addition to this protection, the dialog box offers authorized users access to other tools to control security, the running session's task list, and a menu for orderly shutdown.

Windows NT Server

The version of NT that provides centralized management and security, advanced fault tolerance, and additional connectivity for Windows NT and other Windows workstations. See also *server, Windows NT Workstation.*

Windows NT Workstation

The desktop version of the Windows NT operating system. NT Workstation provides all of the multitasking and memory management benefits of NT to the individual desktop user without the hardware requirements and extra configuration burdens of the NT Server.

WinZip

A program by Niko Mak Computing that provides a simple interface for creating, decompressing, and managing .ZIP archives. WinZip is available at most anonymous FTP sites. See also *anonymous FTP, archive, compress, .ZIP*.

wizard

Microsoft's cutesy name for a utility that helps you configure something.

WordPad

A Windows applet for simple word processing (it replaces the venerable Write). WordPad is basically Microsoft Word 1.0 with a minor facelift.

word wrap

The automatic rendering of text without carriage returns in multiple lines.

workgroup

A collection of computers organized for viewing, security, resource sharing, or collaboration purposes. In a Windows NT network, a workgroup is a set of computers represented by a unique name. See also *domain*.

workstation

A powerful computer with great speed of calculation, enhanced graphics, and communications capabilities, usually networked to a series of other computers for the purpose of sharing resources. The term workstation has a special meaning in the context of a Windows NT network, specifically referring to a computer using the Windows NT Workstation operating system as opposed to the Windows NT Server operating system. See also *domain controller, server, Windows NT Workstation, Windows NT Server*.

Workstation service

A Windows NT program that provides network connections and communications.

World Wide Web (WWW)

A recent Internet service made possible by the combination of hypertext, GUI environments, the HTTP protocol, and HTML. Invented by Tim Berners-Lee at CERN in Switzerland, the WWW was originally a straight character-based implementation of HTTP to transport simple HTML hypertext documents. This was followed shortly after by the first graphical Web "browser," Mosaic, developed by a team of programmers led by Marc Andreeson at the National Center for Supercomputing Applications at the University of Illinois Urbana-Champaign. The Mosaic browser was first developed for UNIX GUIs such as Motif and then ported to the Macintosh and Windows platforms. The introduction of the Windows Mosaic client lit a firestorm of entre-preneurial activity unseen since the introduction of the IBM PC, resulting in a fierce competition for browser technologies and the rapid acknowledgment of the WWW as the next advertising, entertainment, and information distribution frontier. Due to the brisk competition among software companies to develop Web browsers, the WWW is now capable of delivering the same rich multimedia contents as CD-ROM and is only limited by available bandwidth and the processing power of the desktop PC.

WYSIWYG (what you see is what you get)

The beneficial effect of scalable fonts in a GUI word processing or desktop publishing environment is the ability to predict with fairly high accuracy the appearance of a document before it is printed.

X

XMODEM

A simple error-correcting binary file transfer protocol for asynchro-nous serial communications developed by Ward Christenson. See also *file transfer, terminal emulation, YMODEM, ZMODEM.*

Y

YMODEM

An error-correcting binary file transfer protocol for asynchronous serial communications based upon XMODEM. Developed by Chuck Forsberg, YMODEM provides batch file transfer support and greater transfer speed. See also *file transfer, terminal emulation, XMODEM, ZMODEM.*

Z

ZMODEM

An enhanced error-correcting binary file transfer protocol for asynchronous serial communications, written by Chuck Forsberg. ZMODEM provides automatic download, batch file support, filename support, streaming transfers, transfer crash recovery, and enhanced error-correction capabilities compared to earlier protocols. ZMODEM also has more robust timing capabilities that allow it to work with satellite transfers and telnet sessions, where network delays will cause other protocols to fail. ZMODEM is supported by most modern terminal emulation programs, BBS host systems, and UNIX hosts. See also *file transfer, terminal emulation, XMODEM, YMODEM.*

.ZIP

A popular file compression/decompression format for the IBM PC. Requires a .ZIP-compatible program for creating or decompressing .ZIP archives. See also *archive, compress, WinZip.*

INDEX

A

B

C